IN NO TIME

Excel
97

IN NO TIME

Excel 97

Walter Schwabe

Edited by
ROB YOUNG

Prentice Hall Europe

London New York Toronto Sydney Tokyo Singapore Madrid Mexico City Munich Paris

First published in 1997 as Easy – Excel 97 by
Markt&Technik Buch- und Software Verlag GmbH
85540 Haar bei München/Germany
This edition published 1999 by
Prentice Hall Europe
Campus 400, Maylands Avenue
Hemel Hempstead
Hertfordshire, HP2 7EZ

A division of
Simon & Schuster International Group

Translated by Paul Boness and Patricia Cooke
in association with First Edition Translations Limited, Cambridge

Typeset in Stone Sans
by Mike Weintroub

Designed and Produced by Bender Richardson White

Printed and bound in Great Britain
by TJ International Ltd., Padstow, Cornwall

Library of Congress Cataloging-in-Publication Data

Available from the publisher

British Library Cataloguing in Publication Data

A catalogue record for this book is available from the British Library

ISBN 0-13-977687-7

1   2   3   4   5   02   01   00   99   98

4

Contents

1 The first time   16

2 The first calculation   44

6 Business presentation 150

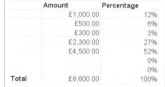

7 Statistics 182

8 One hundred per cent 220

Amount	Percentage
£1,000.00	12%
£500.00	6%
£300.00	3%
£2,300.00	27%
£4,500.00	52%
	0%
	0%
Total £8,600.00	100%

9 Cashing in 238

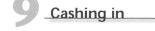

Dear reader,

By choosing this book you have opted for a slightly different learning method. It is rather like a cookery book. If you follow the recipes you will end up with a 'tasty' menu and will gain basic knowledge of food preparation. You can then vary the ingredients and create your own dishes.

Using numerous examples, you will get to know Excel step by step. The aim is to help you over the initial obstacles which beginners always encounter when faced with something new. The chapters are arranged in such a way that you can start with something practical immediately for example, setting up a housekeeping budget, calculating foreign currency, creating a cash book, etc).

I particularly recommend the practical exercises. They not only extend your knowledge but also lead on to other possibilities.

Finally, I should like to thank everyone who has taken part in my Excel beginners' courses. They not only showed me what problems beginners have, but also motivated me to write this book. Above all, I should like to thank those participants who had previously never heard of 'booting up', thought the mouse was a household pest and got more and more into Excel as the course progressed.

I am sure that you the reader will get as much pleasure out of Excel as my 'guinea pigs' did. And at the end of the book you will be able to say, 'Excel – that's easy!'

Yours
Walter Schwabe

On the following three pages you can see how your computer keyboard is arranged. For clarity, only particular blocks of keys are shown at a time. Most of the computer keys work just like typewriter keys. But there are also additional keys which are designed purely for computer operations. See for yourself...

Typewriter keyboard

You use these keys exactly as you would use the keys of a typewriter.
You also use the return key to send commands to the computer.

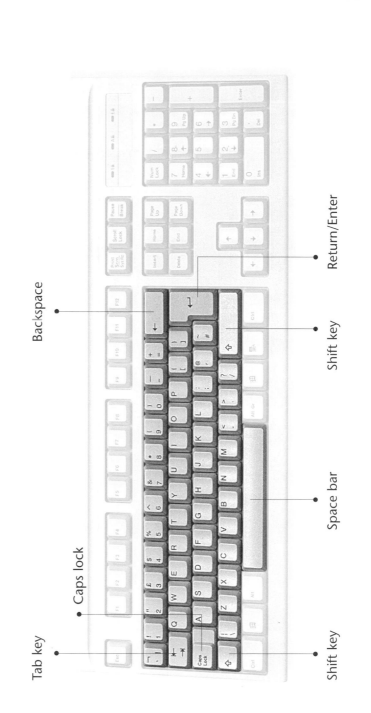

Tab key

Caps lock

Backspace

Return/Enter

Shift key

Space bar

Shift key

11

Special keys, function keys, indicator lights, numeric keypad

The special keys and function keys are used for special computer operations; the Ctrl, Alt and Alt Gr keys are usually used in combination with other keys. The Escape key is used to cancel commands; the Insert and Delete keys are used to insert and delete text respectively.

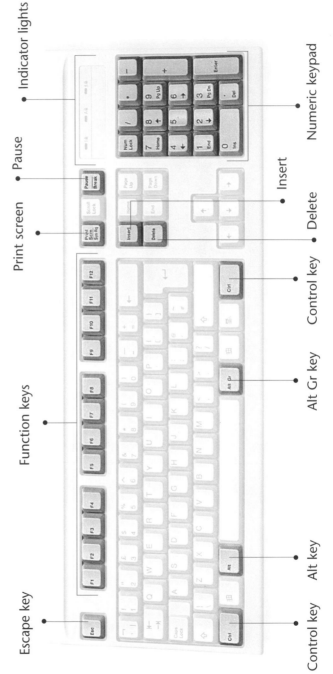

- Indicator lights
- Pause
- Print screen
- Function keys
- Escape key

Control key   Alt key

Control key

Alt Gr key

Insert

Delete

Numeric keypad

Navigation keys

These keys are used to move around the screen

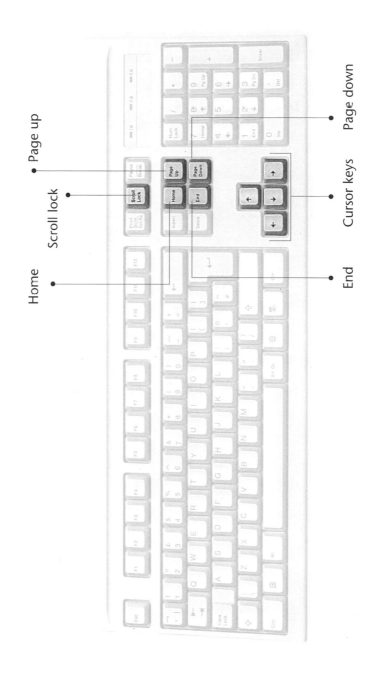

Page up

Scroll lock

Home

Page down

Cursor keys

End

'Click...'
means: quickly
depress a mouse
button once.

Click using the
left mouse
button

Click using the
right mouse
button

'Double-click...'

means: depress the left mouse button twice in quick succession.

Double-click

'Drag...'

means: click on particular items on the screen, using the left mouse button. Keeping the mouse button depressed, move the mouse, and so move the item to another position.

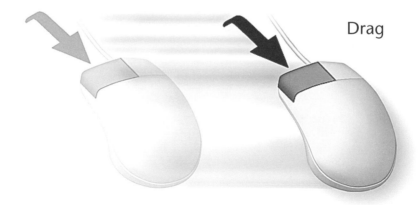

Drag

15

1

What's in this chapter?

There is always a first time for everything in life: the first steps, the first day at school, the first friend, the first disappointment. Just as every seasoned driver had to take driving lessons at one time, the prospective Excel user first has to gain the basic knowledge. So let's get into the car and set off slowly in first gear. You will get to know the Excel screen and what you can do with it. Let's go!

Your are going to learn:

Starting up Excel

Microsoft Excel 97 is a program designed to carry out calculations in tabular form on spreadsheets. The screen shows a table divided into columns and rows. This is where you will normally carry out your calculations.

Before you do your first calculation you have to start up the program. Here is one of the simplest ways: the Excel 97 spreadsheet is a program. As with most programs, to start you first click on the Start button in Windows 95. This is usually located on the lower left edge of the screen on your monitor. After successful installation, Excel 97 is set up as a separate menu entry. You start the spreadsheet with this. You can find further information about installation and an even better way to start up Excel in the Help chapter.

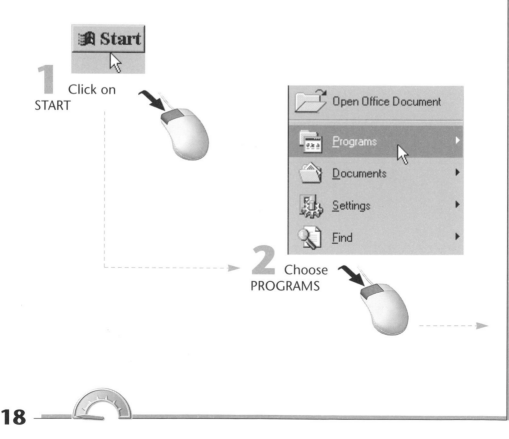

1 Click on START

2 Choose PROGRAMS

Open Office Document

Programs

Documents

Settings

Find

3 Click on
MICROSOFT EXCEL

Setting up Excel as an icon

All roads lead to Rome. But only one of them is the
shortest. You just have to know which one. This is also true
of starting up Excel. The shortest way is to set up Excel as
a separate icon on the user interface of Windows 95.

The user
interface of
Windows is
called the
Desktop.

You have probably already noticed the icons. A
double click and the appropriate program starts up
on the screen. This works exactly the same with
Excel. Move the mouse pointer on to the START
button. Then click the right mouse button and select
OPEN. Since Excel is a program, open Programs with
a double click. Now you will see the icon for Excel.
With the Ctrl button pressed down,
click the icon and drag it on to the Desktop with the
mouse to make a copy. And there it will stay until you
change it.

1 Position the
mouse pointer on
START and press the
right mouse button.

19

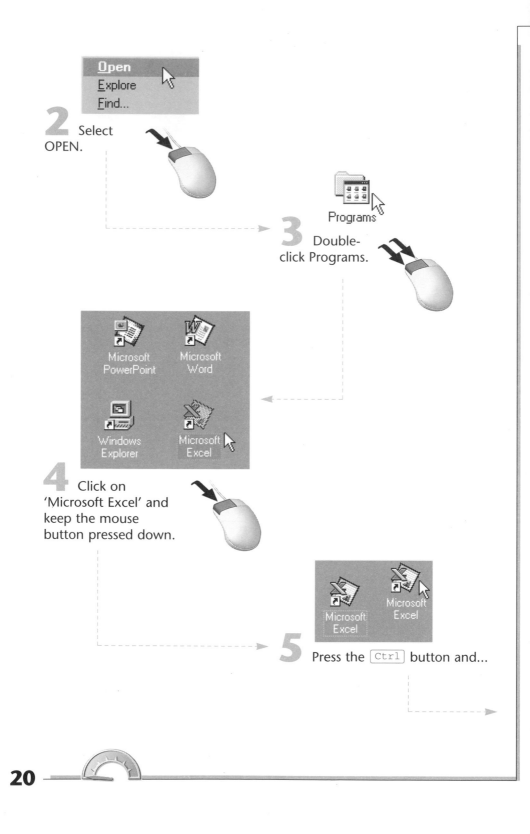

Open
Explore
Find...

2 Select OPEN.

Programs

3 Double-click Programs.

Microsoft PowerPoint   Microsoft Word

Windows Explorer   Microsoft Excel

4 Click on 'Microsoft Excel' and keep the mouse button pressed down.

Microsoft Excel   Microsoft Excel

5 Press the `Ctrl` button and...

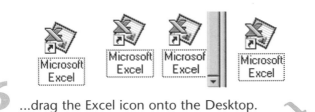

6 ...drag the Excel icon onto the Desktop.

As soon as you release the mouse button the icon is copied to the Windows 95 desktop. A double click on it and Excel is started up.

 With the left mouse button pressed down you can move the icon to any position on the Desktop.

The layout of the Excel 97 screen

After starting up, the Excel 97 user interface is shown.

When you first start, a lively helper reports for duty. This is Clippit, the Office Assistant. He helps you as you manipulate the software and he can be very useful, although occasionally he can get in the way. We will deal with the assistant later. So you should switch him off for the time being. Just click on

A user interface is the total picture that you see on the screen with Excel 97.

the cross with the left mouse button and he will disappear from the screen.

So where are we?

The screen is divided into two main areas: the command area and the work area.

Title bar with
names

Menu bar with
commands

Standard toolbar
with icons

Formatting
bar

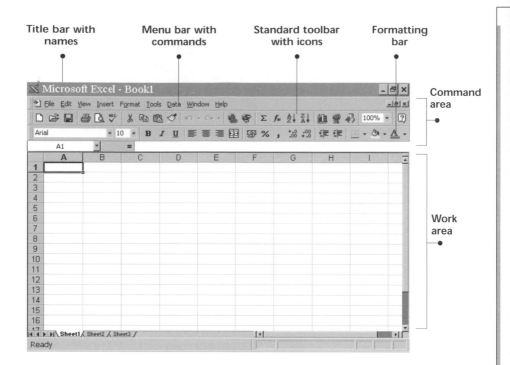

Command
area

Work
area

Right at the top is the command area. This is where commands are selected using the mouse or the keyboard. The second area (the white surface) is the work area. In Excel this is called the worksheet. This is where you will eventually carry out your calculations or textual entries.

Keep up appearances!

The mouse pointer tells you where you are at any particular time. Its appearance alters according to its position on the screen. If you are in the command area it takes the form of an arrow.

 If, on the other hand, you position the mouse pointer in the worksheet it takes on the appearance of a white cross.

The individual bars

The command area contains a number of very distinct bars:

The title bar

Microsoft Excel - Book1 This shows which file you are working on.

In Excel the sheets you work on are called 'files'.

Think of a file in Excel 97 as a document file in which you file away individual worksheets. Likewise in Excel you work with worksheets.

You can label the document file with a name. In Excel this happens when you save the file.

The word Book in the title bar means than it has not been saved yet. It is a name which is automatically given by Excel. (The 'save' function, on the other hand, is another matter.) The number '1' after the term 'file' means that you are working on your first file on the screen.

A practical example:

Practice	Description in Excel
Document file	File or Working file
One sheet of paper in the document file	Worksheet
An unlabelled document file	Unsaved, given the name 'Book'
A labelled document file	Saved and named

The menu bar

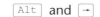

You use the menu bar to call up commands such as OPEN, SAVE, PRINT AND EXIT. You do this by clicking on an entry in the menu bar with the left mouse button and then selecting (clicking on) the desired entry in the open menu.

You can also get into the menu bar by using the keyboard:

Function   **Keyboard shortcut**

Use these keys to get into the   Alt and →
menu. (Directions: first activate the
Alt key, release, then press the
cursor key to the right).

Use the cursor keys to move around   ← → ↓ ↑
in the menu.

Function	Keyboard shortcut

Use the escape key to deactivate the menu bar.	Esc

The standard toolbar

An icon on a toolbar represents a function (for instance, the printer symbol indicates printing).

The standard toolbar contains icons which symbolise commands that can also be carried out via the menu bar.

The real advantage that the standard toolbar has over the menu bar is that you can call up the individual commands more quickly using the mouse.

The formatting toolbar

| Arial ▾ | 10 ▾ | B I U | ≡ ≡ ≡ | % , .00 .00 |

All the commands on the menu bar and standard and formatting toolbars are carried out with a single click of the left mouse button.

This bar is used for formatting, i.e. you can choose a different font, format your figures as percentages, accentuate text by using bold or underlining. We will deal with this later.

25

Selecting and deselecting the toolbars

In Excel 97 you can select and deselect individual toolbars. For this you use the VIEW menu option.

There should be a tick in front of STANDARD and FORMATTING. This means that they are both activated. If you click on one of the menu options you will delesect that toolbar on your screen and the tick will disappear.

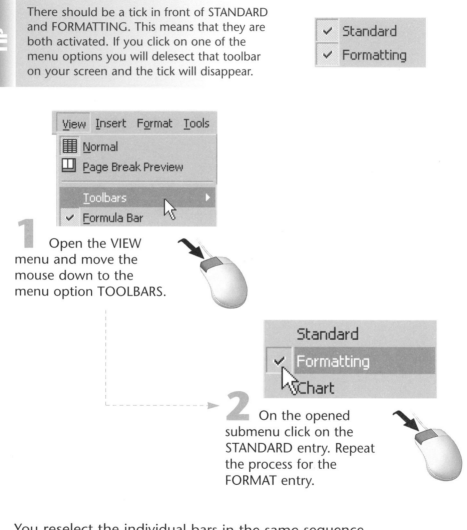

1 Open the VIEW menu and move the mouse down to the menu option TOOLBARS.

2 On the opened submenu click on the STANDARD entry. Repeat the process for the FORMAT entry.

You reselect the individual bars in the same sequence.

You can also place the mouse pointer on a toolbar
and press the right mouse button. A similar menu will
appear which you can also use to select or deselect
the bars.

Moving the bars

The inexperienced beginner can be faced with the apparently
insoluble problem that the toolbars have been moved (this often
happens on computers with more than one user!). The best thing is
to find out for yourself how to move the bars. In this way you can
arrange your work area to suit yourself. When you want to move the
toolbars, look for a raised double-line at the left of the bar. With
mouse button pressed down you can move this line around on the
screen. In this way you can drag a toolbar into the work area to
obtain a better and quicker overview. Dragging is purely a matter of
practice. Now you can arrange your screen to suit your
requirements.

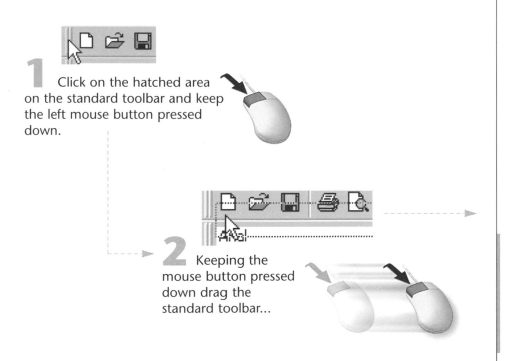

1 Click on the hatched area
on the standard toolbar and keep
the left mouse button pressed
down.

2 Keeping the
mouse button pressed
down drag the
standard toolbar...

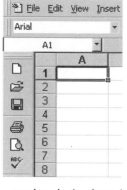

3 ...to the desired position, and then release the mouse button. Do exactly the same thing to put the bar back into its 'old position'.

Dialog boxes and list boxes

Dialog boxes

You are working with a dialog box for the first time. This is how you inform Excel what you would like to change.

Dialog boxes are used for entering data and selecting commands. A 'dialog' takes place between you – as user – and Excel 97.

Customize ? ×

Toolbars | Commands | Options

☐ Large icons

☑ Show ScreenTips on toolbars

Menu animations: (None) ▼

Close

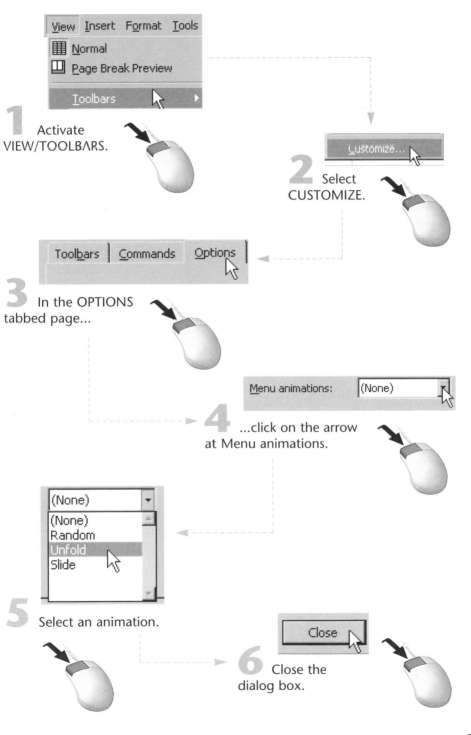

1 Activate VIEW/TOOLBARS.

2 Select CUSTOMIZE.

3 In the OPTIONS tabbed page...

4 ...click on the arrow at Menu animations.

5 Select an animation.

6 Close the dialog box.

Tabbed pages

Tabbed pages are like a card index.

Toolbars | Commands | Options

Instead of browsing through, you simply click on the name of the desired page with the mouse button. This is then automatically brought to the fore.

With or without animation

You subsequently open a given menu command. The result: the animation you chose is implemented. If you want to switch the animation off again, call up the menu command VIEW/TOOLBARS/CUSTOMIZE and select the entry '(None)' from the Menu animations list box on the Options page.

The QuickInfo

Excel offers you an aid for you get to know the individual commands in the standard and formatting bars. Position the mouse pointer on an icon of your choice. After about a second a QuickInfo appears. This is an explanation of what the icon will activate if you click on it.

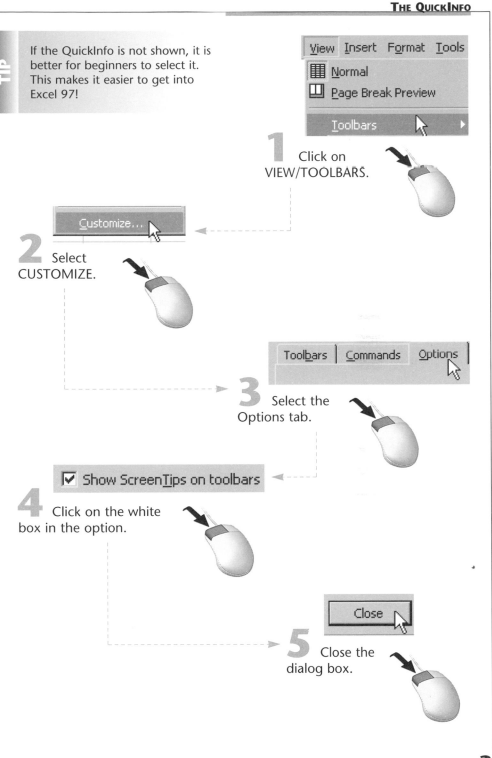

TIP

If the QuickInfo is not shown, it is better for beginners to select it. This makes it easier to get into Excel 97!

View Insert Format Tools

Normal

Page Break Preview

Toolbars ▶

1 Click on VIEW/TOOLBARS.

Customize...

2 Select CUSTOMIZE.

Toolbars | Commands | Options

3 Select the Options tab.

☑ Show ScreenTips on toolbars

4 Click on the white box in the option.

Close

5 Close the dialog box.

A tick appears in this box (known as a check box) after clicking it: the function is activated.

☑ Show Screen**T**ips on toolbars

Place the mouse pointer over an icon, without clicking a mouse button, to select the QuickInfo.

What is a cell?

The worksheet consists of numerous boxes. The individual boxes are formed by the intersections of columns and rows.

The cell names derive from the intersections of the individual columns and rows.

Rows/Columns	Column A	Column B	Column C	Column D
Row 1	Cell A1	Cell B1	Cell C1	Cell D1
Row 2	Cell A2	Cell B2	Cell C2	Cell D2
Row 3	Cell A3	Cell B3	Cell C3	Cell D3

From cell to cell

You move from cell to cell simply by clicking on another cell with the mouse.

You can tell which cell you are in by the bold black border.

1 Click on the top left cell ('A1').

2 Click on another cell.

You can also move from cell to cell with the ⇥ key or with ← → ↓ ↑.

Moving the cursor from one cell to the next.

Description	Key symbol

Left mouse button

Cursor keys   ← → ↓ ↑

Tabstop key   ⇄

Entering the first number

The purpose of a spreadsheet is to perform calculations. Only the Arabic numbers (0,1,2,3,4,5,6,7,8,9) are used for this. The numerical values always appear in the cells. You click on a cell with the left mouse button. Then you enter the figures using the keyboard.

As soon as you enter the first number the cursor flashes in the cell.

The cursor is a position indicator on the screen in the form of a flashing line. It marks the place where the next entry will appear.

| 1234567 |

Once your number ('12343567') is completed, confirm this by pressing the ← key. This tells Excel that the entry is complete and the number should appear in the cell. You know it has been confirmed when the number is moved over to the right.

1234567

As soon as you press the ← key or activate another cell with the left mouse button, ⬚, or ← → ↓ ↑ Excel accepts your information

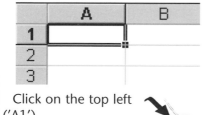

	A	B
1		
2		
3		

1 Click on the top left cell ('A1').

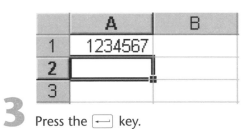

2 Type in the number '1234567' using the keyboard.

3 Press the ⟵ key.

The formula bar

The formula bar is an aid to entry. This is where you can see what you are working on. It is also called the 'entry line', since you make an entry into a cell here.

Information

On the formula bar you can find the name of the cell which is currently activated. In addition you can see the contents of a cell. If you click on the number you have already written, '1234567', you will also see '1234567' on the formula bar. If you go to another cell you will not see anything since you have not yet made any entries in another cell.

The formula bar informs you about:

Term	Example
Cell name	A1
Cell content	1234567

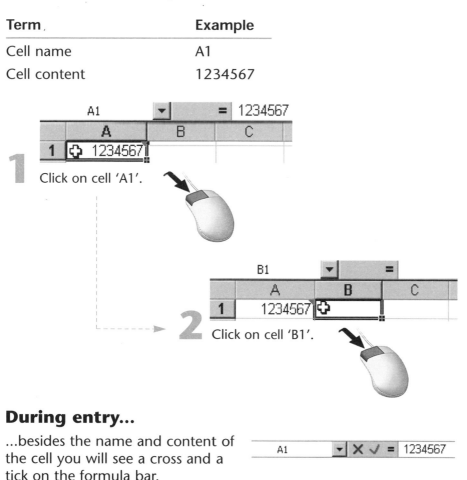

1 Click on cell 'A1'.

2 Click on cell 'B1'.

During entry...

...besides the name and content of the cell you will see a cross and a tick on the formula bar.

If you click on the cross you will erase your earlier entry. If, however, you click on the tick you will complete it (this button does the same thing as the ⏎ key).

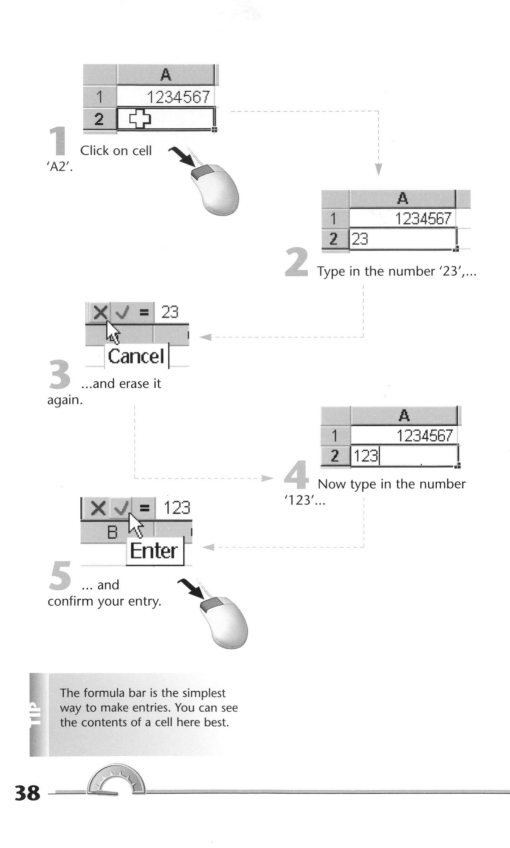

	A
1	1234567
2	🕂

1 Click on cell 'A2'.

	A
1	1234567
2	23

2 Type in the number '23',...

X ✓ = 23

Cancel

3 ...and erase it again.

	A
1	1234567
2	123

4 Now type in the number '123'...

X ✓ = 123

B

Enter

5 ... and confirm your entry.

The formula bar is the simplest way to make entries. You can see the contents of a cell here best.

Closing Excel without saving

You want to stop working on the computer and close Excel 97? Since you have not entered anything of importance it is not necessary to save anything yet. Saving means that you would be able to work on this file again next time you started up Excel. When you leave the program, Excel asks if you would like to save the file. Excel asks this question whenever you want to leave the program without having filed your information. Since this is not necessary at present, you answer No. If you click on the Cancel button you will return to the file.

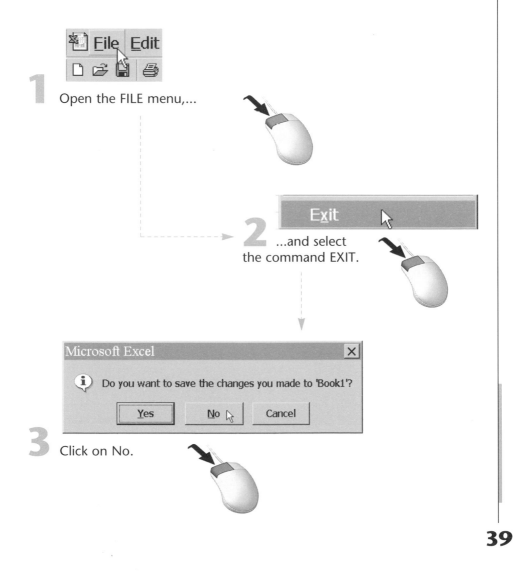

1 Open the FILE menu,...

2 ...and select the command EXIT.

Microsoft Excel

ⓘ Do you want to save the changes you made to 'Book1'?

| Yes | No | Cancel |

3 Click on No.

A further possibility: you can also close Excel with a mouse action. Either double click on the Excel icon on the title bar or click the cross (X) at the top right of the window (also on the title bar). You will again be asked if you want to save the text. If you indicate No, you will leave the program.

Microsoft Excel -

File Edit View Inse

1 Double-click on the Excel icon or simply on the cross.

Microsoft Excel   ☒

ⓘ Do you want to save the changes you made to 'Book1'?

Yes   No   Cancel

2 Click on No.

The Excel trainer

Practice makes perfect. To consolidate what you have learnt, do the following exercises. The answers are in the appendix.

Exercise I

Say which toolbars these are:

| File Edit View Insert Format Tools Data Window Help |

| A1 ▾ X ✓ = 1234567 |

| ☐ ☞ ☐ ☐ ☐ ☐ ABC ✂ ☐ ☐ ☐ ☐ ☐ Σ ƒₓ ☐ ☐ ☐ ☐ ☐ 100% ▾ ☐ |

| Arial ▾ 10 ▾ **B** _I_ U ☰ ☰ ☰ ☐ ☐ % , ☐ ☐ ☐ ☐ ☐ ▾ ☐ ▾ **A** ▾ |

Exercise II

Carry out the following tasks on your screen:

Start up Excel.

Deactivate the formula bar.

Deactivate the standard toolbar.

Deselect the formatting toolbar.

Switch the formula, standard and formatting bars on again.

41

Click on cell 'A1'.

Click on cell 'B2'.

Click on cell 'C3'.

Click on cell 'D4'.

Click on cell 'E5'.

Enter the number '123' in cell A1.

Enter the number '4711' in cell B2.

Enter the number '7' in cell C3.

End Excel without saving.

Exercise III

Answer the following questions (there is only one correct answer for each):

Which key can you use to activate the menu bar?

Alt

Alt Gr

Ctrl

Which sequence of commands do you use to select the QuickInfo?

FORMAT/STYLE/QUICKINFO

VIEW/TOOLBARS/CUSTOMIZE/ QuickInfo list box

VIEW/TOOLBARS/CUSTOMIZE/ Options tab/ switch on QuickInfo

What does your mouse pointer look like when you are in the work area?

How is the name of a cell constructed?

☐ The cell is named first, then the column.

☐ The column is named first, then the row.

☐ The row is named first, then the column.

What's in this chapter?

Now things are starting to happen! In this chapter you will do your first calculations. Admittedly they will be very simple. It will be like being back at school. You will learn how to add up (+), subtract (-), multiply (*) and divide (/), just as you did at primary school. In this respect Excel is like an improved pocket calculator. The real advantage of the software is that if you want to enter new figures you don't have to start the whole calculation again from the beginning. You simply replace the old figures with the new ones. Excel automatically adjusts the result. However, you don't need to search out your dusty old school bag, just work your way through this chapter. When you've finished it you can have your breaktime snack.

	A	B
		SUM
1		66
2		77
3		456
4		599
5	Total	

You already know:

Your are going to learn:

Doing calculations

1+1 = ?

You are now ready to carry out your first calculation. The first calculation is a simple addition of three numbers arranged in a column: 66, 57, 456. You enter each number into a separate cell. To do this you click on the cell, enter the value and confirm by pressing the ⟵ key.

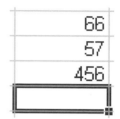

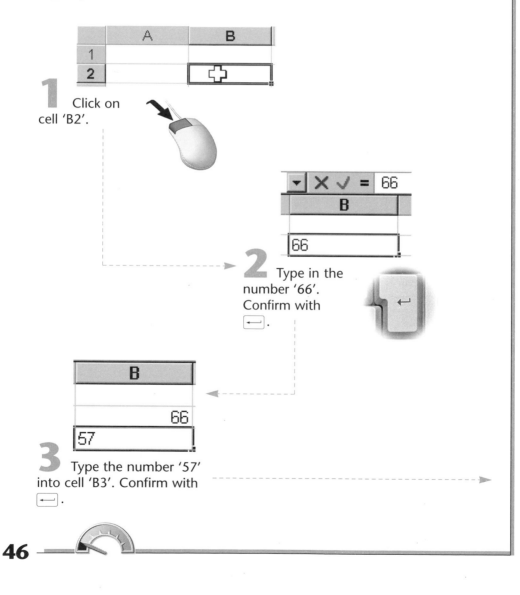

1 Click on cell 'B2'.

2 Type in the number '66'. Confirm with ⟵.

3 Type the number '57' into cell 'B3'. Confirm with ⟵.

4 Type the number '456' into cell 'B4'. Confirm with ⏎.

The result

We want the result of the addition of these three numbers to appear in cell 'B5'. The important thing is to put in an equals sign (=). In this way you are informing Excel that a calculation formula follows.

The equals sign (=) must always be entered before a calculation. In this way the program knows that it is not dealing with an entry, but that it has to carry out a calculation.

You now have to indicate which cells you would like to add up. You inform Excel of this by mouse clicks. You click on the first cell you are adding up. Then you type a plus sign ('+') for the addition using the keyboard. Next you click on the second cell and type another plus sign. Now one more click on the last cell and you confirm the formula with Enter. The result of the calculation is shown.

In general:

Answer = Cell 1 + Cell 2 + Cell 3

In our case:

Cell B5 = Cell B2 + Cell B3 + Cell B4

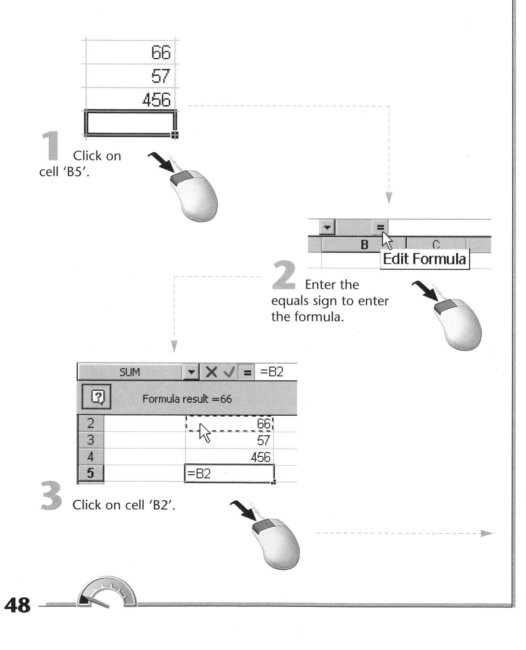

1 Click on cell 'B5'.

Edit Formula

2 Enter the equals sign to enter the formula.

Formula result =66

3 Click on cell 'B2'.

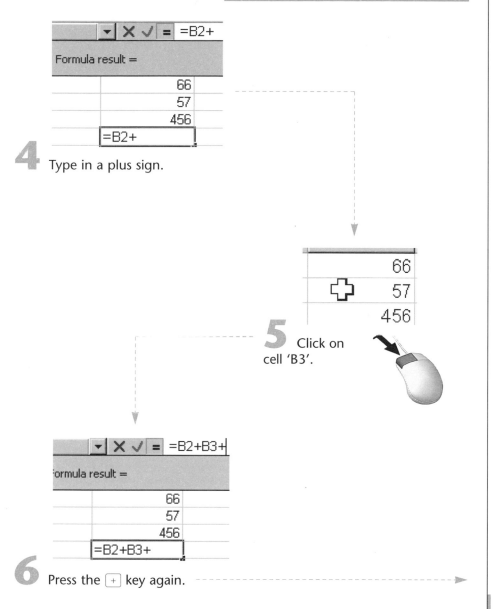

4 Type in a plus sign.

5 Click on cell 'B3'.

6 Press the ⊞ key again.

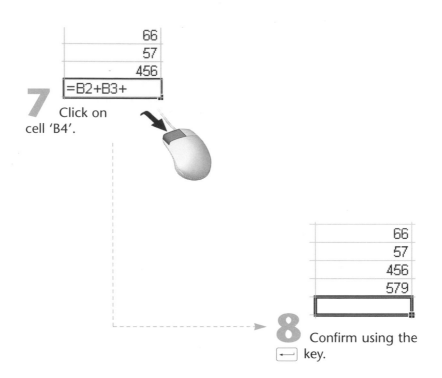

7 Click on cell 'B4'.

8 Confirm using the ⏎ key.

Calculating with Excel

Subtraction, multiplication and division are carried out using exactly the same procedure as addition. Only the sign alters according to the operation.

Mathematical signs in Excel

Type of calculation	Signs in Excel
Addition	+
Subtraction	-
Multiplication	*
Division	/

Entering text

Our little calculation looks rather 'bare', and so we shall label it. However, there is a big difference between the entry of text (letters) and numbers.

Excel can (logically) only calculate with numbers, not with text.

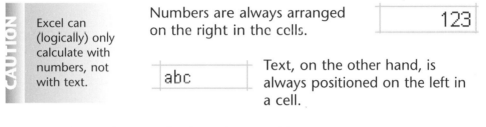

Numbers are always arranged on the right in the cells.

123

Text, on the other hand, is always positioned on the left in a cell.

abc

A number written in the form '123,– –' is not a number for Excel, but text because of the punctuation marks ',– –'. It is therefore left aligned.

123,--

Other mixed forms which are not numbers for Excel are:

-,34

34 °

34,-

£34

34 pounds

Excel differentiates in the cells between numbers (right aligned), text (left aligned) and formulae (equals signs).

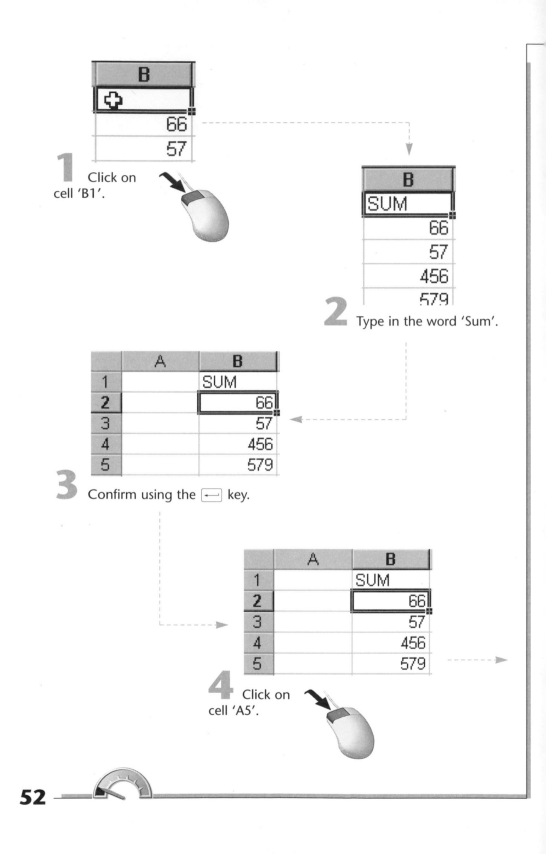

1 Click on cell 'B1'.

2 Type in the word 'Sum'.

3 Confirm using the ⏎ key.

4 Click on cell 'A5'.

	A	B
1		SUM
2		66
3		57
4		456
5	Total	579

5 Type in the word 'Total'.

	A	B
1		SUM
2		66
3		57
4		456
5	Total	579
6		

6 Press the ↵ key.

Changing numbers

The advantage of Excel is that you can change numbers later. You don't have to set up a new calculation every time if only a single value changes. You delete the number by clicking on the appropriate cell and simply type in the new value. You overwrite it, replacing the old entry with the new. The result is adjusted automatically. You can also delete the contents of a cell with the Delete key.

	66
	57
	456
	579

1 Click on cell 'B3'.

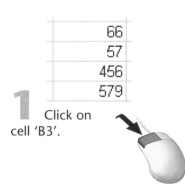

53

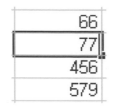

66
77
456
579

2 Type in the number '77'.

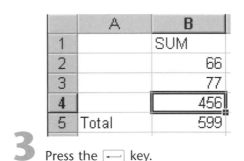

	A	B
1		SUM
2		66
3		77
4		456
5	Total	599

3 Press the ⟵ key.

Saving a calculation

If you leave Excel but would like to carry on with your calculation later, you must save the entries. Otherwise your entries are lost for ever. There are three different ways of doing this.

The first method: click on the button with the diskette symbol on it.

The second method: choose the menu command FILE/SAVE AS.

The third method: leave the program using the menu command FILE/EXIT. You will then be asked if you would like to save the changes. Click on YES.

Whichever of the three possibilities you choose you will always come to the Save As dialog box.

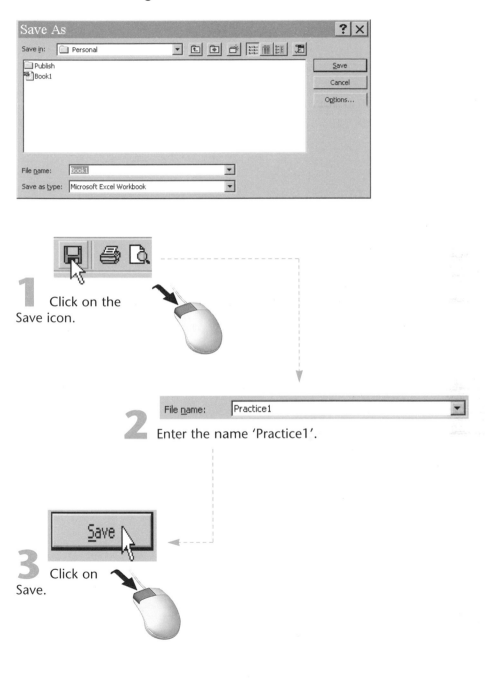

1 Click on the Save icon.

2 Enter the name 'Practice1'.

3 Click on Save.

After saving, you will see the name you have just given on

 Microsoft Excel - Practice1

the title bar. From now on your first calculation is stored under the name 'Practice1'.

Opening a file

Now if you exit Excel, you can call up your first calculation the next time you start up the program. To do this you click on the Open File icon on the standard toolbar or select the menu command FILE/OPEN.

The last four

For the time being, the easiest way is via the FILE menu. You will see the name 'Practice1' right at the bottom. The last four files you have worked on are listed here. If you choose the menu entry PRACTICE1, your first calculation is opened again on the screen.

> If you want to open a new file, use the NEW icon on the toolbar. A 'new file' means that you will be given a new, unused 'worksheet'.

Exit

1 Exit Excel using the menu command FILE/EXIT.

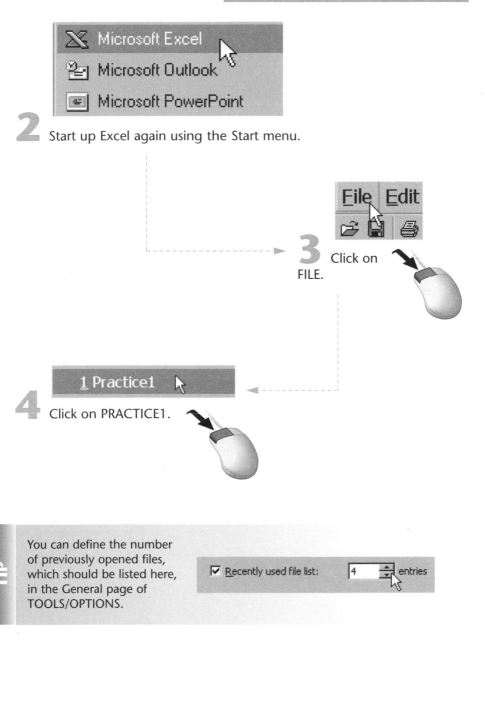

2 Start up Excel again using the Start menu.

3 Click on FILE.

4 Click on PRACTICE1.

You can define the number of previously opened files, which should be listed here, in the General page of TOOLS/OPTIONS.

57

The Excel trainer

Exercise I

Open a new file.

Do the following calculations using Excel:

	A	B	C	D	E	F	G
1	22	2	7546	75	159	45	45
2	34	6	77	98	89	78	56
3	55	3		99			77
4		4					
5							
6							
7	81	78	145				
8	789	99	99				
9	2	77					
10		8					

22+34+55	2*6*3*4	7546/77	75+98+99	159-89
45*78	45*56*77	81+789+2	78+99+77+8	145-99

Exercise II

Save your calculations as 'Practice2'.

Exercise III

Leave Excel via FILE/EXIT.

Exercise IV

Reopen 'Practice1'.

Exercise V

When does Excel recognise the entry as a number (1), and when, as text (2)? It is best to try this out on your screen.

234.56

23 dollars

ABC

−34

34 °

75,−

75 pounds

0.34

+78

Exercise VI

Which signs are used for the different mathematical operations in Excel?

Choose from: −   +   *   /   \   x   X

Division:

Addition:

Multiplication:

Subtraction:

Exercise VII
Which sign has to be inserted before a calculation?

☐ =

☐ No sign has to be given.

☐ ′

Exercise VIII

Open a new file.

Exercise IX
Carry out the following calculations in Excel:

67 – 45

89 x 2

78 : 2

5.6 x 3.5

78 – 13 + 17

83 + 84 + 77

178 – 89 – 43 + 22

Exercise X
Exit Excel without saving.

Exercise XI

Start up Excel again. Open the file 'Practice1' via the menu command FILE/OPEN or via the Open File icon on the toolbar.

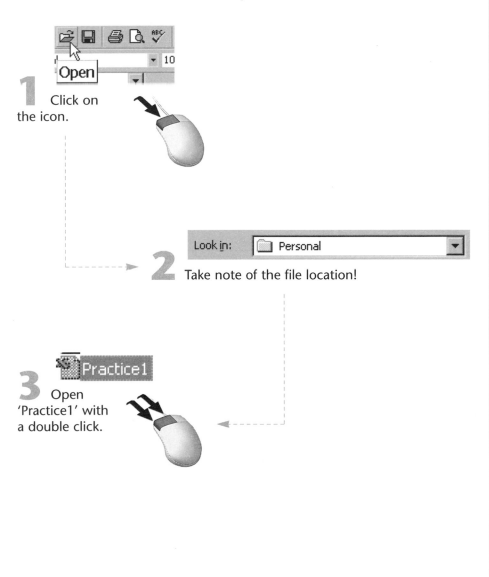

1 Click on the icon.

2 Take note of the file location!

Look in: Personal

3 Open 'Practice1' with a double click.

Practice1

What's in this chapter?

At the end of the month do you wonder where your money has gone? Funds at a low ebb again? Is your economy overheating? And you did so want to spend your next holiday in Florida. Oh well, the Lake District is very pretty, and healthy too. Anyone who ever loses track of their petty cash will find Excel helpful in organising their daily income and expenditure. And so that you have everything in black and white we shall print out our budget.

You already know:

Your are going to learn:

Adjusting columns

Even if an entry is too long to fit into a cell, Excel still accepts it. Here you can see the words 'household budget'. The cell is not quite long enough. The column is too narrow. The 'dget' at the end of budget does not fit in. The phrase could be even longer, for example 'household budget for the month of December'. You can see the complete contents of a cell on the formula bar. But for a better appearance you can adjust the column width.

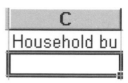

To do this, position the mouse pointer between two columns. It changes its appearance. Now with the mouse button pressed down you can alter the column width until it is the width you require. Then release the mouse button. But there is an even simpler way.

Double click with the left mouse button on the line between two columns and Excel finds the optimum column width i.e. it adjusts the column width to accommodate the longest term (number or words) in the column.

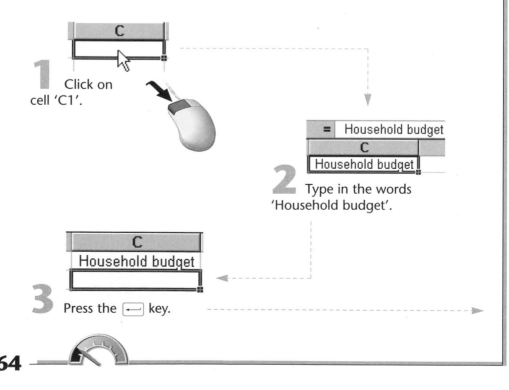

1 Click on cell 'C1'.

2 Type in the words 'Household budget'.

3 Press the ⏎ key.

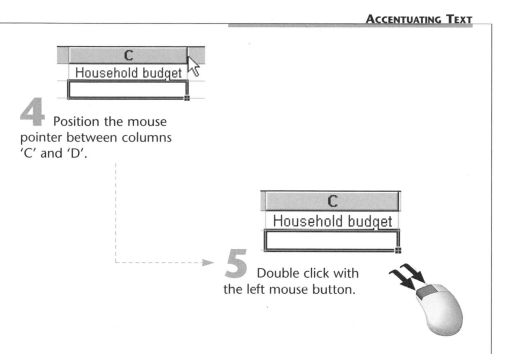

4 Position the mouse pointer between columns 'C' and 'D'.

5 Double click with the left mouse button.

Accentuating text

In Excel you can give prominence to individual words (or numbers). This process is called formatting.

Characters can be formatted for optical emphasis. This is done by bold or italic script, underlining etc.

You will find all the necessary tools in the formatting bar. This is where you can alter the typeface or size. Or you can accentuate the characters by using bold, italics or underlining. Alternatively you can call up the menu command FORMAT/CELLS. You set the formatting on the Font page. Here you will be offered even more possibilities. The characters can be set either as sub- or superscript. Underlining can be double. These accentuations will appear in the final printed document.

C

Hous[ ]d budget

1 Click on cell 'C1'.

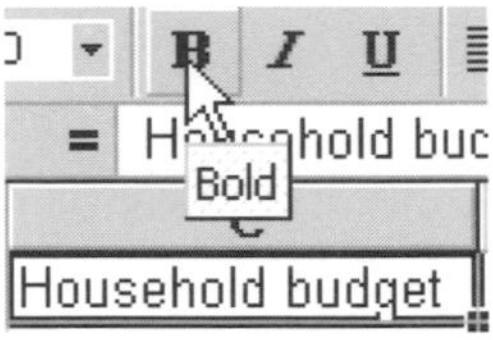

B *I* U
= H[ ]hold buc
Bold

C
Household budget

2 Activate Bold.

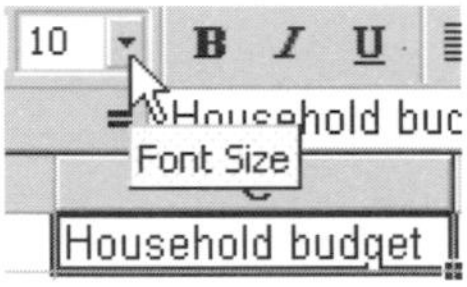

10 ▾ **B** *I* U
= Household buc
Font Size
Household budget

3 Click on the arrow next to the point size.

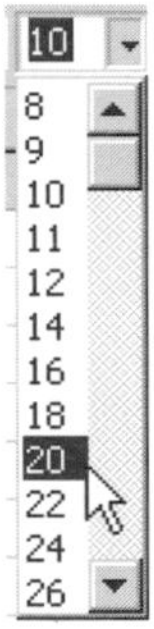

10 ▾
8
9
10
11
12
14
16
18
20
22
24
26

4 Select number '20'.

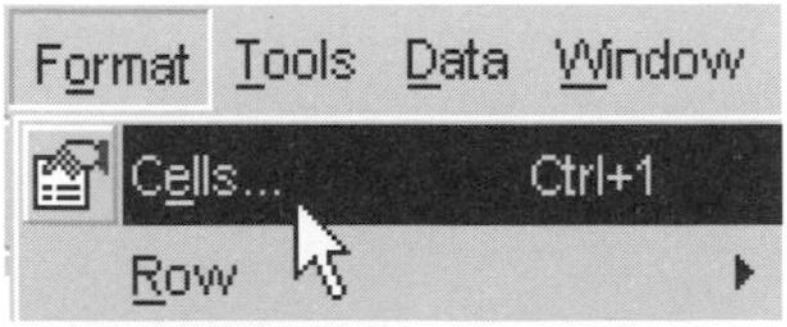

Format	Tools	Data	Window
🖼 Cells...		Ctrl+1	
Row			▶

5 Select the menu command FORMAT/CELLS.

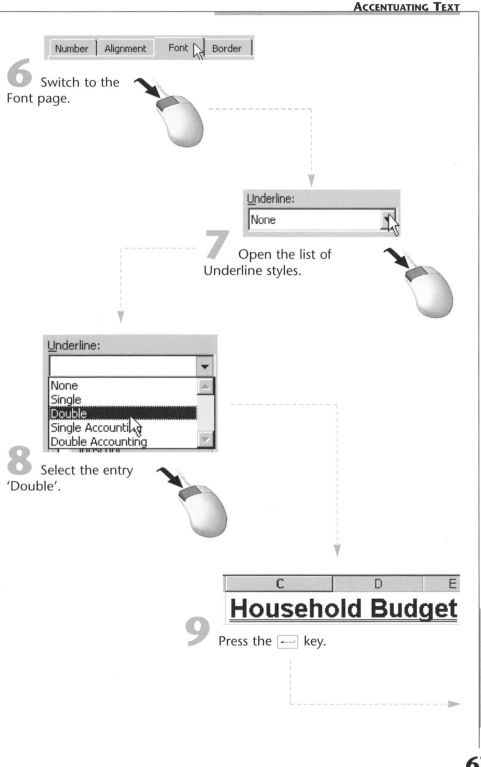

Number	Alignment	Font	Border

6 Switch to the Font page.

Underline:

None

7 Open the list of Underline styles.

Underline:

None
Single
Double
Single Accounting
Double Accounting

8 Select the entry 'Double'.

C	D	E

Household Budget

9 Press the ⬅ key.

67

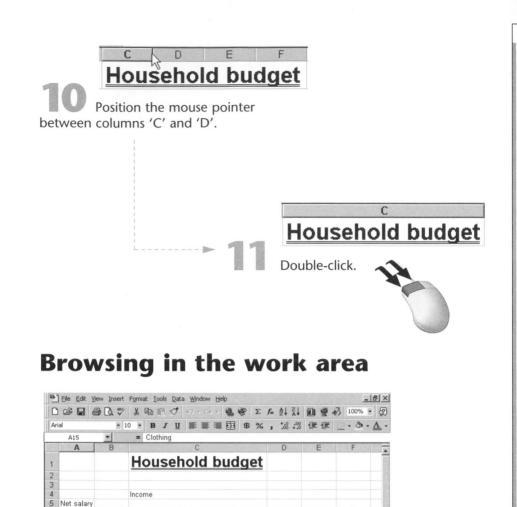

10 Position the mouse pointer between columns 'C' and 'D'.

11 Double-click.

Browsing in the work area

As in this example, you sometimes need to make your entries on the lower edge of the screen. The information even extends beyond this point. You can still see row '16' in this position. But what about the rows after '16'? Of course, this is not the end of the sheet. You are only seeing a section of it on your monitor. You simply browse forward.

To browse through a worksheet more quickly, you use the scroll bars at the bottom and right side of the screen.

To continue your entries you can operate the cursor keys, here ⊥. The bar (called the scroll bar) at the right side of the screen offers a quick way of browsing. You move the oblong box (called the scroll box) up or down, keeping the left mouse button pressed down. Move the box until the desired section of the screen is reached.

Row: 5

Excel indicates in a QuickInfo box the first row of the exposed section of the screen. In this case it is the fifth row. The first four are hidden at the upper edge of the screen.

Or you can click on the arrow on the bar with the left mouse button. Each click browses one row further.

69

File Edit View Insert Format Tools Data Window Help

Arial   ▼ 10 ▼ B *I* U

Clothing

	A	B	C	D	E	F
1			**Household budget**			
2						
3						
4			Income			
5	Net salary					
6	Rent receipts					
7	Interest					
8						
9	Total income					
10						
11			Expenses			
12	Rent					
13	Telephone					
14	Food, Drink					
15	Clothing					
16						

Sheet1 / Sheet2 / Sheet3 /

Enter

1 Enter the following entries into the appropriate cells:

C4: 'Income'
A5: 'Net salary'
A6: 'Rent receipts'
A7: 'Interest'
A9: 'Total income:'
C11: 'Expenses'
A12: 'Rent'
A13: 'Telephone'
A14: 'Food, drink'
A15: 'Clothing'

2 Scroll down,...

3 Row: 5

...until row '5' is shown.

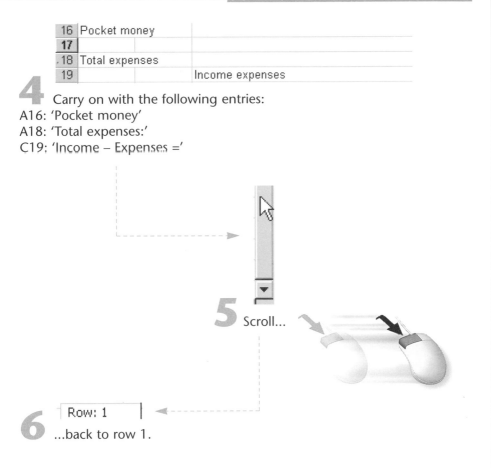

16	Pocket money	
17		
18	Total expenses	
19		Income expenses

4 Carry on with the following entries:

A16: 'Pocket money'
A18: 'Total expenses:'
C19: 'Income – Expenses ='

5 Scroll...

6 Row: 1

...back to row 1.

Using the paintbrush

You now know how to accentuate text or numbers. If you want to use a format several times it is best to use the paintbrush on the formatting toolbar. First click on a cell which has a format you would like to use.

Click once with the left mouse button on the paintbrush symbol and the mouse pointer takes the shape of a paintbrush.

If you activate another cell the formatting is transferred. You only format once with a mouse click on the icon. If you double-click on the paintbrush, you can use it as often as you want. You switch the function off again using the Esc key. Or click on the icon again.

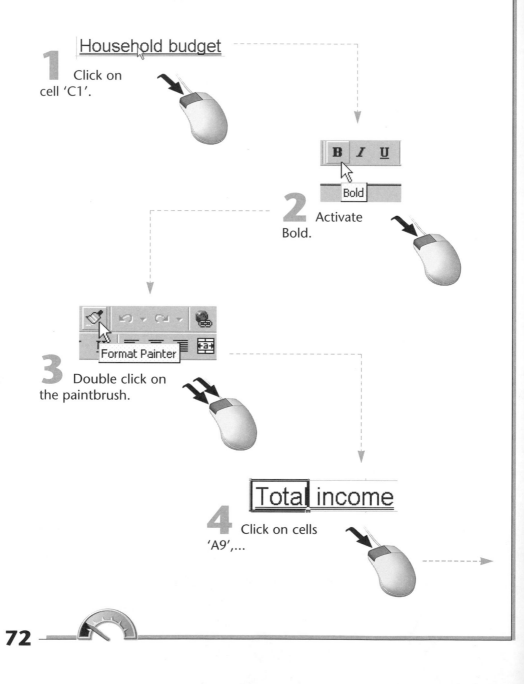

Household budget

1 Click on cell 'C1'.

B *I* <u>U</u>
Bold

2 Activate Bold.

Format Painter

3 Double click on the paintbrush.

Total income

4 Click on cells 'A9',...

Total income	
	Expenses
Rent	
Telephone	
Food, Drink	
Clothing	
Pocket money	
Total expenses	
	Income - Expenses

5 ...'C11', 'A18' and 'A19'. Press the Esc key.

AutoSum

There is a quicker command for arriving at totals. Until now you have used the plus sign '+' for addition. But for cells which are arranged in a column (or next to each other) Excel offers an abbreviated form. So you don't need to put in the '+' after each cell.

Σ

Until now:

Total = Cell 1 + Cell 2 + Cell 3

New way:

Total = Sum (Cell 1; Cell 2; Cell3)

Click on the AutoSum icon on the formatting bar. Excel borders all the cells which contain a number with a dotted line.

Income	
	3200
	1000
	100
=SUM(C5:C8)	

73

If there is an empty cell between the numbers and the total this is also bordered. Since it does not contain a value it causes no problem at present. It does not affect our addition.

You can see that Excel shows 'SUM (C5:C8)'. This means that cells 'C5, C6, C7' and the empty cell 'C8' are being added up. The sign ':' means 'to'. Therefore Excel is adding up all the values in the cells from 'C5' to 'C8'.

Press the ⬅ key once and the total for the cells is produced.

Income

	3200
	1000
	100

Expenses

	1200
	120
	450
	600
	300

1 Enter the following values:

C5: '3200'	C13: '120'
C6: '1000'	C14: '450'
C7: '100'	C15: '600'
C12: '1200'	C16: '300'

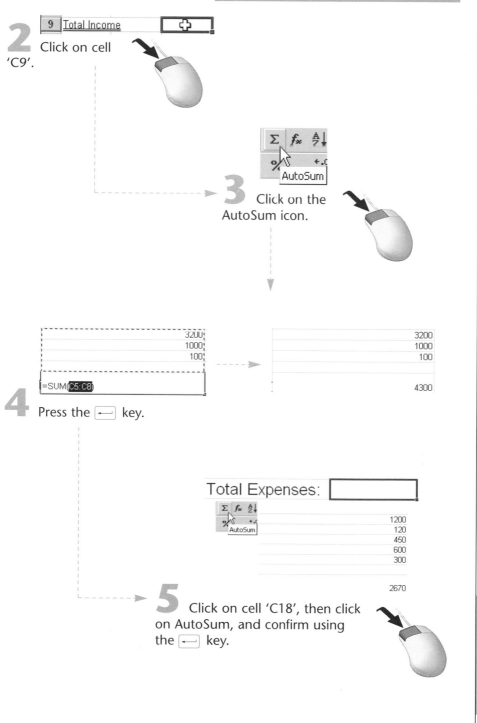

2 Click on cell 'C9'.

9 | Total Income

3 Click on the AutoSum icon.

Σ *fx* A↓
AutoSum

3200
1000
100

=SUM(C5:C8)

3200
1000
100

4300

4 Press the ← key.

Total Expenses:

Σ *fx* A↓
%
AutoSum

1200
120
450
600
300

2670

5 Click on cell 'C18', then click on AutoSum, and confirm using the ← key.

If you want to add up cells which are not next to each other press `Ctrl` and click them with the mouse.

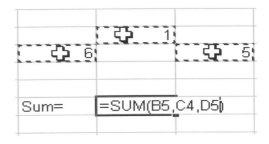

Sum= =SUM(B5,C4,D5)

For our income-expenses calculation click on the cell in which the total should appear. Now do the calculation:

Total = Cell – Cell

First put in the equals sign so that Excel knows that a formula will now appear, or in other words that it has to do a calculation. Then click on the cell with the total income, enter a '-' (minus sign) and activate the cell with the expenses. Finally confirm using the ⏎ key. The result: your income – expenses calculation is carried out.

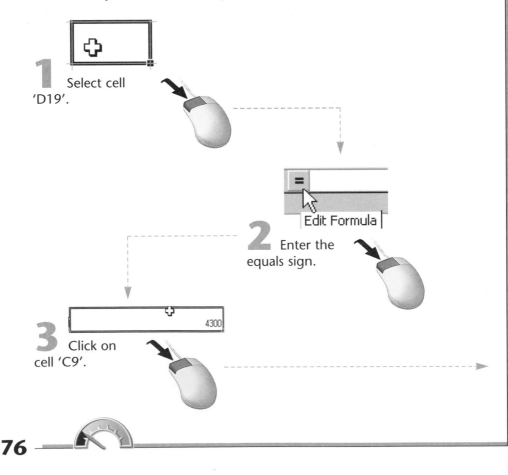

1 Select cell 'D19'.

2 Enter the equals sign.

Edit Formula

3 Click on cell 'C9'.

4300

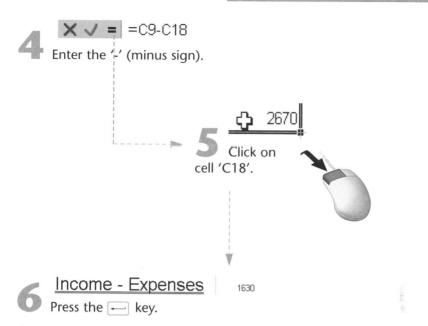

4 ✕ ✓ ≡ =C9-C18
Enter the '-' (minus sign).

5 2670
Click on
cell 'C18'.

6 Income - Expenses   1630
Press the ⟵ key.

In pounds sterling

You are perhaps wondering 'Which currency are we using for our calculations?' Our household budget is not set up in lire or dollars, but in pounds sterling. In order to assign the currency format to several cells at the same time, they must first be marked. Marking is necessary so that Excel knows which cells should have the currency format £.

CAUTION

When marking you must make sure that your mouse pointer is in the form of a white cross. Otherwise you will perform a different function.

If you only want to assign the format to one cell you do not need to mark anything, you just need to click on it.

Click on the Currency icon on the formatting bar and the cells will be assigned a currency format. It is easy to remember: the icon with the notes and coins is the right one.

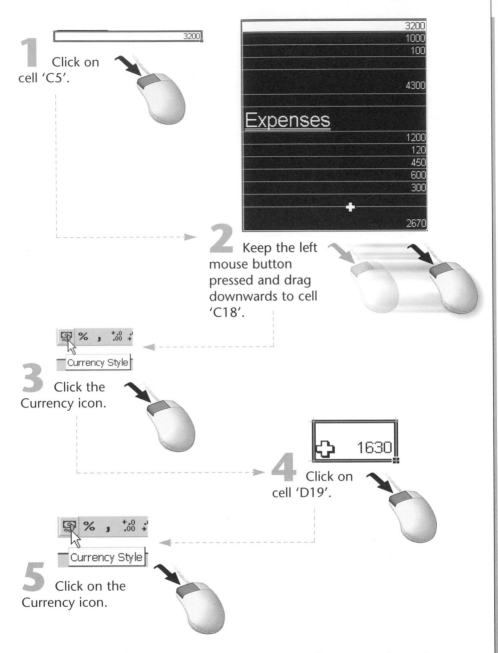

1 Click on cell 'C5'.

2 Keep the left mouse button pressed and drag downwards to cell 'C18'.

Currency Style

3 Click the Currency icon.

1630

4 Click on cell 'D19'.

Currency Style

5 Click on the Currency icon.

If you want to delete the currency again you have to call up the command FORMAT/CELLS. On the Number page choose the 'General' entry under Category.

The print preview

Before you print your household budget you should first check what it looks like on the screen. After all, you don't want to waste any paper. And it could be that you want to change something about the appearance of your calculation.

TIP

Before you print you should always use the print preview.

CAUTION

You cannot make any entries in the print preview.

You will find the print preview under the command of the same name in the FILE menu. It is even quicker via the icon on the standard toolbar. One click and you are in the print preview, that is, you are given a preview of what the document will look like when printed. You can enlarge or reduce the view of the calculation using Zoom. This does not change anything on the subsequent printout.

You get back to the original view by pressing the Esc key or via the Close button.

Print Preview

1 Click on the Print Preview icon.

Household budget

Income

Net salary	£	3,200.00
Rent receipts	£	1,000.00
Interest	£	100.00

Total income   £   4,300.00

Expenses

Rent	£	1,200.00
Telephone	£	120.00
Food, Drink	£	450.00
Clothing	£	600.00
Pocket money	£	300.00

Total expenses   £   2,670.00

Income - Expenses   £ 1,630.00

2 You will see the preview for subsequent printing.

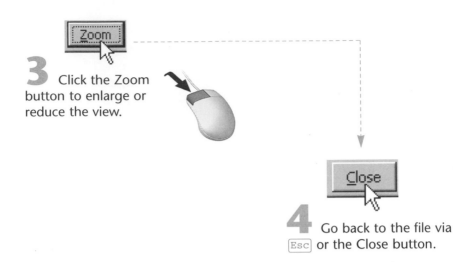

3 Click the Zoom button to enlarge or reduce the view.

4 Go back to the file via Esc or the Close button.

Moving cells

In the print preview it occurred to us that row 19 (Income – Expenses = £1630.00) would look better if it were moved down a row.

To do this you don't need to repeat the entry. Cell contents can be moved using the drag & drop method.

Drag & drop is the method used to move the contents of cells.

You click on a cell, keep the left mouse button pressed down and only release it again when you have reached the cell in which you want to deposit the contents. The appearance of the mouse pointer is crucial to the success of the drag & drop method. It tells you which function you can perform.

 In the worksheet the mouse pointer normally appears as a white cross. As you already know you click on the cells with this.

If, however, you position the mouse pointer on a line of the box it changes to an arrow.

The drag & drop method is only possible if the mouse pointer appears on the worksheet in the form of an arrow.

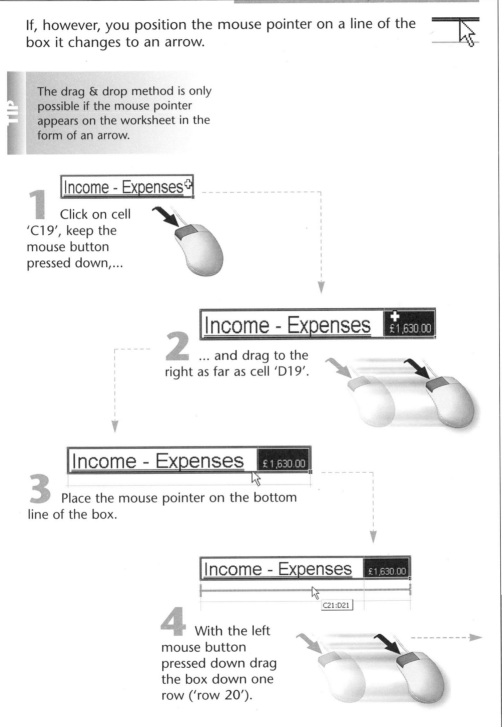

1 Click on cell 'C19', keep the mouse button pressed down,...

2 ... and drag to the right as far as cell 'D19'.

3 Place the mouse pointer on the bottom line of the box.

4 With the left mouse button pressed down drag the box down one row ('row 20').

81

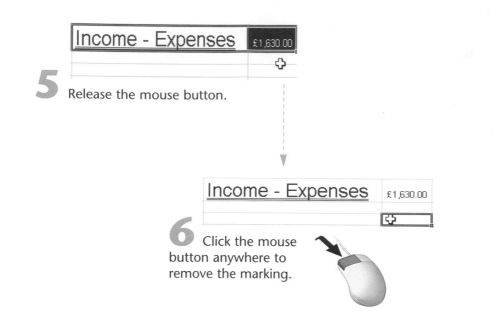

5 Release the mouse button.

6 Click the mouse button anywhere to remove the marking.

If, as a beginner, you have difficulties with the drag & drop method there is an alternative. Mark the cells that you would like to move. Then instead of dragging and dropping with the mouse, click on the icon with the scissors on it (Cut). Next click on the cell in which the contents should appear. Finally click on the Paste icon.

Summary: Moving cell contents

One cell	Click on the cell
More than one cell	Click on one cell
	Mark the cells
Drag & drop	Position the mouse pointer on a line of the box (mouse pointer as arrow!)
	Drag the cell to the new position
	Release mouse button
'Cut' and 'Paste' icons	Click on the scissors (Cut) icon
	Click on new cells
	Click on the Paste icon

The printout

At last you will see your calculation on paper. For this you use the Print icon. The sheet is printed once per click.

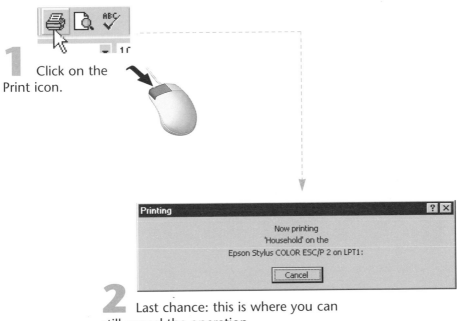

1 Click on the Print icon.

2 Last chance: this is where you can still cancel the operation.

The menu command FILE/PRINT can also be used for printing. And you can specify additional instructions here. For example, you can specify how many copies of your calculation you require or which printer to use, if you have both a black and white and a colour printer.

83

The Excel trainer

Exercise I

Alter the household budget:

Net salary	3500
Rent receipts	1200
Interest	50
Rent, electricity	1050
Telephone	80
Clothing	700
Pocket money	500

Exercise II

 Save the household budget under the name 'Household budget'.

Exercise III

 Open a new file.

Exercise IV

Write the word 'Excel' in cell A1.

Using drag & drop move it into cells B1, C1, D1, E3 and F3.

Exercise V

 Open a new file.

Exercise VI

Do the following calculations using AutoSum:

Receipts

Representative A	£1500.00
Representative B	£200.00
Representative C	£20.00
Representative D	£1300.00
Total:	

Expenses

Monday	£100.00
Tuesday	£300.00
Wednesday	£100.00
Thursday	£20.00
Friday	£200.00
Sunday	£30.00
Total	

Exercise VII

 Open a new file.

Exercise VIII

Set up the following household budget. Format the words 'Household budget' in bold/italics and 14 point. Give the following words the same format using the paintbrush: Expenses, Total, Total expenses, Income, Total income, Surplus income.

Adjust column A to the optimum width with a double click.

	A	B
1	**Household budget**	
2		
3	**Expenses**	**Total**
4	Apartment (rent)	£400.00
5	Additional costs	£150.00
6	Credit card	£100.00
7	Insurance	£60.00
8	Sports club	£25.00
9	Groceries	£200.00
10	Dog food	£25.00
11	Clothes	£140.00
12	Travel (car)	£75.00
13	Miscellaneous	£75.00
14	**Total expenses**	
15		
16	**Income**	
17	Salary (net)	£1,100.00
18	Side income	£120.00
19	**Total income**	
20		
21	**Surplus income**	

Exercise IX

You are familiar with the following icons; match up the icons with the functions and write the appropriate number next to each icon.

1. Currency

2. Italic

3. Print preview

4. Underline

5. Point size

6. Cut

7. Bold

8. New file

9. Print

10. Save file

11. Paste

Exercise X

Exit Excel without saving.

Car leasing compared

What's in this chapter?

In this chapter we are going to make a comparison: what are the most favourable circumstances for obtaining finance, taking out a loan and making a cash purchase? Which is the more advantageous when buying a car: obtaining finance or leasing? It doesn't matter what you compare, you will discover which is the best for you. Let's take the example of buying a car. You just have to find out the prices of vehicles at various car dealers, compare them, get in and drive off. On the road again! And watch out for that tree!

Leasing costs compared

	Vehicle 1	Vehicle 2	Vehicle 3	Vehicle 4
	20000	22000	25000	26500
	5000	5000	8000	12000
List price	5000	8000	9500	8000
Down payment				
Residual value	360	300	300	360
	36	36	36	36
Monthly instalments	12960	10800	10800	12960
Months				
Total monthly instalments	22960	23800	28300	32960
Purchase price				

You already know:

Your are going to learn:

Centring cell contents

The formatting bar gives you the possibility of aligning the contents of a cell (left-aligned, centred or right-aligned).

 The first icon determines that the contents appear on the left. If you click on the second icon the contents are centred. With the third icon the contents of the cell are right-aligned. You can select the icon before or after making an entry.

The personal choice of left-aligned, centred or right-aligned has nothing to do with the recognition of text and numbers in Excel. So, for example, you can have numbers left-aligned in the cells. It is still a number as far as the program is concerned.

≣	Text	123
≣	Text	123
≣	Text	123

As you already know, the software does not recognise the expression '123,-' as a number, but as text because of the punctuation marks '-' (normally text is left-aligned and numbers are right-aligned in cells). If you come up with the idea of formatting the value '123,-' using the Right Align icon, you will not outsmart Excel. It will still be classed as text.

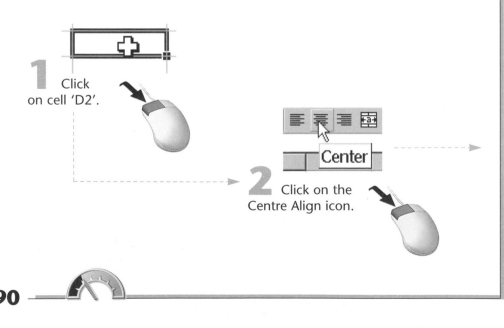

1 Click on cell 'D2'.

Center

2 Click on the Centre Align icon.

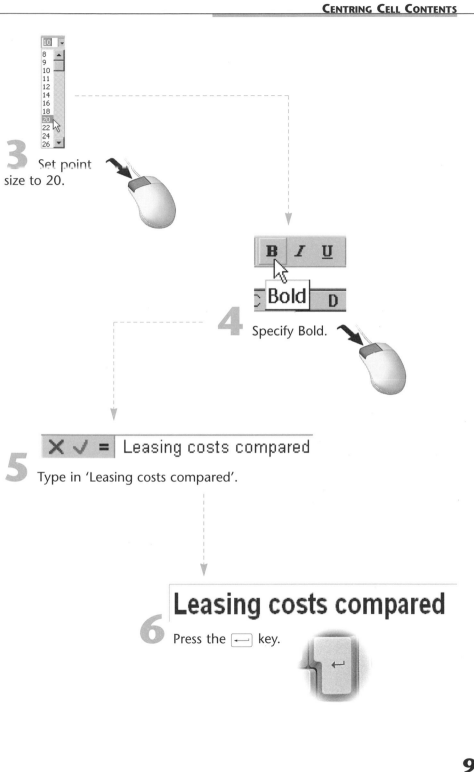

3 Set point size to 20.

4 Specify Bold.

5 Type in 'Leasing costs compared'.

X ✓ = Leasing costs compared

6 Press the ⟵ key.

Leasing costs compared

Colours

Now we shall add colour to our calculation. We 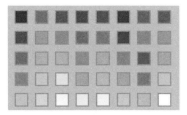 **Leasing costs compared** want to be design-conscious and accentuate the row 'Leasing costs compared' with colour. You simply lay down a background colour (fill colour) and/or select another colour for the characters.

 For the fill colour you choose the 'pouring bucket' icon.

If you click on the arrow next to it you will be given a choice. Just click on the desired colour with the left mouse button and the background in the cells will change. The same procedure applies to the font colour. Look for the 'underlined A' icon on the formatting bar. If you click on the arrow next to this icon you will again be given a choice of colours.

You can use a preset colour scheme by using the menu command Format/AutoFormat. In our example we want to show the inherent possibilities of Excel.

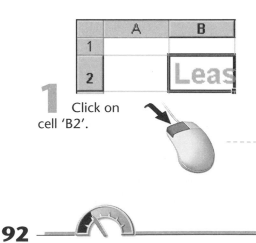

1 Click on cell 'B2'.

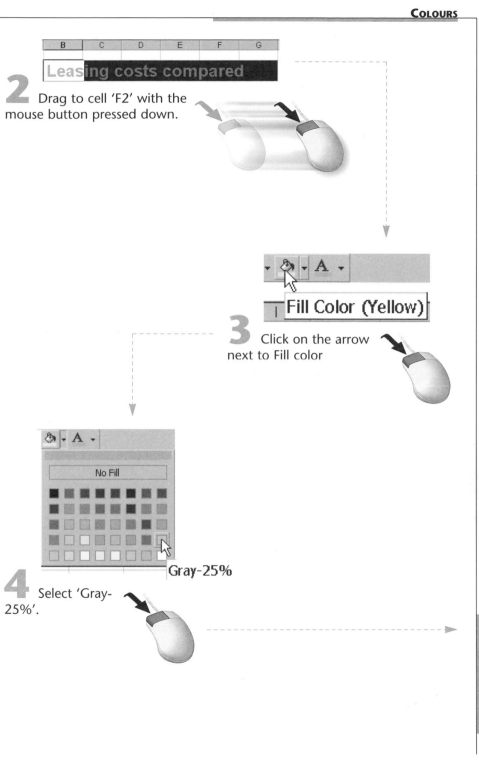

B	C	D	E	F	G

Leasing costs compared

2 Drag to cell 'F2' with the mouse button pressed down.

Fill Color (Yellow)

3 Click on the arrow next to Fill color

No Fill

Gray-25%

4 Select 'Gray-25%'.

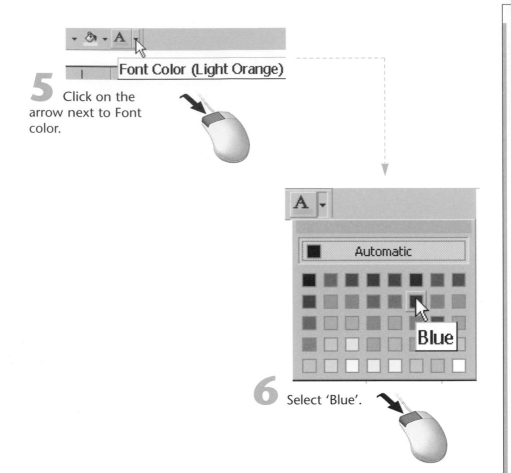

5 Click on the arrow next to Font color.

6 Select 'Blue'.

Erasing colours

Do you want to cancel the fill and type with black characters on a white background again? To do this you have to select the appropriate cell, i.e. you have to click on it. If several cells  are involved they have to be marked. If you click the arrow at Fill you will be given the same choice as before. Don't click on 'white', but choose 'No Fill'. If you would like 'normal' black again as the font colour, click on the arrow at Font Color and choose 'Automatic'.

Automatic cell filling

In our example we would like to make a direct comparison between

| Vehicle 1 | Vehicle 2 | Vehicle 3 | Vehicle 4 |

the prices of four different cars. Therefore we shall take 'Vehicle 1, Vehicle 2, Vehicle 3 and Vehicle 4'. However you don't need to write 'Vehicle 1, Vehicle 2,...' every time; instead you can use an Excel function called AutoFill. In the course of this book we shall keep returning to this function, since it is a great help for making entries and offers still further possibilities. In our calculation you write 'Vehicle 1' and Excel automatically fills in the other cells with 'Vehicle 2, Vehicle 3, Vehicle 4'. And, of course it works just the same with other categories:

Car 1, Car 2, Car 3, Car 4...

District 1, District 2, District 3, District 4...

Salesman 1, Salesman 2, Salesman 3, Salesman 4...

Constituency 1, Constituency 2, Constituency 3, Constiuency 4...

Naturally the number is not restricted to four; you can deal with as many categories as the worksheet has room for. Once again the success of the AutoFill function depends on the appearance of the mouse pointer. It always tells you what you can do or which function you can perform.

 At bottom right in the active cell you will see a small black box. This is used for AutoFill, and is called the handle.

If you position the mouse pointer on this it will change into a cross. This is the only way to inform Excel that a list follows. If you now drag into other cells with the mouse button pressed down they will be filled automatically, and with consecutive numbers. The program informs you what number has been reached in a yellow box. When you release the mouse button the cells are filled automatically.

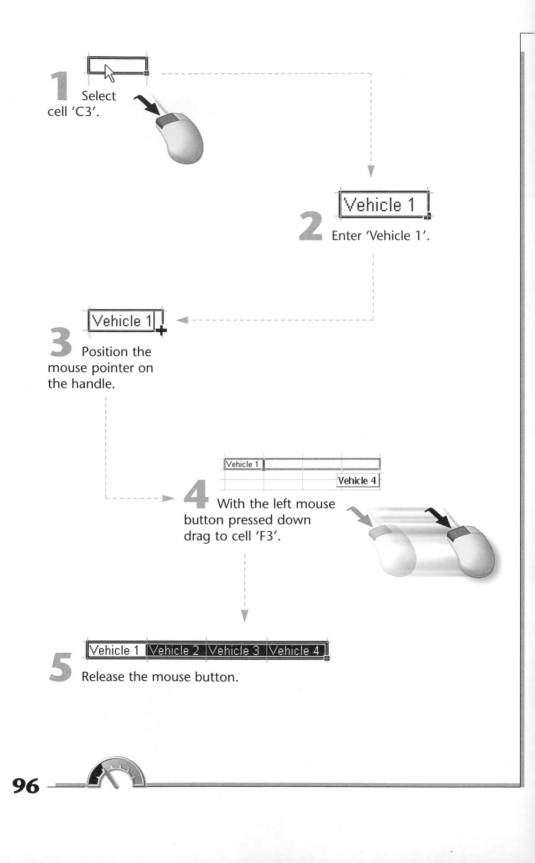

1 Select cell 'C3'.

2 Enter 'Vehicle 1'.

3 Position the mouse pointer on the handle.

4 With the left mouse button pressed down drag to cell 'F3'.

5 Release the mouse button.

1,2,3 ...No problem!

Of course you can also list numbers without text as '1,2,3,4' etc. For example, enter a '1' into a cell, press the `Ctrl` key and keep it pressed. Activate the handle and drag into other cells (a small + appears on the mouse pointer). The numbers '2,3,4' etc. are entered.

Centring headings

First enter the text for our calculation. Then adjust the column – we are using column 'B' – to the optimum width with a double click on the line between columns 'B' and 'C'. The column to the left of the dividing line automatically adjusts to accommodate the longest text.

Now the heading 'Leasing costs compared' does not look quite right. It is no longer centred above our calculation but is set slightly over to the right. This has happened because we adjusted the width of column B. But this time we will not use the Centre Align icon. That would simply align the contents of the cells. Instead click on the Merge and Center icon. Excel then automatically centres the heading above the calculation. When you click on the icon you will see the program 'scanning' the columns on the screen. You will see a slight 'flickering' on the monitor.

	A	B	C	D
1				
2		**Leasing cost**		
3			Vehicle 1	
4		List price		
5		Down payment		
6		Residual value		
7				
8		Monthly installments		
9		Months		
10		Total monthly installments		
11				
12		Purchase price		

1 Enter the following text into the cells:

B4: 'List price:'
B5: 'Down payment:'
B6: 'Residual value:'
B8: 'Monthly instalments:'
B9: 'Months:'
B10: 'Total monthly instalments:'
B12: 'Purchase price:'

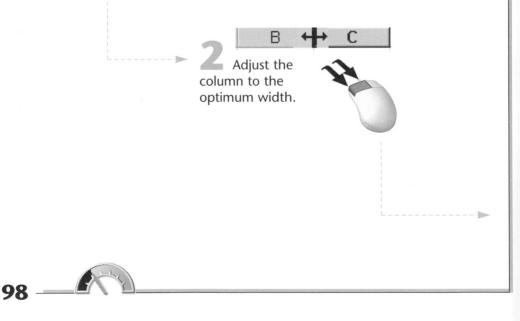

2 Adjust the column to the optimum width.

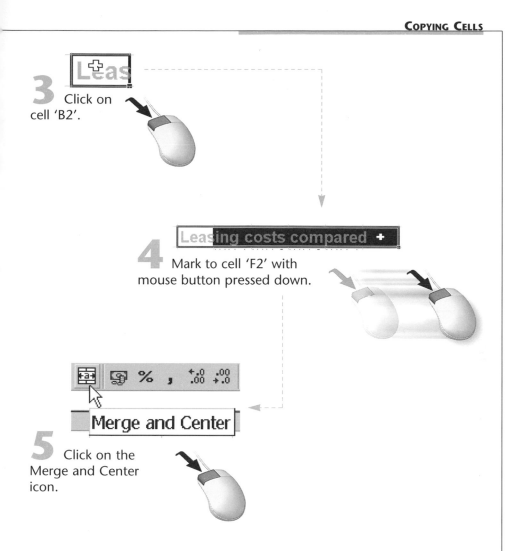

3 Click on cell 'B2'.

4 Mark to cell 'F2' with mouse button pressed down.

5 Click on the Merge and Center icon.

Copying cells

First we enter the numerical values (which you have obtained from your car dealer!). The leasing period is 36 months for all four vehicles. We will obviously make use of that, namely with the AutoFill function. However, we can only use this function for copying because the cells in our example are next to each other. Other ways of copying are available, but we shall deal with them in later chapters. For that reason the heading ought to say 'Copying cells using the AutoFill function'.

Position the mouse pointer on the handle and drag over the target cells. The result: the contents of the first cell are pasted (copied) into the others.

	A	B	C	D	E	F
1						
2		**Leasing costs compared**				
3			Vehicle 1	Vehicle 2	Vehicle 3	Vehicle 4
4		List price	20000	22000	25000	26500
5		Down payment	5000	5000	8000	12000
6		Residual value	5000	8000	9500	8000
7						
8		Monthly instalments	360	300	300	360
9		Months	36			
10		Total monthly instalments				
11						
12		Purchase price				

1 Enter the following numbers into the cells.

C4: '20,000'   E4: '25,000'

C5: '5,000'   E5: '8,000'

C6: '5,000'   E6: '9,500'

C8: '360'   E8: '300'

C9: '36'   F4: '26,500'

D4: '22,000'   F5: '12,000'

D5: '5,000'   F6: 8,000'

D6: '8,000'   F8: '360'

D8: '300'

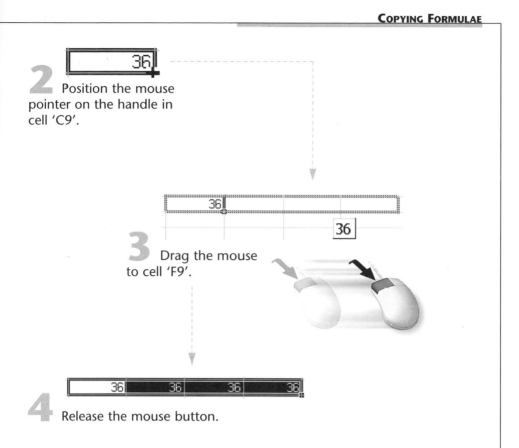

2 Position the mouse pointer on the handle in cell 'C9'.

3 Drag the mouse to cell 'F9'.

4 Release the mouse button.

Copying formulae

It is difficult to compare how expensive or how reasonable the individual vehicles actually are. The financial arrangements are too different. We have to determine the cells 'Total monthly instalments' and 'Purchase price'. We shall deal with the total monthly instalments first. For this the monthly instalment has to be multiplied by the number of instalments. Quite a simple sum:

Total monthly instalments = monthly instalment * months

C10 = C8 * C9

101

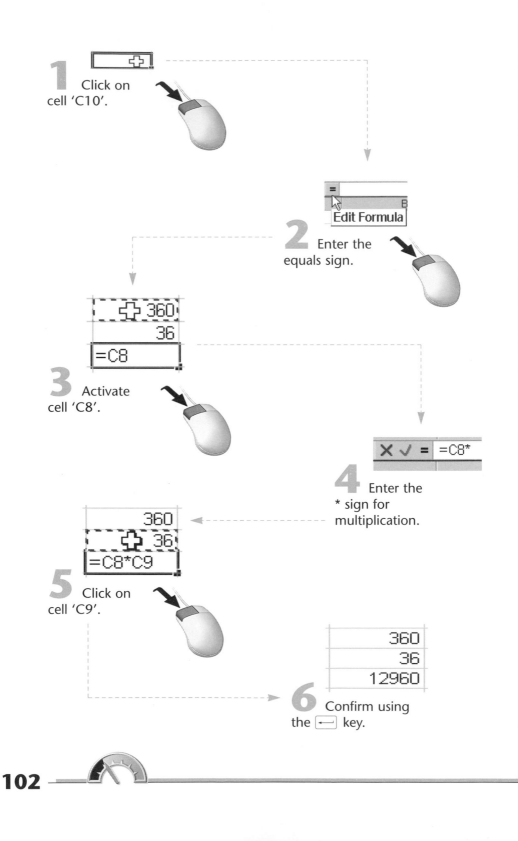

1 Click on cell 'C10'.

2 Enter the equals sign.

Edit Formula

3 Activate cell 'C8'.

360
36
=C8

4 Enter the * sign for multiplication.

X ✓ = =C8*

5 Click on cell 'C9'.

360
36
=C8*C9

6 Confirm using the ⏎ key.

360
36
12960

What sort of reference?

Relative references

With all four vehicles the total monthly instalments are obtained by multiplying the monthly instalments by the number of months.

As it happens the necessary data are in the same rows:

Row 8: Monthly instalments

Row 9: Months

Row 10: Total monthly instalments

List price	20000	22000	25000	26500
Down payment	5000	5000	8000	12000
Residual value	5000	8000	9500	8000
Monthly instalments	360	300	300	360
Months	36	36	36	36
Total monthly instalments	12960	10800	10800	12960

Up to now we have copied cell contents in Excel. But it is also possible to duplicate formulae. Excel is even so clever that it calculates the columns instantly.

Activate a cell in which there is already a formula, then position the mouse pointer on the handle so that it changes into a cross again. Now drag with the mouse button into the other cells. The result: Excel inserts the correct answer into the appropriate cells. And of course you don't have to copy formulae from cells to the right, you can also copy to the left, up and down.

You always duplicate formulae which relate to adjacent cells. In Excel these cells are called 'relative references'.

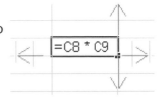

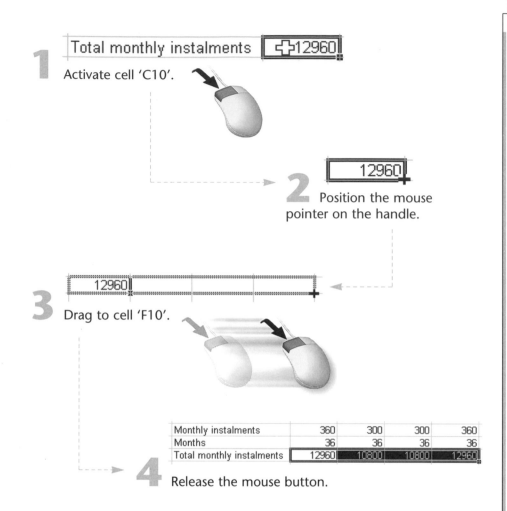

1 Activate cell 'C10'.

Total monthly instalments   ⊕12960

2 Position the mouse pointer on the handle.

12960

3 Drag to cell 'F10'.

12960

4 Release the mouse button.

Monthly instalments	360	300	300	360
Months	36	36	36	36
Total monthly instalments	12960	10800	10800	12960

Purchase price

First we have to enter a formula for the calculation. We are assuming that you will keep the car at the end of the leasing period. The purchase price is the down payment plus the residual value plus the total monthly instalments.

Purchase price = down payment + residual value + total monthly instalments

Cell C12 = Cell C5 + Cell C6 + Cell C10

We can only make partial use of the AutoSum since only two cells are next to each other (i.e. one on top of the other).

C12 = Sum (C5:C6) + C10.

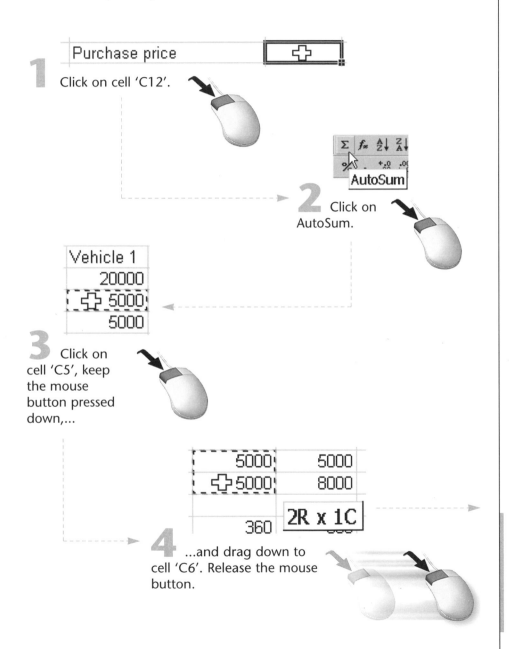

1 Click on cell 'C12'.

2 Click on AutoSum.

3 Click on cell 'C5', keep the mouse button pressed down,...

4 ...and drag down to cell 'C6'. Release the mouse button.

5 X ✓ = =SUM(C5:C6)

Click on the
formula bar just after ')'.

6 X ✓ = =SUM(C5:C6)+

Enter a plus sign (+).

| 36 | 36 |
| 12960 | 10800 |

=SUM(C5:C6)+C10

7 Click on cell
'C10'.

✓ = =SUM(C5:C6)+C10

B

Enter

8 Confirm your entry.

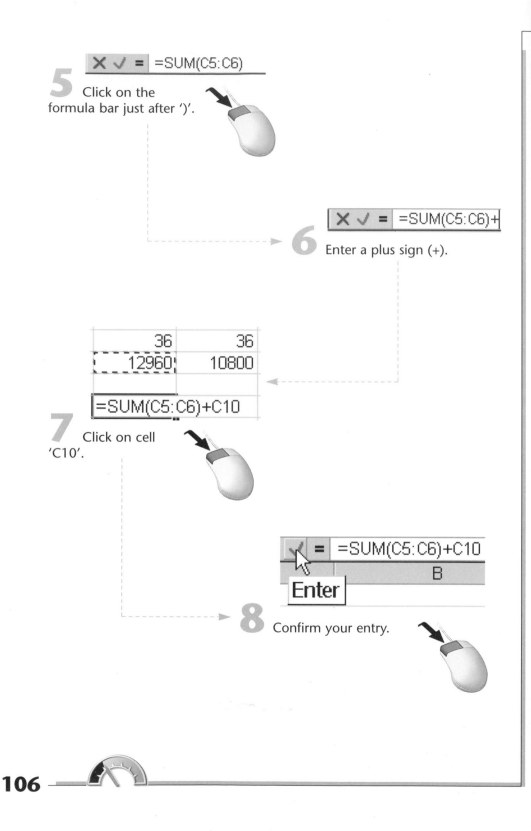

Copying formulae

Since the purchase price calculation applies to all the vehicles – i.e. cells – you only need to copy the formula.

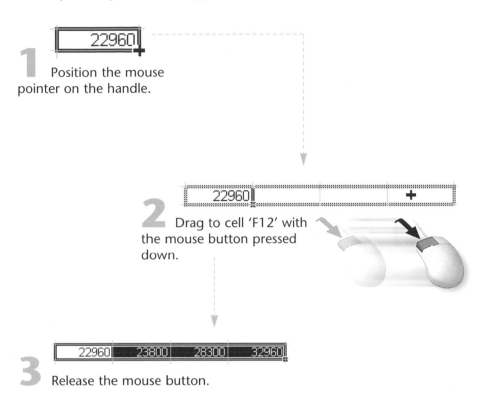

1 Position the mouse pointer on the handle.

2 Drag to cell 'F12' with the mouse button pressed down.

3 Release the mouse button.

...on with the calculation!

At the moment Vehicle 1 seems to be the most favourable option. Up to now, however, we have only ascertained the purchase price of the cars. But our calculation calculates the leasing cost, i.e. the additional expense of the vehicle. That is the difference between the purchase price and the list price.

Leasing cost = purchase price – list price

107

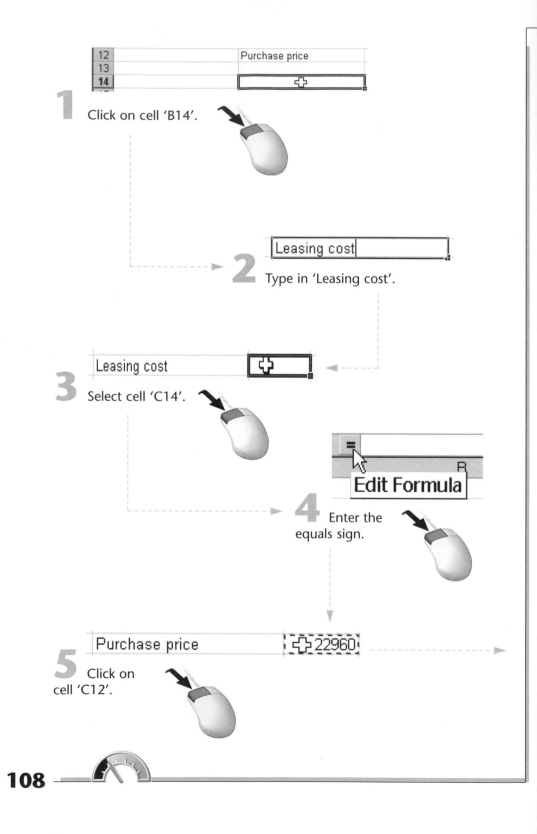

12	Purchase price
13	
14	✛

1 Click on cell 'B14'.

Leasing cost|

2 Type in 'Leasing cost'.

Leasing cost   ✛

3 Select cell 'C14'.

=   R

Edit Formula

4 Enter the equals sign.

Purchase price   ✛22960

5 Click on cell 'C12'.

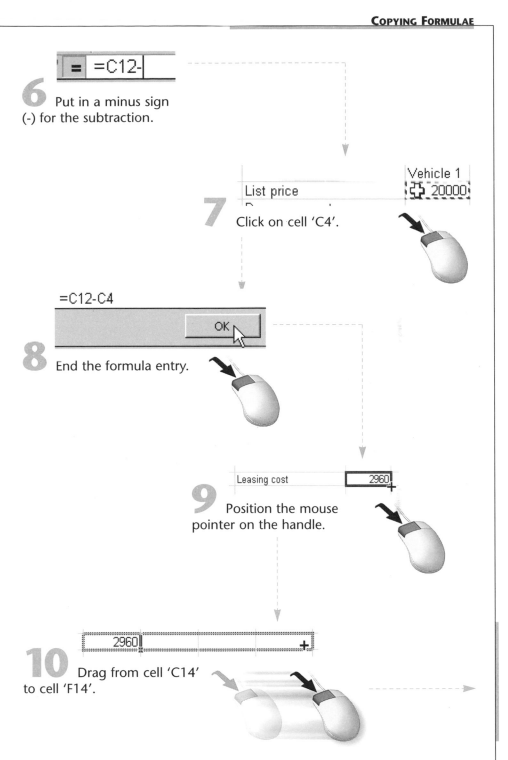

= | =C12-|

6 Put in a minus sign (-) for the subtraction.

List price   Vehicle 1   20000

7 Click on cell 'C4'.

=C12-C4

OK

8 End the formula entry.

Leasing cost   2960

9 Position the mouse pointer on the handle.

2960   +

10 Drag from cell 'C14' to cell 'F14'.

11
	2960	1800	3300	6460

Release the mouse button.

12
Leasing cost		2960	1800	3300	➕ 6460

Mark cells 'B14' to 'F14'.

No Fill

Gray-25%

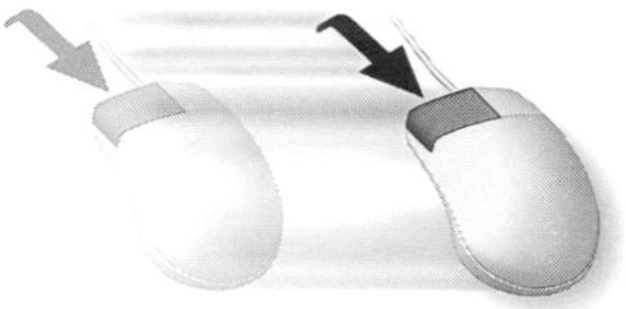

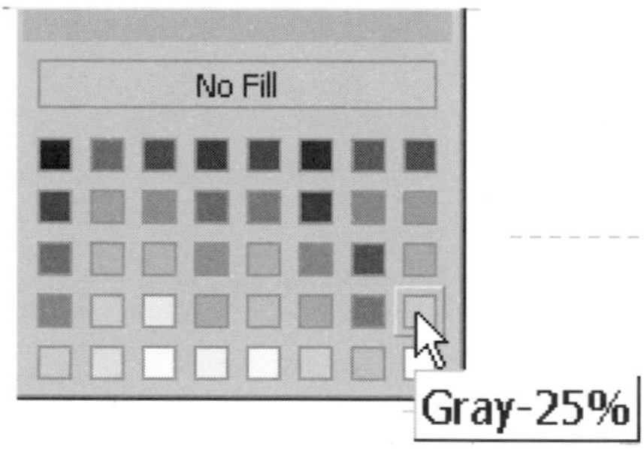

13 Give the cells a background of 'Gray-25%'.

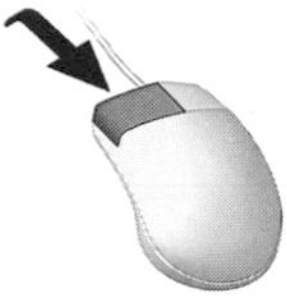

Vehicle 1	Vehicle 2	Vehicle 3	Veh ➕ 4

14 Mark cells 'C3' to 'F3',...

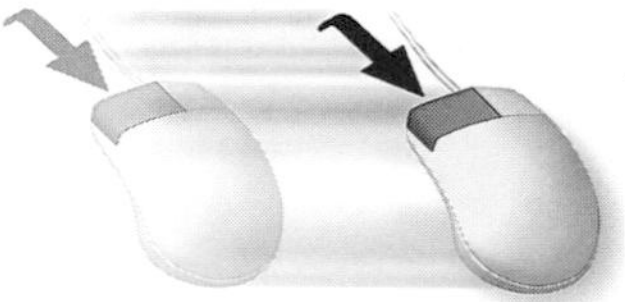

Align Right

15 ... and Right Align them.

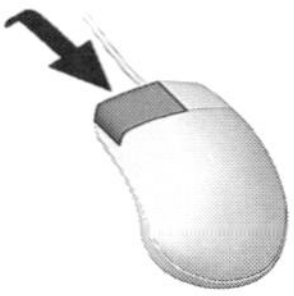

Save

16 Click on the Save icon.

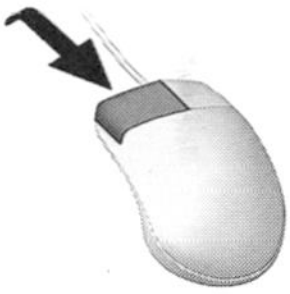

File name:	Leasing	▼
Save as type:	Microsoft Excel Workbook	▼

17 Enter the name 'Leasing' in the File Name box.

Save
Cancel

18 Save the file.

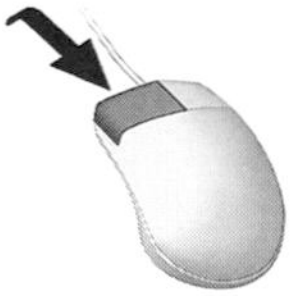

Our calculation is finished. Have fun buying your car!

The Excel trainer

Naturally you need to practise copying formulae. You can do this with our practice exercise.

	District 1	District 2	District 3	Total
Representative 1	2000	400	800	3200
Representative 2	700	800	900	2400
Representative 3	1000	1000	800	3200
Total	3700	2200	2500	

As mentioned earlier, formulae can be copied not only from left to right, but also from top to bottom (and vice versa). Here are the instructions step by step.

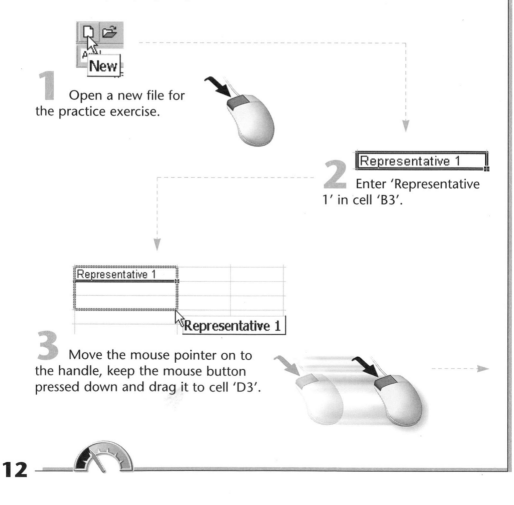

1 Open a new file for the practice exercise.

2 Enter 'Representative 1' in cell 'B3'.

3 Move the mouse pointer on to the handle, keep the mouse button pressed down and drag it to cell 'D3'.

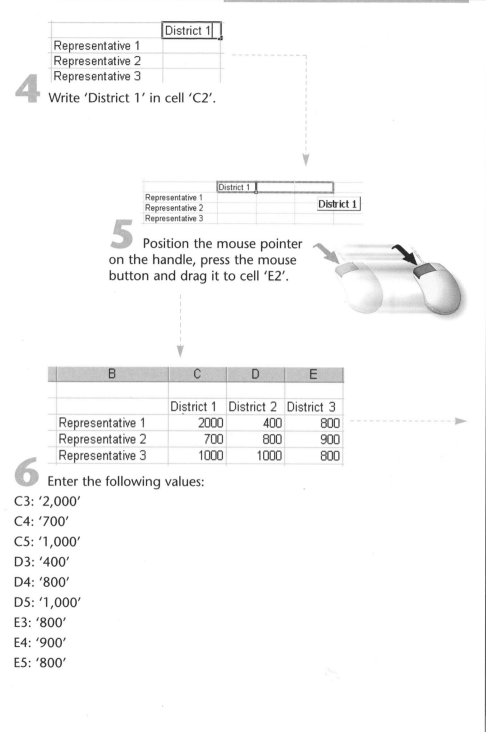

	District 1
Representative 1	
Representative 2	
Representative 3	

4 Write 'District 1' in cell 'C2'.

	District 1		District 1
Representative 1			
Representative 2			
Representative 3			

5 Position the mouse pointer on the handle, press the mouse button and drag it to cell 'E2'.

	B	C	D	E
		District 1	District 2	District 3
	Representative 1	2000	400	800
	Representative 2	700	800	900
	Representative 3	1000	1000	800

6 Enter the following values:

C3: '2,000'

C4: '700'

C5: '1,000'

D3: '400'

D4: '800'

D5: '1,000'

E3: '800'

E4: '900'

E5: '800'

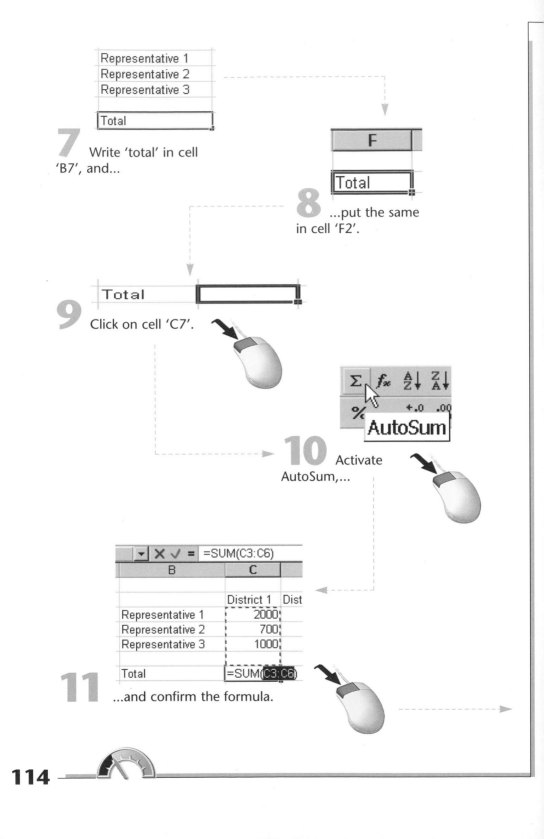

Representative 1	
Representative 2	
Representative 3	
Total	

7 Write 'total' in cell 'B7', and...

F	
Total	

8 ...put the same in cell 'F2'.

Total	

9 Click on cell 'C7'.

Σ f_x A↓ Z↓
   Z↓ A↓
%   +.0 .00
AutoSum

10 Activate AutoSum,...

	=SUM(C3:C6)
B	**C**
	District 1	Dist
Representative 1	2000
Representative 2	700
Representative 3	1000
Total	=SUM(C3:C6)

11 ...and confirm the formula.

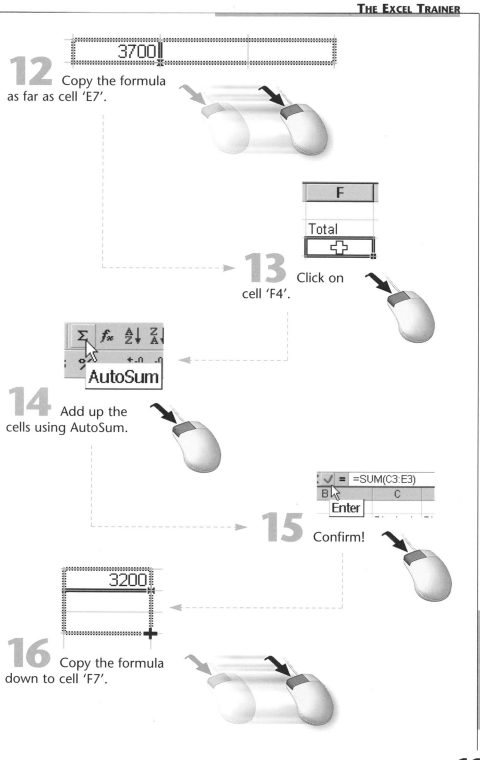

12 Copy the formula as far as cell 'E7'.

13 Click on cell 'F4'.

14 Add up the cells using AutoSum.

15 Confirm!

16 Copy the formula down to cell 'F7'.

Calculating exchange rates

What's in this chapter?

Do you like travelling? Then it would be interesting to know how many pounds there are to the dollar, franc, 100 yen or 1,000 lire. After the next calculation you will be permanently informed how much ten, twenty, thirty or fifty pounds is worth. If the exchange rate changes, you don't have to work out what you will get for your money every time. And you can also calculate interest for a savings account, loans or a credit arrangement, the value of securities or even the Euro. If the interest rate or price changes, enter the new rate and Excel will calculate the individual amounts.

You already know:

Your are going to learn:

Entering foreign currencies

Our calculation tells us how many US dollars we will receive for our money. Of course you already know that you cannot calculate with text. If, for example, you enter '1$' for one dollar, the contents of the cell will be aligned on the left. This means that Excel does not consider the entry to be a number for calculation, but text.

$$\boxed{\$ \quad 1.00}$$

The cell must be, as it were, converted – formatted – to dollars. If you click on the Currency Style icon on the formatting bar you will be given the £ sign for pounds sterling. But what about the other currencies? To indicate these call up the menu command Format/Cells. Since we are working with numbers, select the Number tab. Under Category you will see a selection of possible formats. In our practice calculation we are working with currency therefore you need the Currency line. Click on the down arrow in the Symbol list box. Here you will find the currencies of various countries, for example Germany, Spain and France. And obviously the US dollar is here too.

Exact to a decimal point

On the Number page you can also set the decimal places (1; 1.2; 1.23; 1.234 etc) of numbers up to a maximum of 30: 1.234567890123456789 01234567890.

Since we won't use any decimal places for our calculation of dollars we shall change this to '0'.

Decimal places: |0|

Sample
1$

The preview window is a great help. Here you can see what your number looks like as soon as you confirm your format with OK.

At Negative numbers you determine whether a negative figure should be presented in red or with a minus sign (or both). We don't need to use this in our calculation at the moment, but it would be useful in a calculation of income and expenditure or profit and loss. You can see whether you are dealing with figures in the black or in the red.

Negative numbers:

-£1,234
£1,234
-£1,234
-£1,234

Instead of getting to the Number tabbed page by the more arduous route of the FORMAT/CELLS menu, you can use the considerably quicker key combination Ctrl + 1 (first press the 1 key, keep it pressed, then type Ctrl and release both keys).

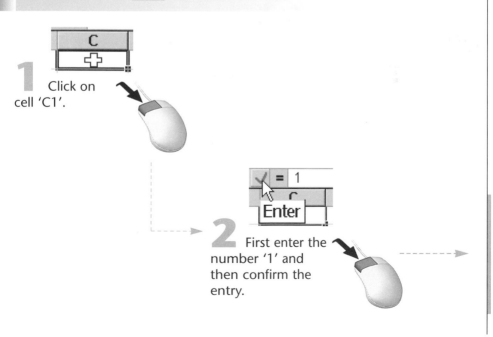

1 Click on cell 'C1'.

= 1

Enter

2 First enter the number '1' and then confirm the entry.

119

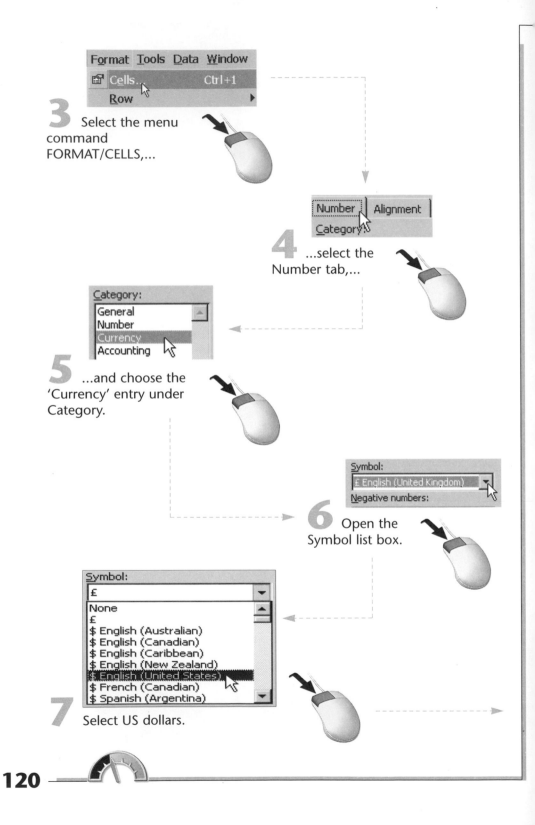

Format Tools Data Window

🖺 Cells...   Ctrl+1

Row   ▸

3 Select the menu command FORMAT/CELLS,...

Number | Alignment
Category

4 ...select the Number tab,...

Category:

General
Number
Currency
Accounting

5 ...and choose the 'Currency' entry under Category.

Symbol:

£ English (United Kingdom) ▼

Negative numbers:

6 Open the Symbol list box.

Symbol:

£   ▼

None   ▲
£
$ English (Australian)
$ English (Canadian)
$ English (Caribbean)
$ English (New Zealand)
$ English (United States)
$ French (Canadian)
$ Spanish (Argentina)   ▼

7 Select US dollars.

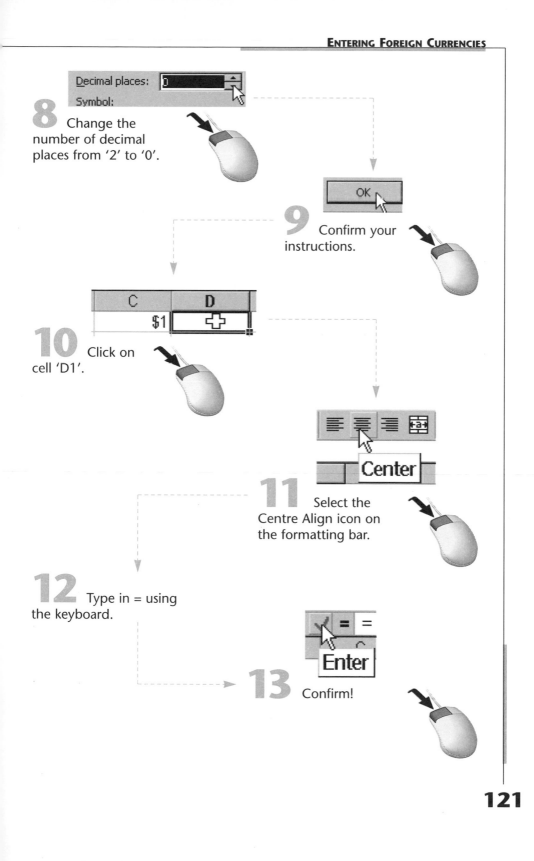

Decimal places:
Symbol:

8 Change the number of decimal places from '2' to '0'.

OK

9 Confirm your instructions.

C	D
$1	

10 Click on cell 'D1'.

Center

11 Select the Centre Align icon on the formatting bar.

12 Type in = using the keyboard.

Enter

13 Confirm!

121

In pounds and pence

To enter a number in the £ format, you use the Currency Style icon on the formatting bar. Once entered, the number automatically has two decimal places (£1.50). However you know from the TV news that in foreign currency dealing the dollar is set with three decimal places (£1.503).

Naturally we shall do that too. You can follow the longer menu route via FORMAT/CELLS/Number tab and enter '3' at Decimal places.

But it's quicker and more convenient to go via the icons on the formatting bar. There are two to choose from. One is used to decrease the number of decimal places, the other to increase it. Since we have only two decimal places (£1.50) after the point, we need to add one (£1.503).

+.0 .00	0.606	Increase Decimal
.00 +.0	0.6	Decrease Decimal

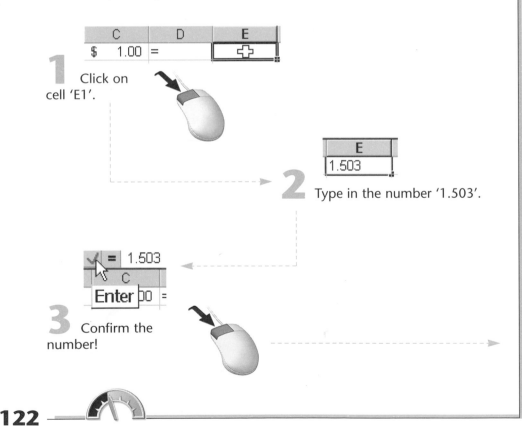

1 Click on cell 'E1'.

	C	D	E
	$ 1.00	=	✚

E
1.503

2 Type in the number '1.503'.

✓ =	1.503
	C
Enter	00 =

3 Confirm the number!

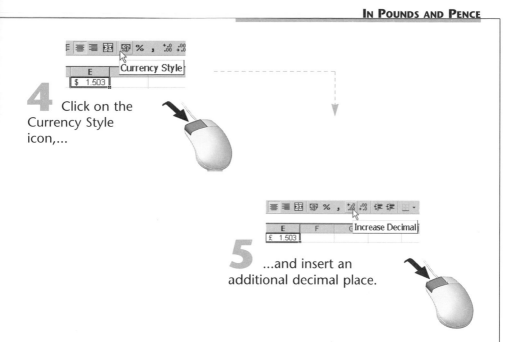

4 Click on the Currency Style icon,...

5 ...and insert an additional decimal place.

Transferring formats

First enter the dollar values. We will not take the longer menu route to give the numbers the 'dollar' format, but instead we shall use the paintbrush icon on the standard toolbar. We can transfer the currency format with this and save time. The $ symbol is already present in a cell. This cell must be selected. Click on the Format Painter icon and 'pass over' the cells which should also have dollar values.

5	10
6	20
7	30
8	50

1 Enter the following numbers:

A5: '10'

A6: '20'

A7: '30'

A8:'50'

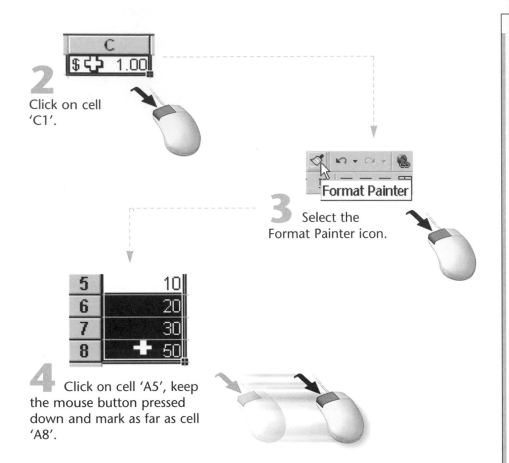

2 Click on cell 'C1'.

3 Select the Format Painter icon.

4 Click on cell 'A5', keep the mouse button pressed down and mark as far as cell 'A8'.

Copying and pasting

We need the equals sign four times altogether (it could be even more!). You can enter them one after the other. But why take so much trouble when it's soooo easy! We copy from the cell which already has the (centred) equals sign into another cell. After that we use the handle and all the cells will contain the (centred) equals sign.

$10	=
$20	=
$30	=
$50	=

Copying is similar to cutting. With cutting the original disappears; with copying, on the other hand, the original is retained.

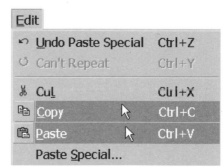

1st possibility: you can duplicate via the menu. However that is the longest route. Click on the cell to be copied and call up the menu command EDIT/COPY. Then click on the target cell and select the menu command EDIT/PASTE (six mouse actions altogether!).

2nd possibility: the icons on the standard toolbar offer a shorter route. To take this route you click on the cell to be copied, activate the Copy icon and insert into the target cell using the Paste icon (four mouse actions in all!)

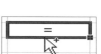

3rd possibility: the drag & drop method is undoubtedly the quickest copying procedure. This method only requires two mouse actions. Click on the cell to be copied. Now position the mouse pointer on a line of the active cell, press the Ctrl key and keep it pressed. Then operate the left mouse button and keep this pressed down too. A small cross or plus sign (+) appears on the mouse pointer. This means that Excel's copying function is active. Now move the mouse pointer on to the target cell and release the mouse button and the Ctrl key. The result: the cell contents have been copied.

Copying cell contents using drag & drop is carried out in a similar way to the cut function. But the Ctrl key must be pressed too.

125

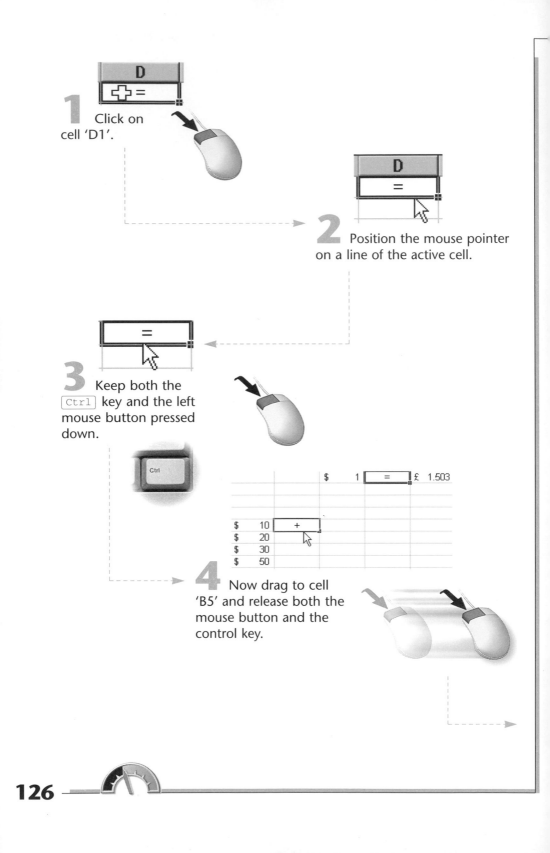

1 Click on cell 'D1'.

2 Position the mouse pointer on a line of the active cell.

3 Keep both the `Ctrl` key and the left mouse button pressed down.

| | | | $ | 1 | = | £ 1.503 |

$	10	+		
$	20			
$	30			
$	50			

4 Now drag to cell 'B5' and release both the mouse button and the control key.

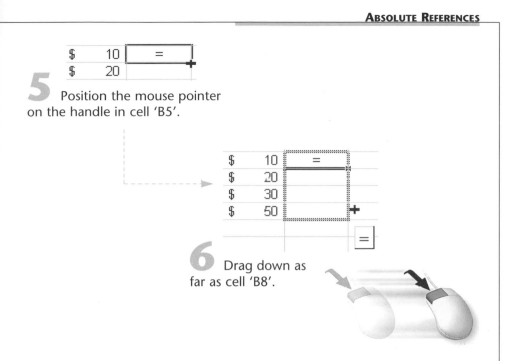

5 Position the mouse pointer on the handle in cell 'B5'.

6 Drag down as far as cell 'B8'.

Absolute references

All that is missing now is the formula for the calculation. If a dollar is worth £1.503, then £10, £20, £30 or £50 would be worth 10, 20, 30, or 50 times this amount.

 1 dollar = £1.503

10 dollars = £1.503 * 10

20 dollars = £1.503 * 20

30 dollars = £1.503 * 30

50 dollars = £1.503 * 50

Since in Excel we not only calculate with numbers but also with cells, our formulae are worded as follows:

	A	B	C	D	E
1			$ 1	=	£ 1.503
2					
3					
4					
5	$ 10	=			
6	$ 20	=			
7	$ 30	=			
8	$ 50	=			

C5 = E1 * A5

C6 = E1 * A6

C7 = E1 * A7

C8 = E1 * A8

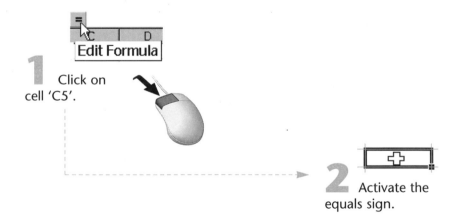

1 Click on cell 'C5'.

2 Activate the equals sign.

Now you have the problem that the formula bar is concealing the cells you would like to work with i.e.'C1' to 'E1'.

Moving the formula bar

The information is in the first row. So that we can see it better we shall move part of the formula bar. Click on the grey area with the left mouse button, keep the mouse button pressed down and drag the bar – as in the drag & drop method- to another position in the work area where it will not be in the way. With every new start, i.e. when you click on the equals sign, the formula bar is back in its original position

| [?] | Formula result = | OK | Cancel |

1 Click on the grey area, keep the mouse button pressed down,...

| [?] | Formula result = | OK | Cancel |
| 2 |

2 ... and drag the bar to a position in the work area...

| | $1 | = | £ 0.606 |

$10	=	=
$20	=
$30	=
$50	=

| [?] | Formula result = | OK | Cancel |

3 ... where it is not in the way.

129

Copying formulae

... and on with the calculation. We shall enter the formula mentioned above. For the first row it reads:

C5 = E1 * A5

Since the formula is identical for all cells (relative references), we can copy it into the lower cells using the handle.

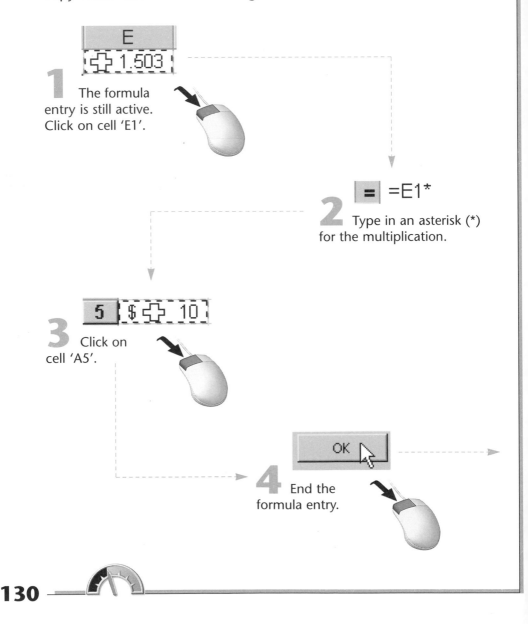

1 The formula entry is still active. Click on cell 'E1'.

2 Type in an asterisk (*) for the multiplication.

3 Click on cell 'A5'.

4 End the formula entry.

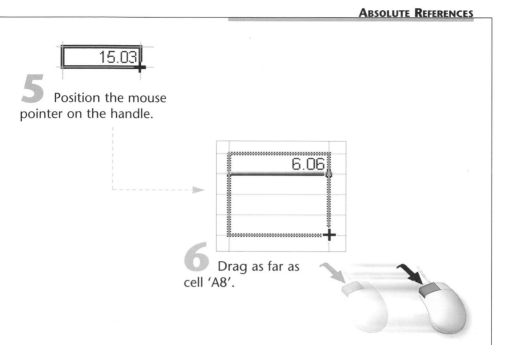

5 Position the mouse pointer on the handle.

6 Drag as far as cell 'A8'.

No values or incorrect values?

But what's happened? Three of the cells have been given no value or rather a '0'. That can't be right! Only the value in the first cell is correct. Why has that happened? When copying formulae Excel always counts 'one more'.

$	10	=	15.03
$	20	=	0
$	30	=	0
$	50	=	0

Thus the subsequent cells relate to 'A6 and E2, A7 and E3, A8 and E4'. This is correct for column 'A', but not for column 'E'.

131

Cell references

The value for one dollar is only in one and the same cell (here 'E1'). Every copied formula relates to this cell. Therefore it would be wrong to 'count up' here. The program must be informed that it should always take the value from one particular cell.

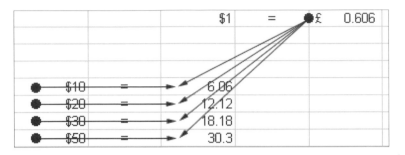

This is done by means of the dollar sign, which in this connection has nothing to do with the currency. '$E$1' means that the value concerned is always in cell E1. In this way Excel does not 'add one' when copying formulae.

If, when copying, several formulae relate to one and the same cell, it must be entered with the dollar sign $ (be sure not to confuse this with the currency).

You can add the dollar sign before or after entry. If you have already entered the cell name you only need to press the F4 key.

When copied formulae relate to one particular cell the technical term for this in Excel is absolute reference or absolute references.

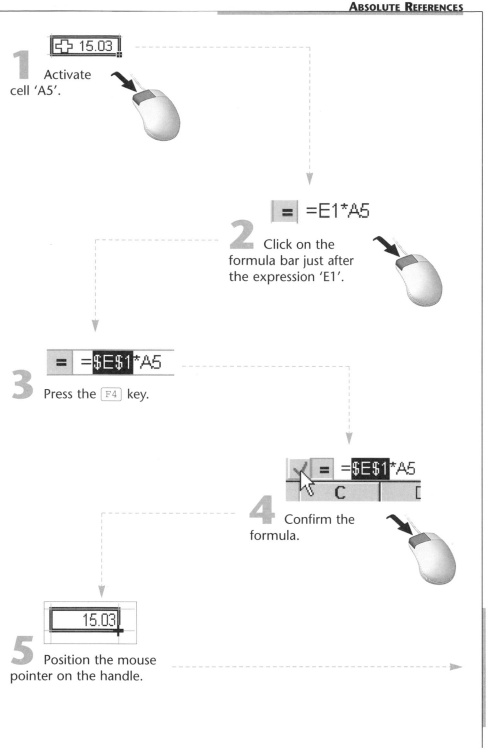

1 Activate cell 'A5'.

⊕ 15.03

2 Click on the formula bar just after the expression 'E1'.

= =E1*A5

3 Press the F4 key.

= =$E$1*A5

4 Confirm the formula.

✓ = =$E$1*A5

5 Position the mouse pointer on the handle.

15.03

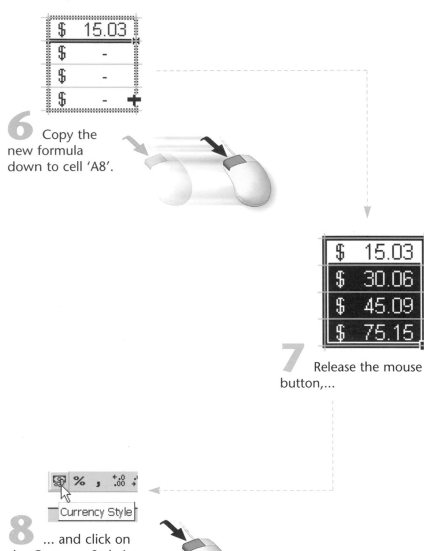

6 Copy the new formula down to cell 'A8'.

7 Release the mouse button,...

8 ... and click on the Currency Style icon.

Currency Style

Creating your own currency formats

Let's move on to the second calculation. The first step merely reinforces what you have just learnt and is good training for the Excel student. Here we enter numbers, mark them and format them in the currency £.

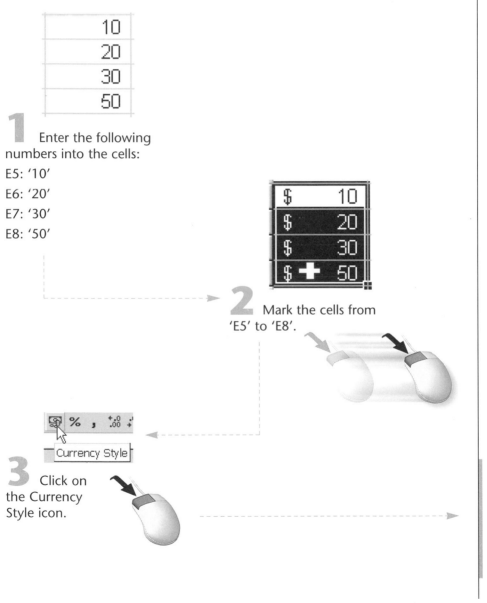

1 Enter the following numbers into the cells:

E5: '10'

E6: '20'

E7: '30'

E8: '50'

2 Mark the cells from 'E5' to 'E8'.

Currency Style

3 Click on the Currency Style icon.

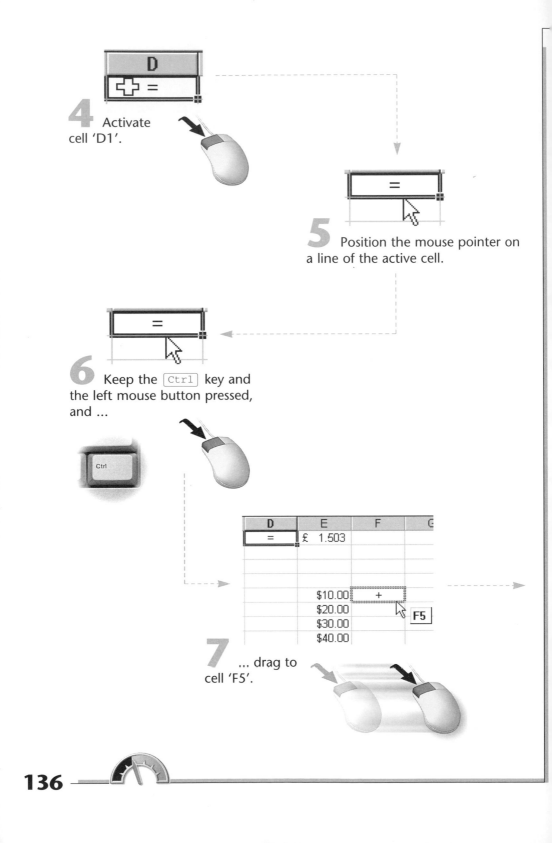

4 Activate cell 'D1'.

5 Position the mouse pointer on a line of the active cell.

6 Keep the `Ctrl` key and the left mouse button pressed, and ...

7 ... drag to cell 'F5'.

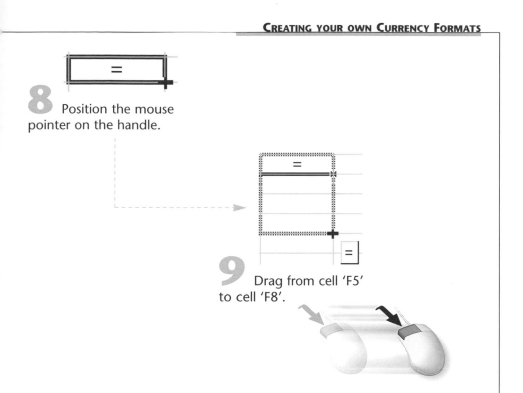

8 Position the mouse pointer on the handle.

9 Drag from cell 'F5' to cell 'F8'.

Pounds in dollars

Back to the calculation: we would like to know how many dollars we would receive for one, ten, twenty, thirty or fifty pounds.

Excel accepts everything you enter, i.e. the program cannot check whether a formula gives the correct answer.

> Before you enter the formula make sure that the mathematical procedure is logical and correct!

In our currency example we are using the rule of three. If the dollar is equivalent to £1.503, for one pound you will receive one dollar divided by £1.503.

1 dollar = £1.503

£1 = 1 dollar/£1.503

Accordingly for ten, twenty, thirty or fifty pounds you will receive a multiple of this.

£10 = 1 dollar/£1.503 * 10
£20 = 1 dollar/£1.503 * 20
£30 = 1 dollar/£1.503 * 30
£50 = 1 dollar/£1.503 * 50

$10.00	=	$ 6.65
$20.00	=	$ 13.31
$30.00	=	$ 19.96
$40.00	=	$ 33.27

Since the exchange rate for the calculation is in one cell – 'E1' – we shall use absolute references and enter this via the dollar sign (be sure not to confuse it with the currency format!).

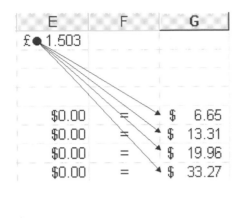

E	F	G
£ 1.503		
$0.00	=	$ 6.65
$0.00	=	$ 13.31
$0.00	=	$ 19.96
$0.00	=	$ 33.27

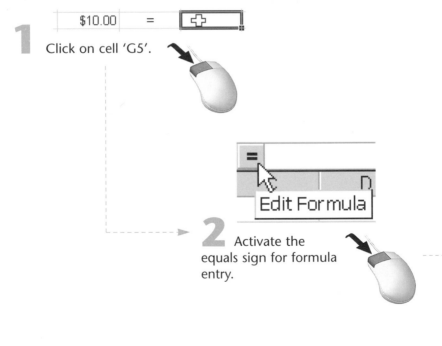

$10.00	=	✛

1 Click on cell 'G5'.

Edit Formula

2 Activate the equals sign for formula entry.

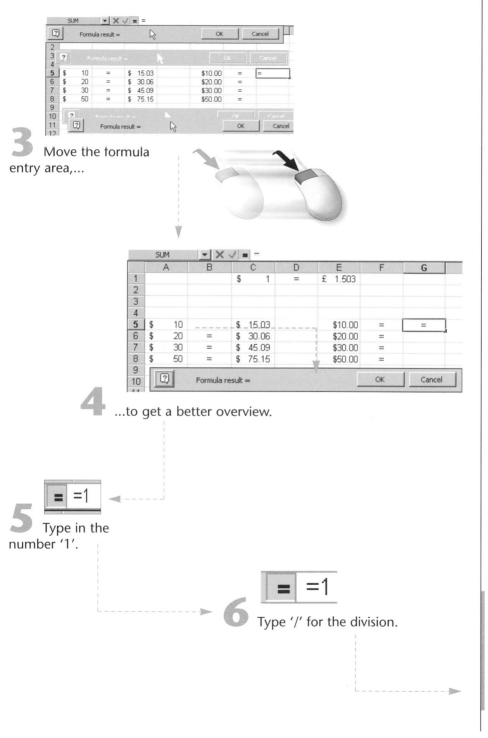

3 Move the formula entry area,...

4 ...to get a better overview.

5 Type in the number '1'.

6 Type '/' for the division.

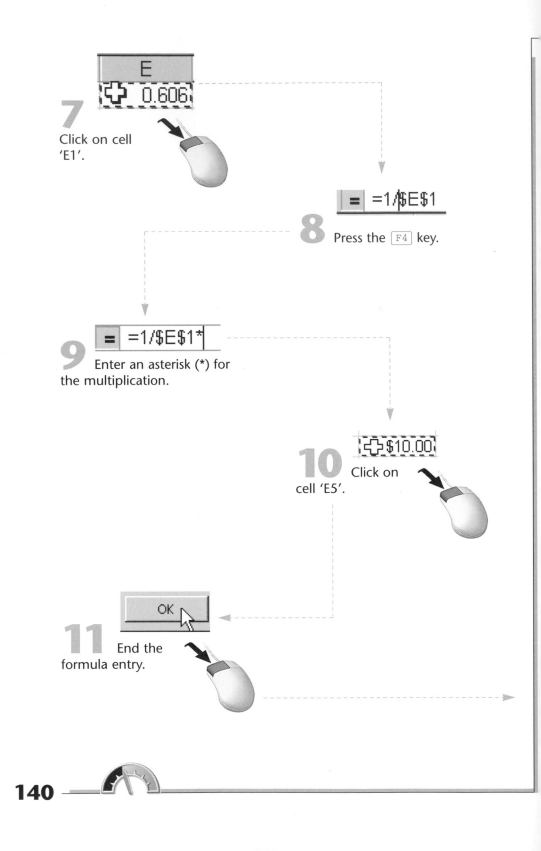

7 Click on cell 'E1'.

= =1/$E$1

8 Press the F4 key.

9 = =1/$E$1*

Enter an asterisk (*) for the multiplication.

10 Click on cell 'E5'.

$10.00

OK

11 End the formula entry.

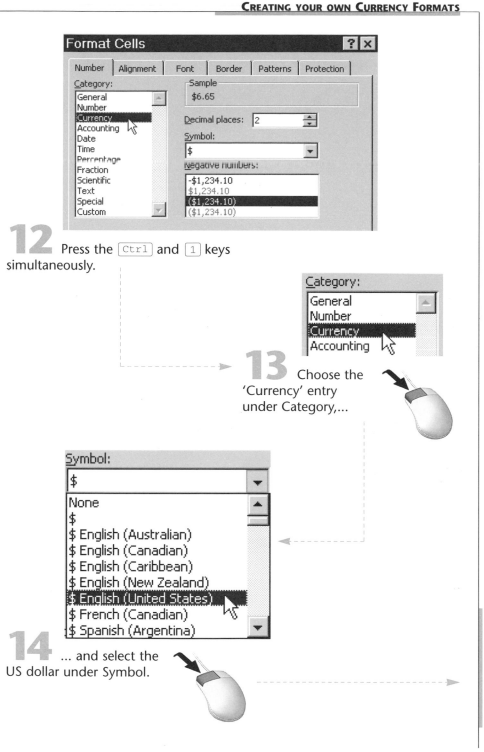

Format Cells [?][X]

| Number | Alignment | Font | Border | Patterns | Protection |

Category:
- General
- Number
- **Currency**
- Accounting
- Date
- Time
- Percentage
- Fraction
- Scientific
- Text
- Special
- Custom

Sample
$6.65

Decimal places: 2

Symbol:
$

Negative numbers:
- -$1,234.10
- $1,234.10
- ($1,234.10)
- ($1,234.10)

12 Press the [Ctrl] and [1] keys simultaneously.

Category:
- General
- Number
- **Currency**
- Accounting

13 Choose the 'Currency' entry under Category,...

Symbol:
$

- None
- $
- $ English (Australian)
- $ English (Canadian)
- $ English (Caribbean)
- $ English (New Zealand)
- **$ English (United States)**
- $ French (Canadian)
- $ Spanish (Argentina)

14 ... and select the US dollar under Symbol.

141

15 Confirm your instructions.

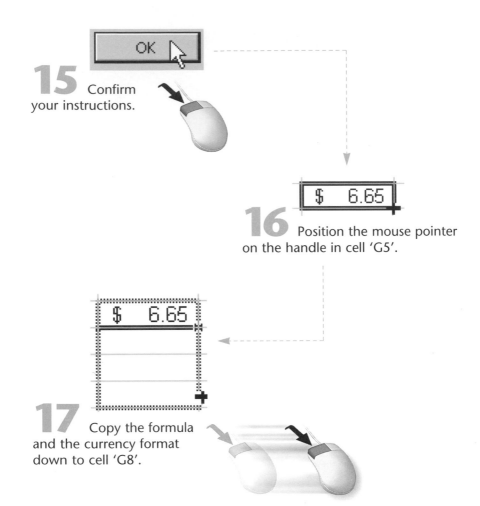

$ 6.65

16 Position the mouse pointer on the handle in cell 'G5'.

$ 6.65

17 Copy the formula and the currency format down to cell 'G8'.

Creating your own number formats

In Excel you can design your own forms of presentation. Up to now we have only used the style '$1' for the dollar, but this can look a little inelegant.

$	6.65
$	13.31
$	19.96
$	33.27

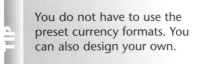

Other formats such as 'dollar, US dollar, US $ etc.' can be set up in Excel (in theory 'lucky dollar' would also be possible). In our example we are simply placing the dollar sign after the number, so that instead of '$1' we are using the style '1$'. You will not find this form in the currency Category.

You set your own currency formats via the FORMAT/CELLS menu by choosing the Custom category on the Number page.

Simply click on the style you fancy for your currency (0.00) at Symbol. Then enter the currency sign for dollars '$'. The preview window is very helpful. It always shows you what the figure looks like when you confirm your instructions with OK.

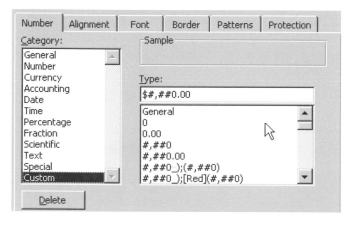

1 Activate cell 'G5'.

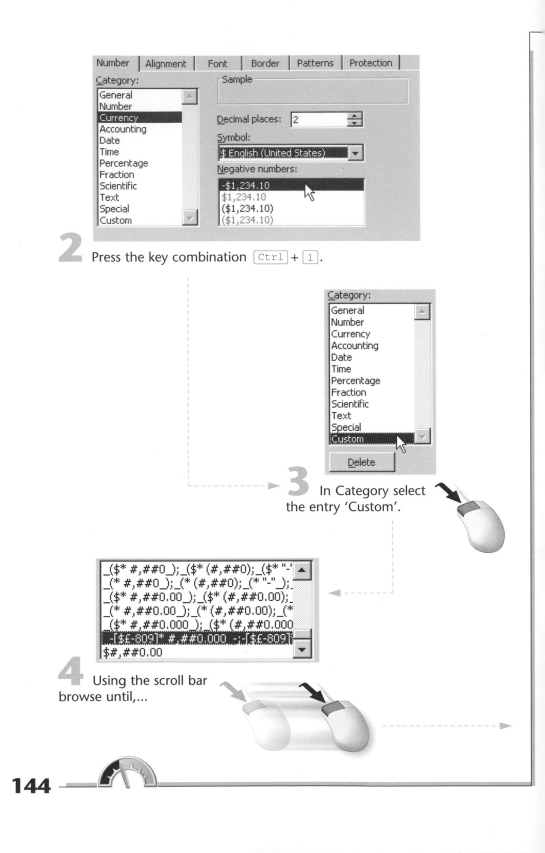

| Number | Alignment | Font | Border | Patterns | Protection |

Category:

General
Number
Currency
Accounting
Date
Time
Percentage
Fraction
Scientific
Text
Special
Custom

Sample

Decimal places: 2

Symbol:
$ English (United States)

Negative numbers:

-$1,234.10
$1,234.10
($1,234.10)
($1,234.10)

2 Press the key combination ⌨Ctrl⌨ + ⌨1⌨.

Category:

General
Number
Currency
Accounting
Date
Time
Percentage
Fraction
Scientific
Text
Special
Custom

Delete

3 In Category select
the entry 'Custom'.

_($* #,##0_);_($* (#,##0);_($* "-'
_(* #,##0_);_(* (#,##0);_(* "-"_);.
_($* #,##0.00_);_($* (#,##0.00);_
_(* #,##0.00_);_(* (#,##0.00);_(*
_($* #,##0.000_);_($* (#,##0.000
-[$£-809]* # ##0.000_-;-[$£-809]
$#,##0.00

4 Using the scroll bar
browse until,...

144

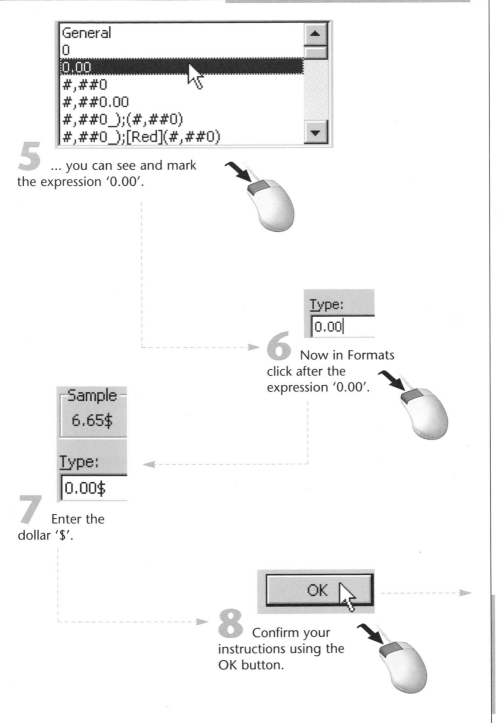

```
General
0
0.00
#,##0
#,##0.00
#,##0_);(#,##0)
#,##0_);[Red](#,##0)
```

5 ... you can see and mark the expression '0.00'.

Type:
```
0.00
```

6 Now in Formats click after the expression '0.00'.

Sample
```
6.65$
```

Type:
```
0.00$
```

7 Enter the dollar '$'.

OK

8 Confirm your instructions using the OK button.

9 Position the mouse pointer on the handle in cell 'G5'.

10 Copy the new currency format down to cell 'G8'.

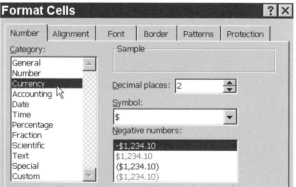

Deleting number formats again

Number formats cannot be deleted as easily as cell contents using the `Delete` key. The format remains in the cell until another is selected.

You need the Format Cells dialog box (menu command FORMAT/CELLS or `Ctrl` + `1`) and the Number tab). In Category select either General or Number. Then activate a 'normal' number

Format Cells ? X

| Number | Alignment | Font | Border | Patterns | Protection |

Category:
- General
- Number
- Currency
- Accounting
- Date
- Time
- Percentage
- Fraction
- Scientific
- Text
- Special
- Custom

Sample

Decimal places: 2

Symbol:
$

Negative numbers:
- -$1,234.10
- $1,234.10
- ($1,234.10)
- ($1,234.10)

format. As soon as you confirm your instructions by OK or with the `←` key the cells receive your self-defined format.

Number formats can only be removed via the Number page in the Format Cells dialog box.

Some examples of number formats:

Format	Concept	Number
0	Whole number	7
0.00	Two regular decimal places	7.77
#,##0	Whole number with comma to indicate a thousand	7,777
-#,##0	Negative whole number with 'thousand comma'	-7,777
#,##0.00	Whole number with 'thousand comma' and two decimal places	7,777.77

The Excel trainer

I. Save the calculation under the name 'Currency'.

II. Change the exchange rate of the dollar:

$1 = £1.725

$1 = £1.843

$1 = £1.456

III. Now you have to do some independent work. Do the exercises without instructions and think carefully about the formulae. The steps you need to take can be found alongside the answers which are given directly after each exercise.

Exercise 1:

	B	C
1	**Delay charge**	
2		
3	Delay surcharge	$20.00
4	Processing charge	$5.00
5		
6		
7	Amount total	Amount to pay
8		
9	$725.00	
10	$800.00	
11	$900.00	
12	$1,000.00	
13	$2,500.00	
14	$10,000.00	

Answer:

C11		=	=$C$3+$C$4+B11

	B	C
1	**Delay charge**	
2		
3	Delay surcharge	$20.00
4	Processing charge	$5.00
5		
6		
7	Amount total	Amount to pay
8		
9	$725.00	$750.00
10	$800.00	$825.00
11	$900.00	$925.00
12	$1,000.00	$1,025.00
13	$2,500.00	$2,525.00
14	$10,000.00	$10,025.00

Amount to pay
=$C$3+$C$4+B9
=$C$3+$C$4+B10
=$C$3+$C$4+B11
=$C$3+$C$4+B12
=$C$3+$C$4+B13
=$C$3+$C$4+B14

Change the delay surcharge to £10.00, £15.00, £30.00.
Change the processing charge to £10.00, £15.00, £20.00.

Exercise 2:

	A	B	C
1		**Savings bank**	
2			
3		*Interest on savings*	
4			
5		Interest factor	0.03
6			
7	Amount saved	Interest	Amount paid
8	£1,000.00	£30.00	£1,030.00
9	£2,000.00	£60.00	£2,060.00
10	£3,000.00	£90.00	£3,090.00
11	£5,000.00	£150.00	£5,150.00
12	£10,000.00	£300.00	£10,300.00

Answer:

C9   = =SUM(A9:B9)

	A	B	C
1		**Savings bank**	
2			
3		*Interest on savings*	
4			
5		Interest factor	0.03
6			
7	**Amount saved**	**Interest**	**Amount paid**
8	$1,000.00	$30.00	$1,030.00
9	$2,000.00	$60.00	$2,060.00
10	$3,000.00	$90.00	$3,090.00
11	$5,000.00	$150.00	$5,150.00
12	$10,000.00	$300.00	$10,300.00

Interest	Amount paid
=$C$5*A8	=SUM(A8:B8)
=$C$5*A9	=SUM(A9:B9)
=$C$5*A10	=SUM(A10:B10)
=$C$5*A11	=SUM(A11:B11)
=$C$5*A12	=SUM(A12:B12)

Change the interest factor to 0.02; 0.025; 0.01.

149

What's in
this chapter?

A picture is worth a thousand words. And
numbers make a better impression if they are
'polished' a little. Where the facts and figures
may appear to convey little, Excel uses charts to
bring the information to life. They catch the
reader's eye and back up the analyses. One
glance tells you
everything. Sober
business figures are
presented in an
impressive way and
scarcely need further
explanation. And if
the facts change,
it's easy to alter
the figures and
charts.

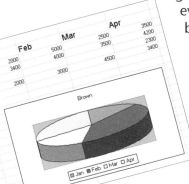

You already know:

Your are going to learn:

151

AutoFill

Before you learn something new we shall first repeat what we already know. Write the heading (Representative: sales in £), format it in bold and enlarge it. The reader knows immediately what it is about.

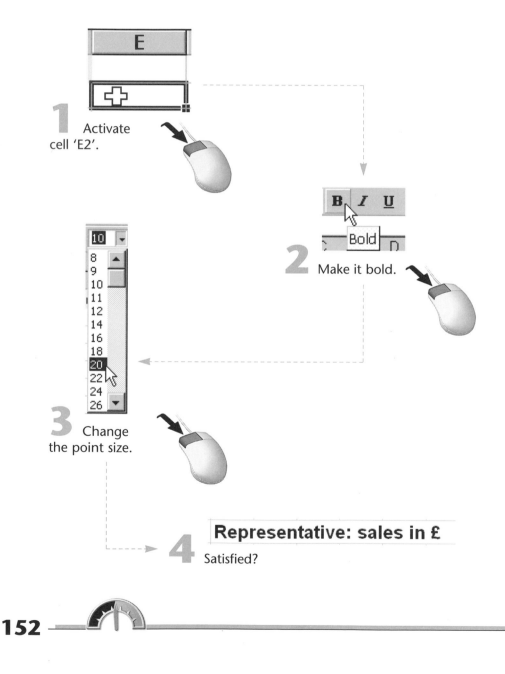

1 Activate cell 'E2'.

2 Make it bold.

3 Change the point size.

4 Satisfied?

Representative: sales in £

April, April

All this repetition. Time is money! Excel offers a quick way of making entries. If you want to enter the months of the

Jan	Feb	Mar	Apr
January	February	March	April
Mon	Tue	Wed	Thu
Monday	Tuesday	Wednesda	Thursday

year you don't have to waste time putting them in individually, you simply need to enter the first month. You can either write 'January' in full or use the abbreviation 'Jan'. If you now position the mouse pointer on the handle and drag into other cells with the mouse button pressed down, Excel will automatically fill in the other months. If you start with 'April' and fill in the cells to the right it will carry on with 'May, June, July...'. If, however, you drag to the left the list will read:'March, February, January, December...'. It also works with cells in a vertical column. You can also use the AutoFill function for the days of the week.

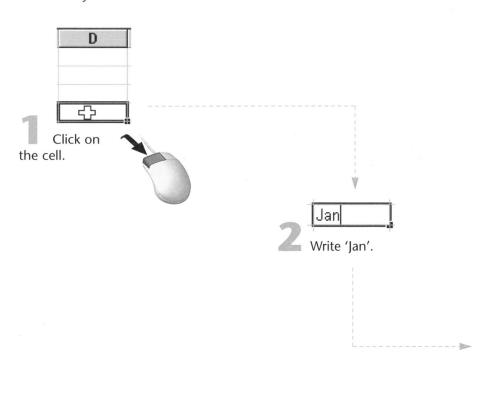

1 Click on the cell.

2 Write 'Jan'.

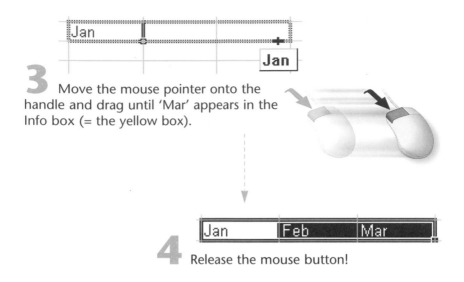

3 Move the mouse pointer onto the handle and drag until 'Mar' appears in the Info box (= the yellow box).

4 Release the mouse button!

Do it yourself!

The entries for months and days are already preset by Excel. But they can be changed or supplemented by you. You will find the lists for AutoFill in the AutoFill list box after selecting the menu command TOOLS/OPTIONS.

You can also specify your own sequence here. Let us assume that you would always use the same names – eg Brown, Jones, Smith – in your lists. What could be more obvious than to put these names into a list of your own. To do this click on the entry 'New List' under Custom Lists. The cursor will now flash at List entries. This is where you enter the names or terms. They can be separated from each other by a comma or by pressing the ⏎ key. When you have finished your entry click on InsAddert. Your information has been included in the user list and is ready to be inserted into a worksheet.

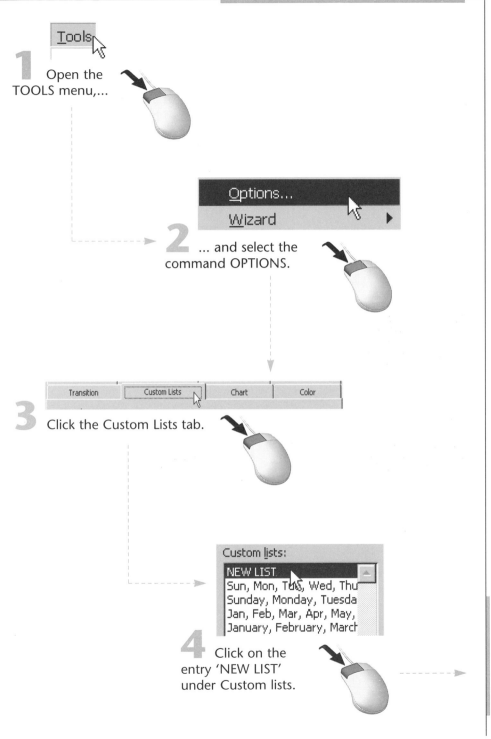

Tools

1 Open the
TOOLS menu,...

Options...

Wizard ▶

2 ... and select the
command OPTIONS.

| Transition | Custom Lists | Chart | Color |

3 Click the Custom Lists tab.

Custom lists:

NEW LIST
Sun, Mon, Tue, Wed, Thu
Sunday, Monday, Tuesda
Jan, Feb, Mar, Apr, May,
January, February, March

4 Click on the
entry 'NEW LIST'
under Custom lists.

155

List entries:

5 The cursor will flash ready for use under List entries.

List entries:

Brown
Jones
Smith

6 Type in:
'Brown' ⏎
'Jones' ⏎
'Smith'.

Add

7 Click on the Add button

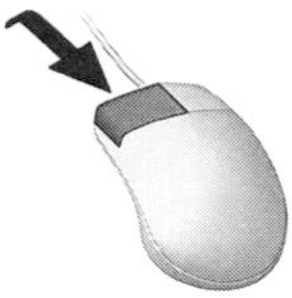

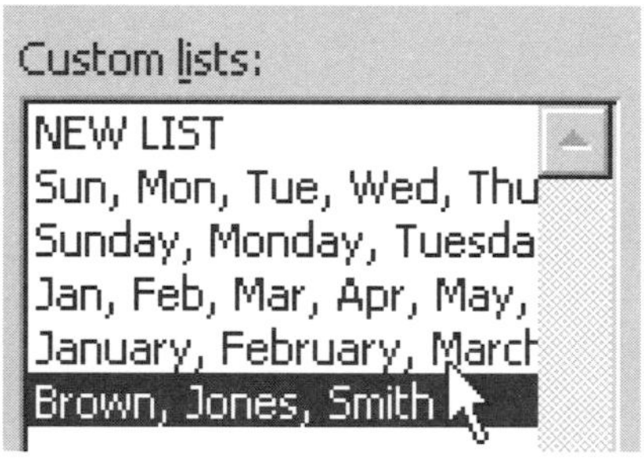

Custom lists:

NEW LIST
Sun, Mon, Tue, Wed, Thu
Sunday, Monday, Tuesda
Jan, Feb, Mar, Apr, May,
January, February, March
Brown, Jones, Smith

8 Your entries have been included in the Custom lists.

OK

9 Close the dialog box via OK.

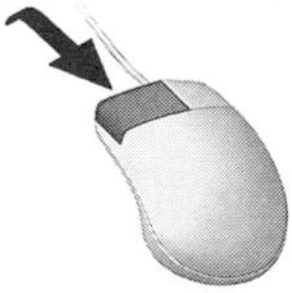

Brown, Jones, Smith

Now that we have made our own list, we need to try it out. To do this you have to write at least one name. Then, as you already know, position the mouse pointer on the handle and drag it over the other cells. As soon as you release the mouse button these cells are filled in.

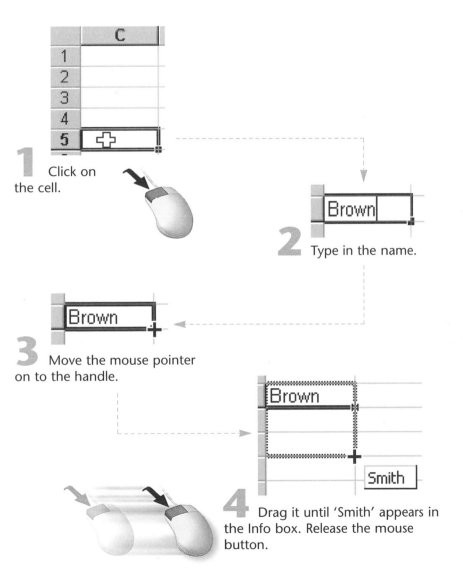

1 Click on the cell.

2 Type in the name.

3 Move the mouse pointer on to the handle.

4 Drag it until 'Smith' appears in the Info box. Release the mouse button.

Deleting a list

If you want to delete a list again, that's no problem. Once again you need the Custom Lists page (from TOOLS/OPTIONS). Simply click on the list you want to delete and click on the Delete button. You will be told that the list will be deleted for good as soon as you confirm with OK.

View	Calculation	Edit	General
Transition	Custom Lists	Chart	Color

Custom lists: List entries:

```
NEW LIST                    Brown                      Add
Sun, Mon, Tue, Wed, Thu     Jones
Sunday, Monday, Tuesda      Smith                      Delete
Jan, Feb, Mar, Apr, May,
January, February, March
Brown, Jones, Smith
```

Microsoft Excel   ☒

⚠ List will be permanently deleted.

OK   Cancel   Import

Inserting a chart

We'll use a short sales figures presentation to demonstrate the construction of a chart. Various values are to be compared. There are many different possibilities, but it would take more than one chapter to describe them.

So that Excel knows what the chart is supposed to refer to, the whole presentation must be marked. On the standard toolbar you will find the Chart Wizard icon (or in the menu under INSERT/CHART). If you click on this you can start on the chart straight away.

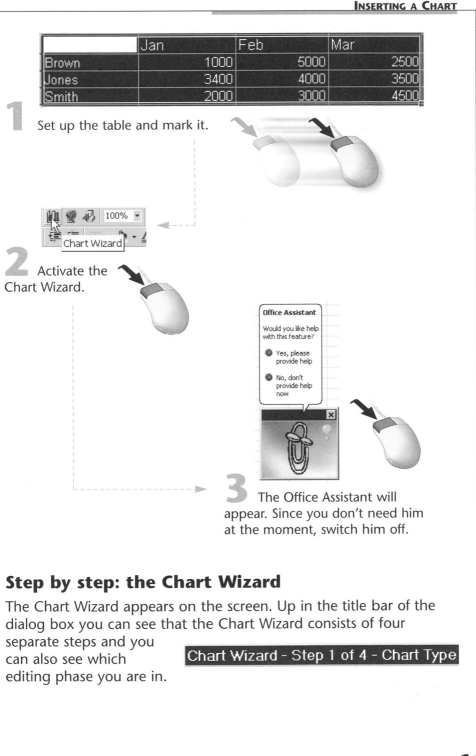

	Jan	Feb	Mar
Brown	1000	5000	2500
Jones	3400	4000	3500
Smith	2000	3000	4500

1 Set up the table and mark it.

2 Activate the Chart Wizard.

Chart Wizard

100%

Office Assistant

Would you like help with this feature?

● Yes, please provide help

● No, don't provide help now

3 The Office Assistant will appear. Since you don't need him at the moment, switch him off.

Step by step: the Chart Wizard

The Chart Wizard appears on the screen. Up in the title bar of the dialog box you can see that the Chart Wizard consists of four separate steps and you can also see which editing phase you are in.

Chart Wizard - Step 1 of 4 - Chart Type

159

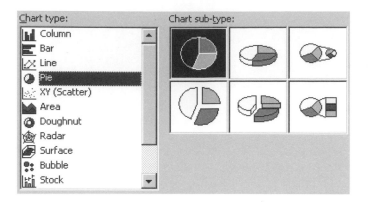

You can select the various graphic forms at Chart Type. There are column charts, line charts, pie charts, scatter charts etc. And there are subtypes of these. At 'Pie Chart', for example, you can select from several variations which are shown at Subtype.

By clicking on Press and hold to view sample you will be shown what the numbers will look like in the preview chart.

When you have decided on a type you pass on to the next step in the Chart Wizard with Next.

Some chart types:

Chart type	Use
Columns	Compares individual values by means of different-size columns.
Bars	Like the column chart, but the rows are horizontal.
Lines	Shows trends and developments over a certain period of time and mainly suited to the representation of time-dependent processes.

Chart type	Use
Pie	Shows the distribution of the individual data as fractions of a whole.
XY Scatter	Use when the numbers in a dependence relate to each other (speed: petrol consumption; receipts: costs).
Area	Similar to the line chart, used to represent developments over time. This type shows the volume of changes more clearly.
Volume/Hi-Lo Close	Designed for 'dabblers in the stock market and speculators', shows developments in stock market prices.

What does it relate to?

In the second step in the Chart Wizard you determine which row should be considered – here there are 'Representatives' and 'Months'. If you activate the Row option you will see the sales of one representative for the individual months. If you selected the Columns option the chart would show the sales of the individual representatives for one month.

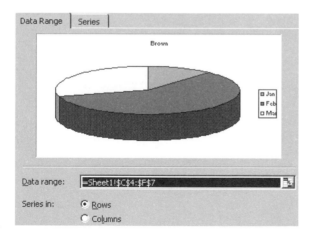

Click on Next and you will come to the third step in the Chart Wizard.

Information on the chart

WHAT'S THIS?

A legend contains explanations about the areas within a chart.

This is where you indicate, among other things, where the legend should appear on the chart.

□ Brown
■ Jones
□ Smith

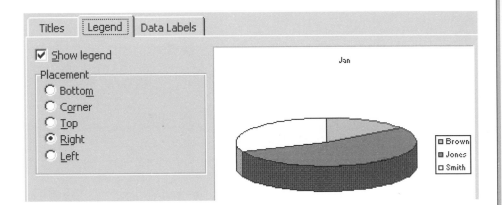

Whither the chart?

In the last step you determine where the chart should appear. With larger tables it can be on a separate new sheet. In that case at Insert Chart you activate: 'As new sheet'. Since our table is not too extensive, we can include the chart on the same sheet as the original table. To do this activate 'As object in' by a mouse click. It is generally preset by Excel.

Chart Wizard - Step 4 of 4 - Chart Location 🔧 ✕

Place chart:

○ As new sheet: | Chart1 |

● As object in: | Sheet1 | ▼

🔧 | Cancel | | < Back | | Next > | | Finish |

You can get back to the previous steps of the Chart Wizard using the Back button and then if need be you can make further alterations.

You will get to know other possibilities of the Chart Wizard in the Excel Trainer at the end of this section.

Cancel stops the Chart Wizard and you return to the worksheet without a chart. When you click on Finish, Excel inserts the chosen chart.

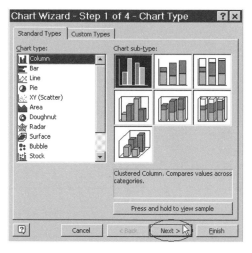

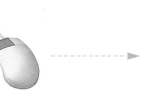

1 Excel offers you a chart suggestion. Confirm it using Next.

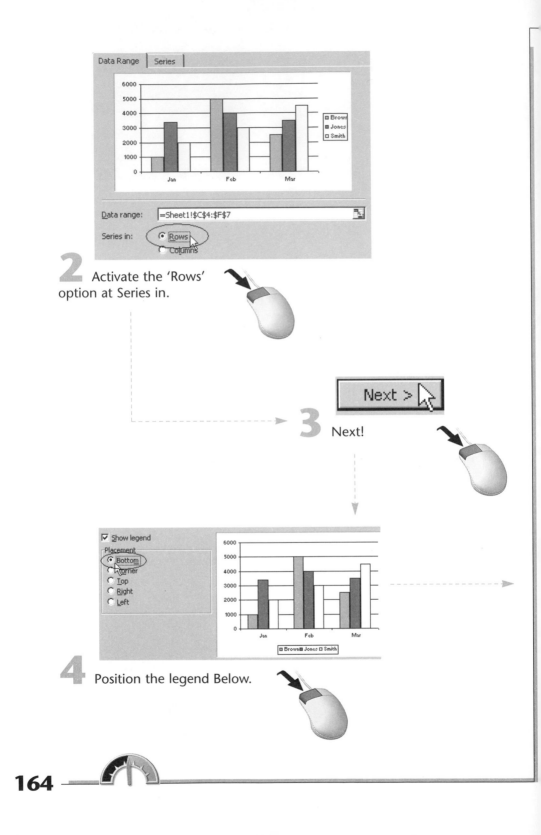

2 Activate the 'Rows' option at Series in.

Next >

3 Next!

4 Position the legend Below.

164

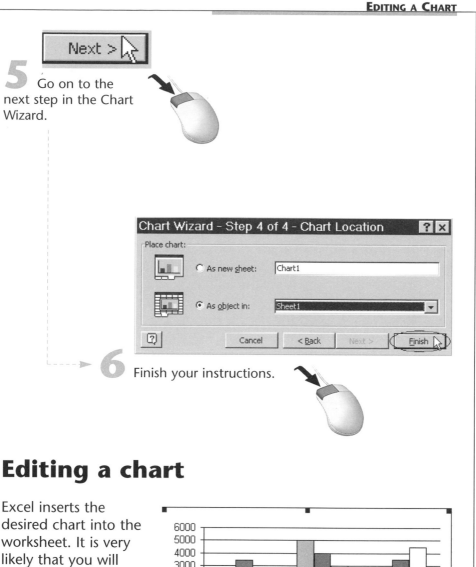

5 Go on to the next step in the Chart Wizard.

6 Finish your instructions.

Editing a chart

Excel inserts the desired chart into the worksheet. It is very likely that you will have to use the scroll bar to see it. If you click in the graphic, small black squares will appear. This shows you the size of 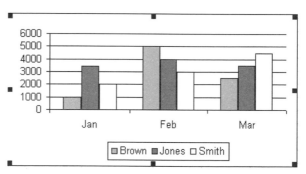 your chart. You can only edit the chart when you can see the squares.

165

If you move the mouse pointer onto a column a piece of information appears about the data the column represents. (Here: Representative Jones, Sales

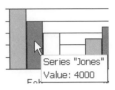

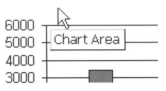

4000). Let the mouse pointer 'roam around' in the chart and various pieces of information will be shown.

Moving the chart

You can move the chart, and position it next to the table containing the figures. Move the mouse pointer inside the graphic until a 'Chart Area' QuickInfo message appears. If you press the left

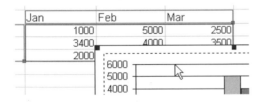

mouse button and keep it pressed the mouse pointer turns into a multi-arrow shape. With the mouse button pressed down you can now position the chart wherever you want to in the worksheet.

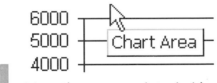

1 Move the mouse pointer inside the chart until 'Chart Area' appears.

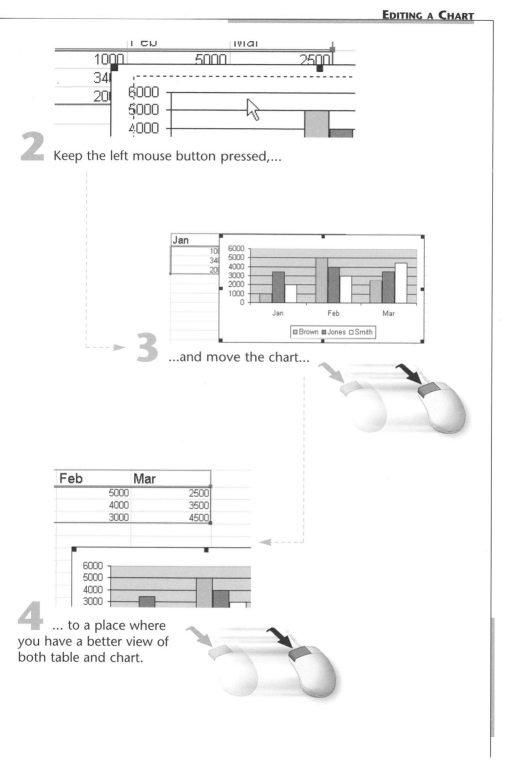

2 Keep the left mouse button pressed,...

3 ...and move the chart...

4 ... to a place where you have a better view of both table and chart.

Changing the size of the chart

If you move the mouse pointer onto the black squares at the edge of the graphic you can enlarge or reduce the chart in the direction of the arrows. Hence the squares are called dragging points.

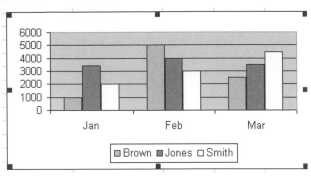

Using the dragging points inside the graphic you can change the size of the chart in the direction of the arrows with the mouse button pressed down.

In our example you use the dragging point at bottom right. Use the scroll bar to reach it if necessary. With the left mouse button pressed down, reduce the size of the chart.

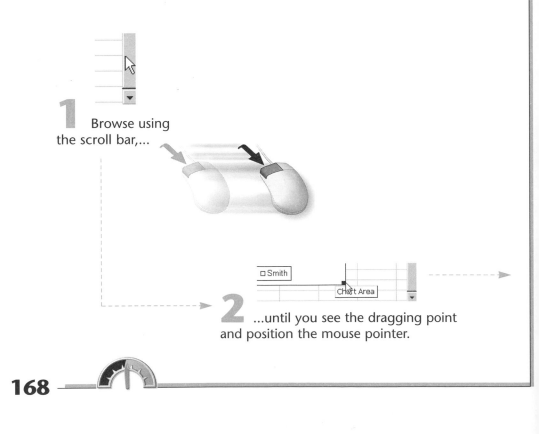

1 Browse using the scroll bar,...

2 ...until you see the dragging point and position the mouse pointer.

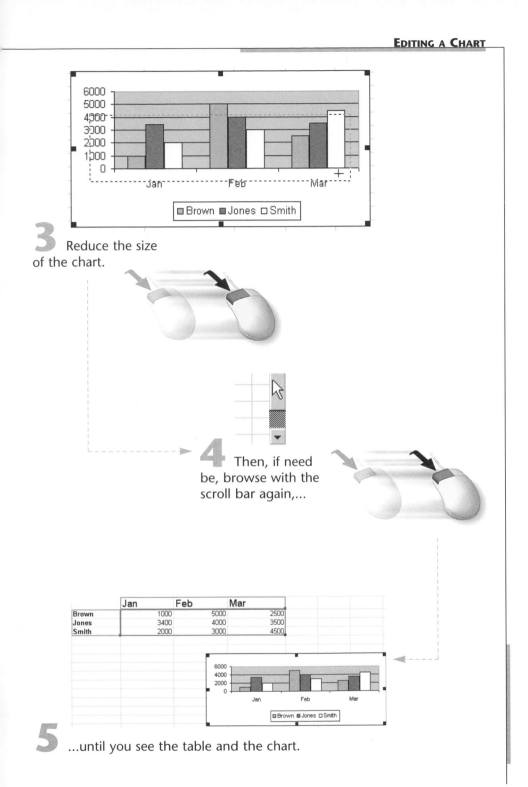

3 Reduce the size of the chart.

4 Then, if need be, browse with the scroll bar again,...

	Jan	Feb	Mar
Brown	1000	5000	2500
Jones	3400	4000	3500
Smith	2000	3000	4500

5 ...until you see the table and the chart.

Changing a chart

If you double-click in the chart, Excel will give a coloured background to the table relating to it. The program is informing you that the graphic relates to these values.

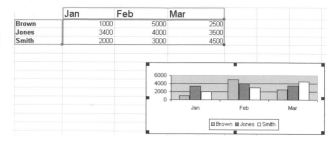

	Jan	Feb	Mar
Brown	1000	5000	2500
Jones	3400	4000	3500
Smith	2000	3000	4500

However, the individual pieces of data can also be edited from this point.

Peanuts: changing numbers

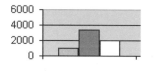

A true-life example: Mr Brown is feeling rather upset. There is a mistake in his sales figures for January. He made not £1,000 but £4,000. His sales figures for the month of January do look a little 'modest'. 'Keep calm, Mr Brown, we'll deal with it!'

To change figures in a completed chart you don't need to produce a new graphic. You simply change the relevant number in the table. Excel automatically adjusts the chart – in this case the column.

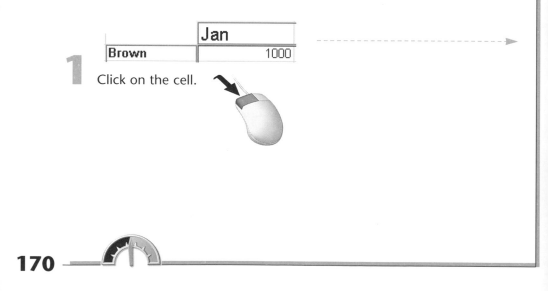

	Jan
Brown	1000

1 Click on the cell.

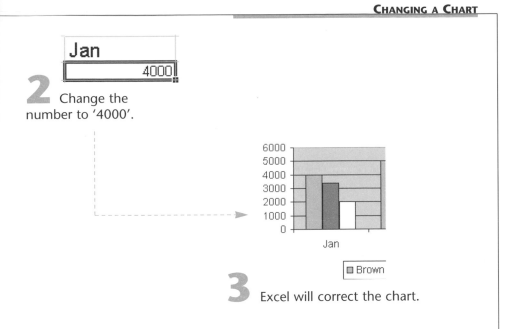

Jan

2 Change the number to '4000'.

3 Excel will correct the chart.

As you see, Excel registers the higher sales figure. You can see the chart before alteration on the left and after, on the right. Mr Brown's column rose from £1,000 to £4,000. This operation can also be carried out the other way round.

You can change the figures on the chart. To do this simply click on the relevant column. With the mouse button pressed down you can drag the sales figure to 'dizzying' heights (if you want to). The value in the table is adjusted to match.

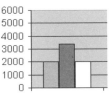

A new month

Of course, the sales figures extend beyond the three months we have given. The figures for the month of April are also available. First enter the values. Naturally we don't enter the word 'April'. We use the AutoFill function. To do this click on the month 'Mar' and drag the handle into the next cell.

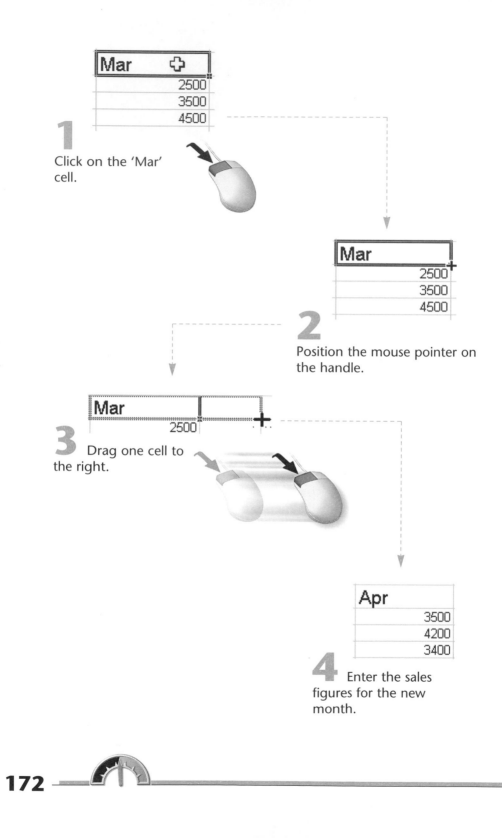

1 Click on the 'Mar' cell.

2 Position the mouse pointer on the handle.

3 Drag one cell to the right.

4 Enter the sales figures for the new month.

New sales figures are available. Does that mean we have to set up a new chart? No! You simply drag the information into the graphic. To do this mark the new month. Move the mouse pointer onto the edge of the marking. It will change into an arrow. Now you can use the drag & drop method. Press the left mouse button, keep it pressed and simply drag into the

chart. You will see a small plus (+) on the mouse pointer as soon as you are in the graphic. Release the mouse button anywhere. The values for the new month are now included in the chart.

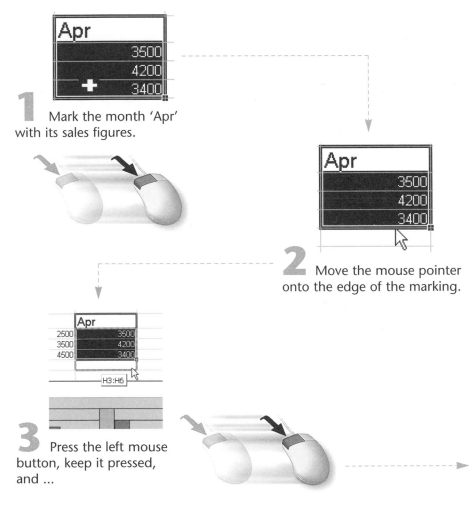

1 Mark the month 'Apr' with its sales figures.

2 Move the mouse pointer onto the edge of the marking.

3 Press the left mouse button, keep it pressed, and ...

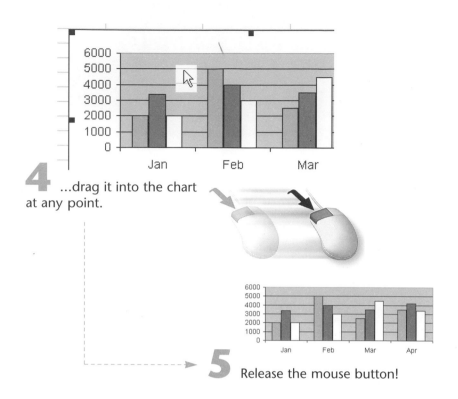

4 ...drag it into the chart at any point.

5 Release the mouse button!

A new person

In the same way that you added a new month you will now add a new representative. First enter the data, mark it and drag the information into the chart using drag & drop.

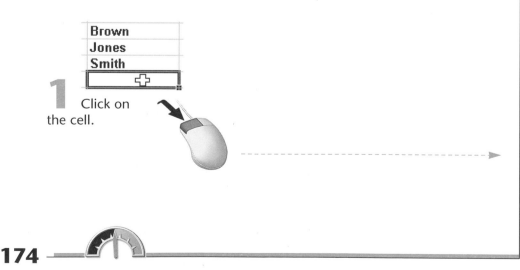

Brown
Jones
Smith

1 Click on the cell.

	Jan	Feb	Mar	Apr
Brown	2000	5000	2500	
Jones	3400	4000	3500	
Smith	2000	3000	4500	
Mark				

2 Type in the data.

| Mark | | | | ✚ | 2300 |

3 Mark it.

4500	3400
	2300

4 Place the mouse pointer on the edge of the marking until it turns into an arrow.

| | | | 2300 |

D8:H8

5 Drag into the graphic with the mouse button pressed down.

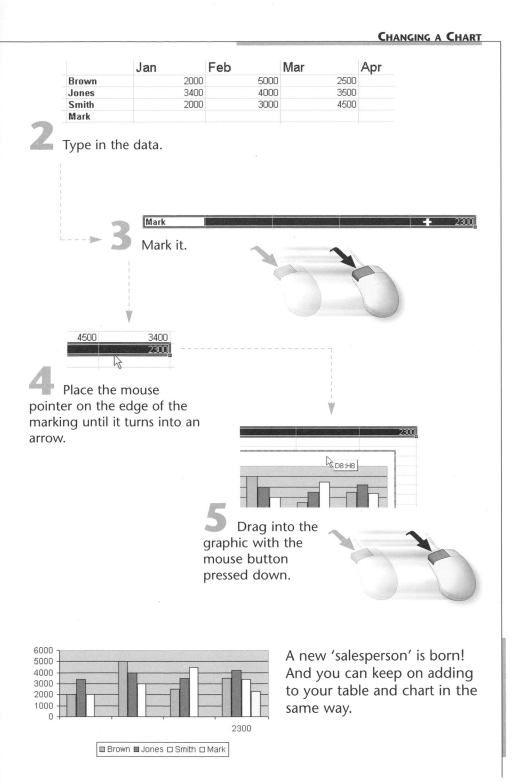

A new 'salesperson' is born! And you can keep on adding to your table and chart in the same way.

2300

☐ Brown ■ Jones ☐ Smith ☐ Mark

175

Sorting cells

From A to Z

Things can get a bit disorderly when you enter new
representatives. The list is no longer sorted in
alphabetical order. To correct this, find the appropriate
buttons on the standard toolbar. With AZ you sort in ascending
order; with ZA, in descending order.

You just need to click on any cell. Excel then knows that you want to
sort this column. The sales figures relating to the various
representatives are also taken into consideration. As soon as you click
on a button, Excel changes the order on the chart.

	Jan
Brown	2000
Jones	3400
Smith	2000
Mark	

1 Activate any table cell
in the column.

Sort Ascending

2 Click on the
Sort Ascending
button.

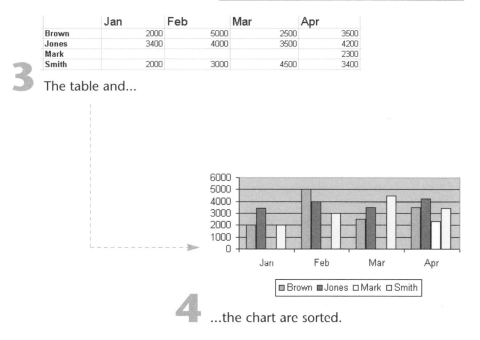

	Jan	Feb	Mar	Apr
Brown	2000	5000	2500	3500
Jones	3400	4000	3500	4200
Mark				2300
Smith	2000	3000	4500	3400

3 The table and...

4 ...the chart are sorted.

Another type

If you would like to change the type of chart later, for example you want to change columns to bars, choose the command CHART TYPE in the CHART menu.

TIP

Before you use the menu command CHART/CHART TYPE you must make sure that the graphic is active i.e. that the dragging points are visible.

177

The Excel trainer

Now you can all reduce your fat intake! We're dealing with the percentages of various constituents of a food (it's not beer!). The Excel trainer will show you some new ways of producing charts. This type is the pie chart. The constituents are shown as percentages.

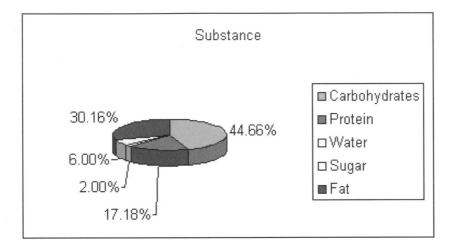

Carbohydrates	44.66%
Protein	17.18%
Water	2.00%
Sugar	6.00%
Fat	30.16%

1 Set up the table shown here.

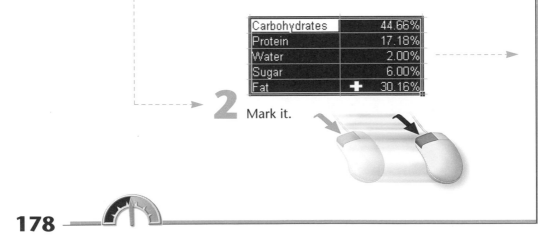

2 Mark it.

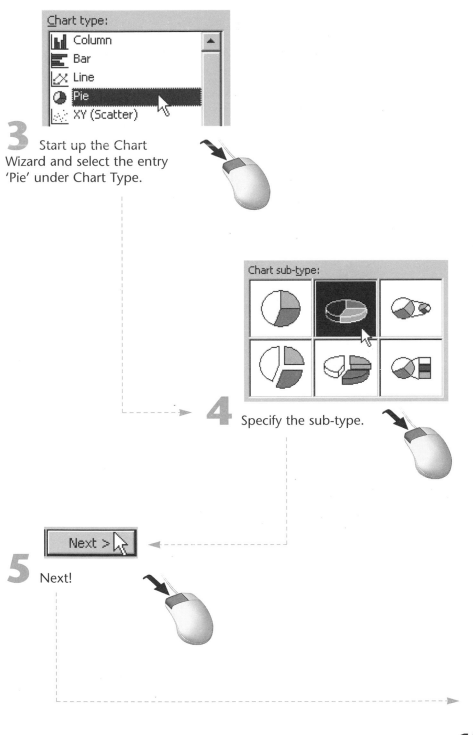

Chart type:

- Column
- Bar
- Line
- Pie
- XY (Scatter)

3 Start up the Chart Wizard and select the entry 'Pie' under Chart Type.

Chart sub-type:

4 Specify the sub-type.

Next >

5 Next!

179

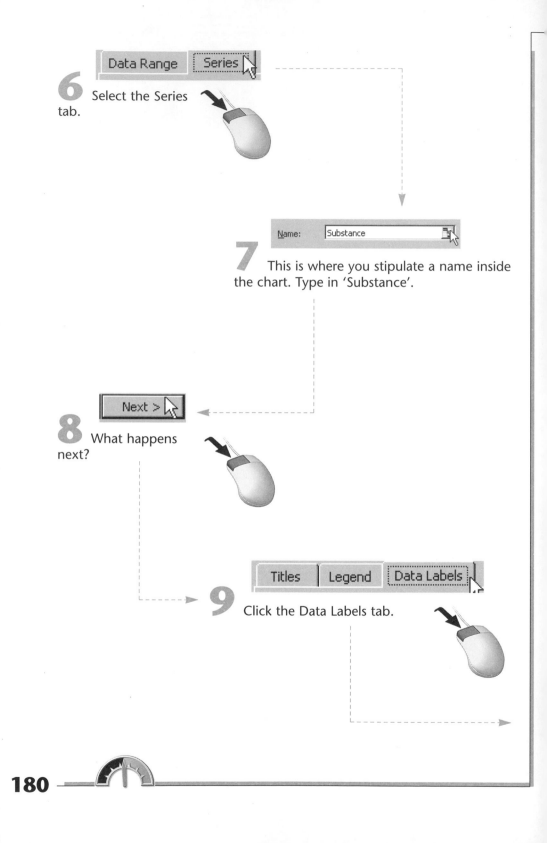

Data Range | Series

6 Select the Series tab.

Name: | Substance

7 This is where you stipulate a name inside the chart. Type in 'Substance'.

Next >

8 What happens next?

Titles | Legend | Data Labels

9 Click the Data Labels tab.

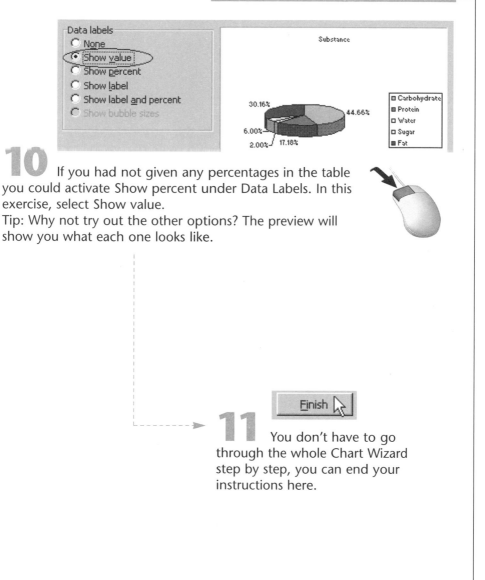

10 If you had not given any percentages in the table you could activate Show percent under Data Labels. In this exercise, select Show value.

Tip: Why not try out the other options? The preview will show you what each one looks like.

11 You don't have to go through the whole Chart Wizard step by step, you can end your instructions here.

What's in this chapter?

There are people who can make statistics out of anything. But what are statistics? Suppose, for example, a man drinks three bottles of wine in a restaurant. You and I have not benefited. But statistically, the man, you and I have knocked back a bottle of wine each. Cheers – your very good health!

Football teams	Goals		Statistics	
			Maximum goals	38
			Minimum goals	23
Manchester United	31		Average goals	30
West Ham	23			
Manchester City	24		Number of teams	7
Wimbledon	32		Teams having 30 or more	5
Leeds United	32			
Arsenal	31			
Tottenham	38			

You already know:

Your are going to learn:

Statistical analyses

Who has the highest sales – and the lowest? Statistical analyses are no problem with Excel. In this chapter we shall be using football teams and goals scored as an example. Of course, this system can be extended to other things: production, sales figures, cost analyses, etc.

First, enter the names of the football teams. If there is not enough room in one column, adjust the width by placing the mouse pointer between the column headings (on the column heading border) and double-clicking. Excel will automatically adjust the column width to accommodate the longest entry.

Football teams	Goals
Manchester United	
West Ham	
Manchester City	
Wimbledon	
Leeds United	
Arsenal	
Tottenham	

1 Enter the football teams.

2 Set the optimum column width by double-clicking on the column heading border.

Football teams	Goals		Statistics	
Manchester United			Most goals	
West ham			Least goals	
Manchester City				
Wimbledon			Average goals	
Leeds United				
Arsenal			Number of teams	
Tottenham			Teams having scored more than 20 goals	

3 Three cheers for statistics! Enter the statistical analysis.

Football teams	Goals		Statistics	
Manchester United	29		Most goals	
West ham	19		Least goals	
Manchester City	21			
Wimbledon	30		Average goals	
Leeds United	29			
Arsenal	30		Number of teams	
Tottenham	34		Teams having scored more than 20 goals	

4 Goal! What use are goal statistics without goals?

Naming cells

For future work with Excel it makes sense to name the range to be analysed. In this case, it is the range of goals, which we are going to call 'goals'. This will make things easier later on. Then you will only need to enter 'goals' for statistical analyses, not the range of cells.

To do this, select the range of cells, click on the Name box and enter the name.

185

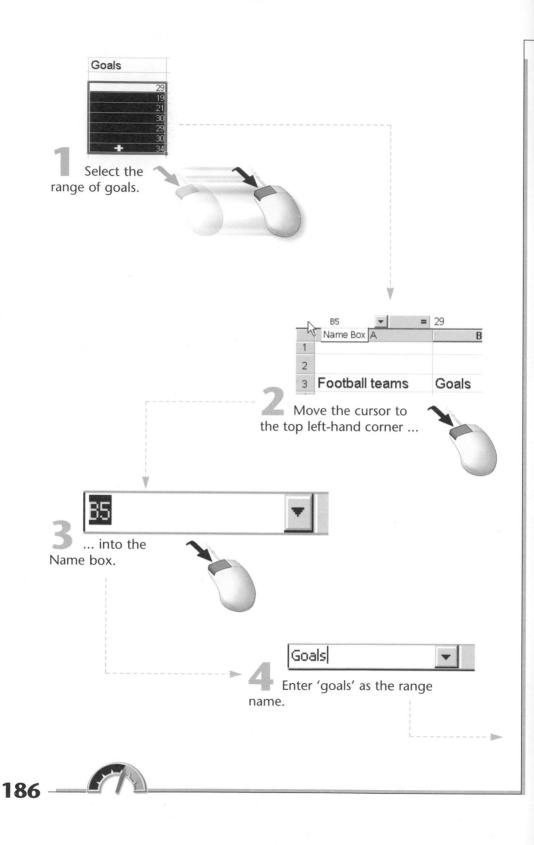

Goals

	29
	19
	21
	30
	29
	30
✚	34

1 Select the range of goals.

B5	▼	=	29
Name Box	A		B

1		
2		
3	**Football teams**	**Goals**

2 Move the cursor to the top left-hand corner ...

B5 ▼

3 ... into the Name box.

Goals ▼

4 Enter 'goals' as the range name.

	A	B
	Goals ▼	= Goals
1		
2		
3		
4	**Football teams**	**Goals**
5		
6	Manchester United	29
7	West Ham	19
8	Manchester City	21
9	Wimbledon	00
10	Leeds United	29
11	Arsenal	30
12	Tottenham	34

5 Press the ⏎ key

Inserting a function

Various functions are available in Excel. First, we would like to find out who has scored the most goals. Instead of 'most' we can also say 'maximum'. 'MAX' is the name of the Excel function which you now need. The Function Wizard contains all the functions. You can run them with this button on the standard toolbar.

The Function Wizard will guide you and help you to create functions.

You are spoiled for choice under Function category in the following dialog box. The first option you will see is Most Recently Used. This is where you will find the functions which you used last time.

Unfortunately, there wasn't a last time. But once you have used 'MAX', you can retrieve it here too.

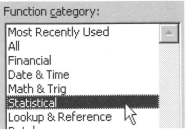

Function category:

Most Recently Used
All
Financial
Date & Time
Math & Trig
Statistical
Lookup & Reference

Every function is available under the option All, so you can always use this selection.

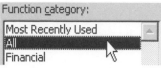

Lower down, you will see terms such as 'Financial', 'Date & Time' and 'Math & Trig'. You will also find them in the individual special categories too, depending upon what they do. Unfortunately, you won't always know which function belongs to which category, but in our case it's still relatively easy, because the 'MAX' function belongs to the 'Statistical' range. Once you have selected the category with a click of the mouse, give your attention to choosing the right function. There are plenty to choose from. You can view them all with the scroll bar. But there is a simpler way. Just click on the first function. A broken yellow line will appear. The 'MAX' function starts with the letter 'M'. if you type in an 'M', the blue highlighter under Function Name will automatically jump to the first word beginning with an 'M' which just happens to be 'MAX', the function we were looking for.

To find a function faster, just type its first letter.

Unfortunately, you cannot type in the second letter. If, for example, you type in the 'A', Excel will jump back to the functions which start with 'A'.

You will also find information on what the respective function does at the bottom of the dialog box.

Here is the explanation of the MAX (= Maximum) function:

> **MAX(number1,number2,...)**
>
> Returns the largest value in a set of values. Ignores logical values and text.

The maximum

Run the function by double-clicking on 'MAX'. The step 2 dialog box will appear. Enter the range from which the maximum is to be calculated against Number1. In our case enter 'goals'. You will be able to see the result immediately. In this case it is '34'. Finish will insert the result of the function in your worksheet.

```
┌─MAX─────────────────────────────────────────────────────────────┐
│                                                                  │
│   Number1 │Goals│              [■] = {"Goals";0;29;19;21         │
│                       ↖                                          │
│   Number2 │                    [■] = number                      │
│                                                                  │
│                                           = 34                   │
│ Returns the largest value in a set of values. Ignores logical values and text. │
│                                                                  │
│     Number1: number1,number2,... are 1 to 30 numbers, empty cells, logical values, or │
│              text numbers for which you want the maximum.        │
│   [?]          Formula result =34              [  OK  ]   [ Cancel ] │
└──────────────────────────────────────────────────────────────────┘
```

Statistics	
Most goals	[⊕]
Least goals	
Average goals	
Number of teams	
Teams having scored more than 20 goals	

1 Select the cell in which the maximum is to appear.

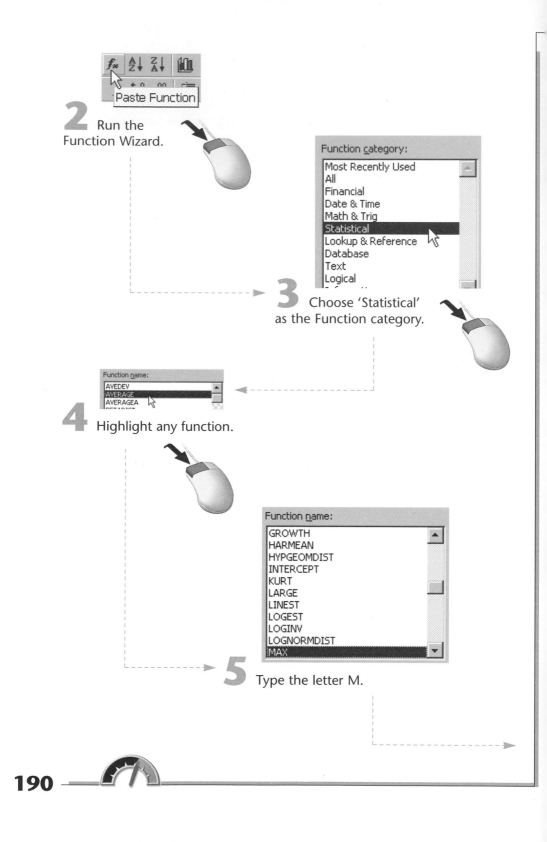

Paste Function

2 Run the Function Wizard.

Function category:

Most Recently Used
All
Financial
Date & Time
Math & Trig
Statistical
Lookup & Reference
Database
Text
Logical

3 Choose 'Statistical' as the Function category.

Function name:

AVEDEV
AVERAGE
AVERAGEA

4 Highlight any function.

Function name:

GROWTH
HARMEAN
HYPGEOMDIST
INTERCEPT
KURT
LARGE
LINEST
LOGEST
LOGINV
LOGNORMDIST
MAX

5 Type the letter M.

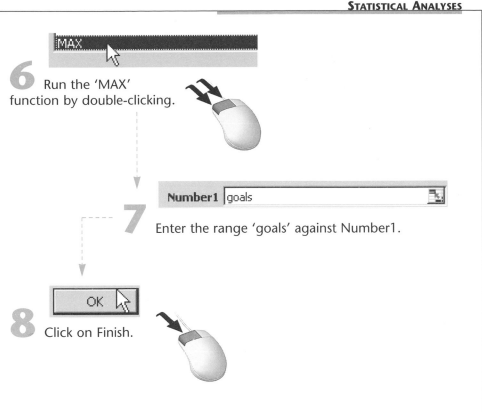

6 Run the 'MAX' function by double-clicking.

7 Enter the range 'goals' against Number1.

8 Click on Finish.

Number1	goals

| = | =MAX(Goals) |

Excel will now insert the highest number from the selected range of cells. You will see the formula 'Max(goals)' in the formula bar. This means that it shows the maximum from the 'goals' range of cells.

Most goals		34
Least goals		
Average goals		
Number of teams		
Teams having scored more than 20 goals		

The minimum

If there is a maximum, there must be a minimum too. We would like to determine the least number of goals. The method is almost analogous to determining the maximum. First, the line on which the result is to appear must be selected. Click on the Function Wizard button and select 'Statistical' under Function Category. Click on any function name and type the letter M. Excel will jump to the first

191

function which starts with an 'M', which is 'MAX'. But we don't need this one. We need 'MIN', for minimum. If you now typed in an 'I' as the second letter, the functions which start with 'I' would be displayed. This is not what we want! Just press the ⊡ key several times until the function 'MIN' is highlighted. Apply it by double-clicking. Then enter the range of cells (goals) against Number1 and click on Finish.

MAX

| Number1 | Goals | | = {"Goals";0;29;19;21 |
| Number2 | | | = number |

= 34

Returns the largest value in a set of values. Ignores logical values and text.

Number1: number1,number2,... are 1 to 30 numbers, empty cells, logical values, or text numbers for which you want the maximum.

Formula result = 34

OK Cancel

| Most goals | | 34 |
| Least goals | | |

1 Select the cell in which the minimum is to appear.

2 Run Function Wizard.

Paste Function

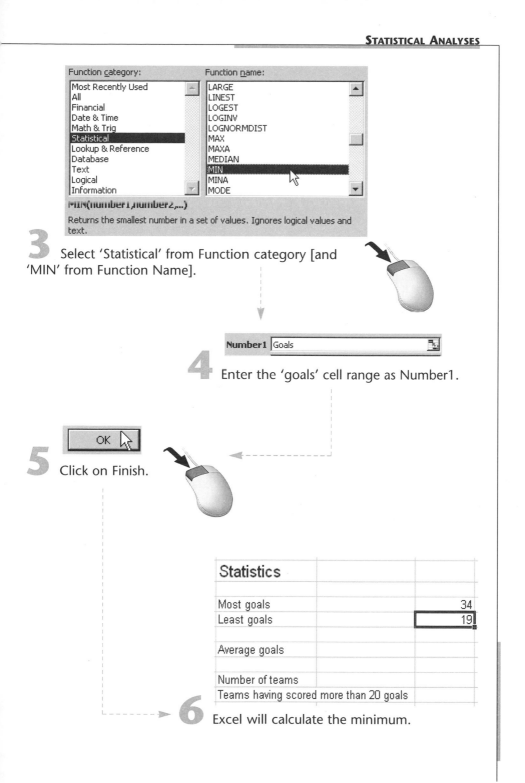

Function category:	Function name:
Most Recently Used	LARGE
All	LINEST
Financial	LOGEST
Date & Time	LOGINV
Math & Trig	LOGNORMDIST
Statistical	MAX
Lookup & Reference	MAXA
Database	MEDIAN
Text	MIN
Logical	MINA
Information	MODE

MIN(number1,number2,...)

Returns the smallest number in a set of values. Ignores logical values and text.

3 Select 'Statistical' from Function category [and 'MIN' from Function Name].

Number1 | Goals

4 Enter the 'goals' cell range as Number1.

OK

5 Click on Finish.

Statistics		
Most goals		34
Least goals		19
Average goals		
Number of teams		
Teams having scored more than 20 goals		

6 Excel will calculate the minimum.

How's it going? Average!

In the next cell we want to calculate the goal average. The procedure is, however, the same as for the maximum and minimum. The statistical expression for 'average' is Average. Run the Function Wizard and select 'AVERAGE' under Function Name. Enter the range to be analysed ('goals') against Number1.

MAX

Number1 Goals	= {"Goals";0;29;19;21
Number2	= number

= 34

Returns the largest value in a set of values. Ignores logical values and text.

Number1: number1,number2,... are 1 to 30 numbers, empty cells, logical values, or text numbers for which you want the maximum.

Formula result =34   OK   Cancel

Statistics		
Most goals		34
Least goals		19
Average goals		

1 Click on the appropriate cell.

f_x A↓ Z↓

2 Click on the Function Wizard button.

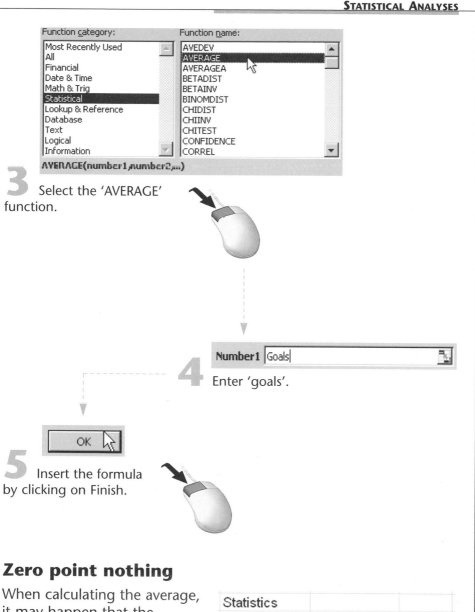

Function category:	Function name:
Most Recently Used	AVEDEV
All	AVERAGE
Financial	AVERAGEA
Date & Time	BETADIST
Math & Trig	BETAINV
Statistical	BINOMDIST
Lookup & Reference	CHIDIST
Database	CHIINV
Text	CHITEST
Logical	CONFIDENCE
Information	CORREL

AVERAGE(number1,number2,...)

3 Select the 'AVERAGE' function.

Number1 Goals

4 Enter 'goals'.

OK

5 Insert the formula by clicking on Finish.

Zero point nothing

When calculating the average, it may happen that the number calculated has decimal places. You can delete them in stages with the Decrease Decimal button on the standard toolbar. One decimal place will disappear

Statistics		
Most goals		34
Least goals		19
Average goals		27.4285714
Number of teams		
Teams having scored more than 20 goals		

195

with every click of the mouse and Excel will round the figures up or down as appropriate. If, on the other hand, you want to increase the number of decimal places, use the Increase Decimal button.

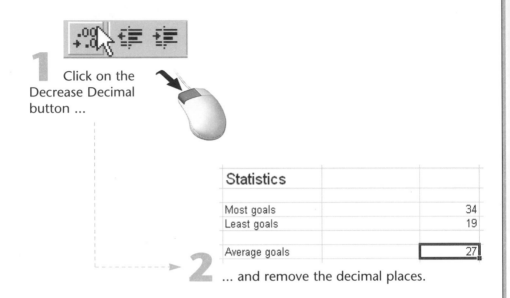

1 Click on the Decrease Decimal button ...

Statistics		
Most goals		34
Least goals		19
Average goals		27

2 ... and remove the decimal places.

What's the score, then?

The 'COUNTA' function is used to determine how many teams are specified. You can select 'COUNT', but this will only count cells of which the content consists of only numbers. 'COUNTA' will count all the cells, whatever their content, whether words or numbers.

MAX		
Number1 Goals		= {"Goals";0;29;19;21
Number2		= number

= 34

Returns the largest value in a set of values. Ignores logical values and text.

Number1: number1,number2,... are 1 to 30 numbers, empty cells, logical values, or text numbers for which you want the maximum.

Formula result =34   OK   Cancel

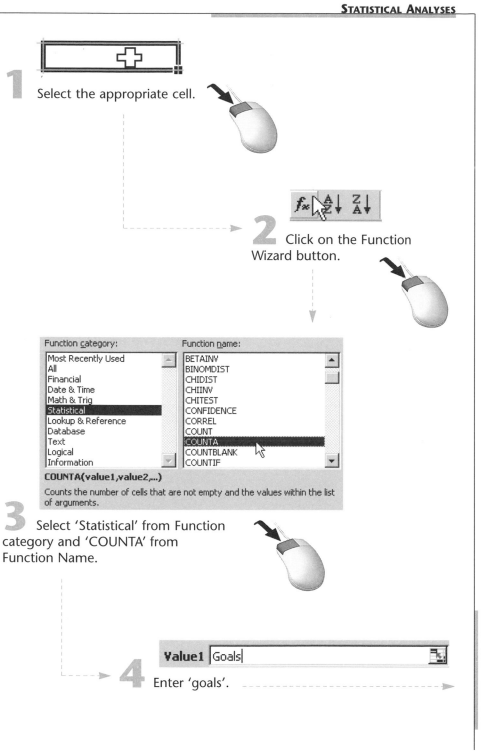

1 Select the appropriate cell.

2 Click on the Function Wizard button.

Function category:

Most Recently Used
All
Financial
Date & Time
Math & Trig
Statistical
Lookup & Reference
Database
Text
Logical
Information

Function name:

BETAINV
BINOMDIST
CHIDIST
CHIINV
CHITEST
CONFIDENCE
CORREL
COUNT
COUNTA
COUNTBLANK
COUNTIF

COUNTA(value1,value2,...)

Counts the number of cells that are not empty and the values within the list of arguments.

3 Select 'Statistical' from Function category and 'COUNTA' from Function Name.

Value1 Goals

4 Enter 'goals'.

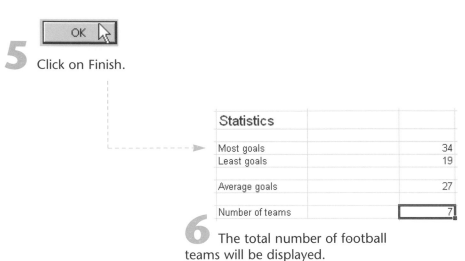

5 Click on Finish.

Statistics		
Most goals		34
Least goals		19
Average goals		27
Number of teams		7

6 The total number of football teams will be displayed.

If only the word 'if' didn't exist

Now for the last function in our example. The entry is now a bit more specific. We are looking for the number of goals over 20. Excel is only to count them if this criterion is fulfilled. The same procedure which you know from the other functions applies here too. The range is the same as in the other functions ('goals'). Now enter '>20' against criteria. Excel will count all the cells with a content greater than '20'. (i.e. 21, 22, 23, etc.).

COUNTIF

    Range `Goals`   = {"Goals";0;29;19;21

    Criteria `>20`   =

                            =

Counts the number of cells within a range that meet the given condition.

    Criteria is the condition in the form of a number, expression, or text that defines which cells will be counted.

Formula result =   OK   Cancel

Here are the characters for possible retrievals based on the number '20' in the summary:

Search criterion	Character	Result
Greater than 20	>20	21, 22, 23, ...
Greater than or equal to 20	>= 20	20, 21, 22 ...
Less than 20	<20	19, 18, 17, ...
Less than or equal to 20	<=20	20, 19, 18 ...

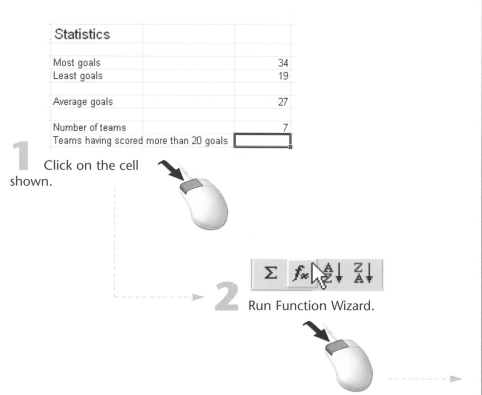

Statistics

Most goals		34
Least goals		19
Average goals		27
Number of teams		7
Teams having scored more than 20 goals		

1 Click on the cell shown.

2 Run Function Wizard.

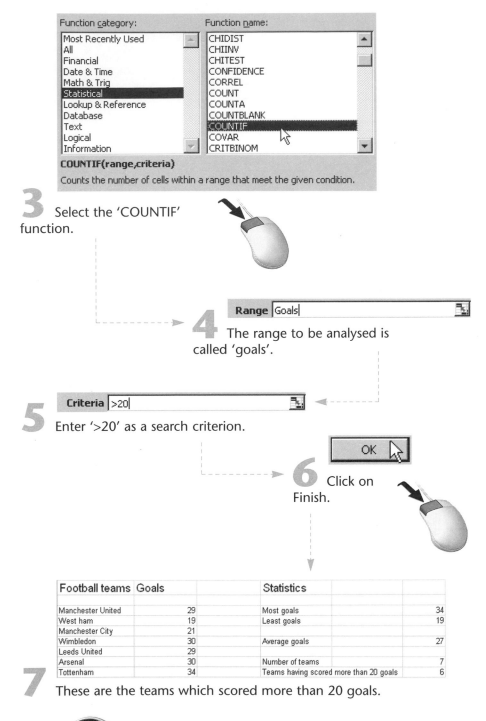

Function category:

- Most Recently Used
- All
- Financial
- Date & Time
- Math & Trig
- Statistical
- Lookup & Reference
- Database
- Text
- Logical
- Information

Function name:

- CHIDIST
- CHIINV
- CHITEST
- CONFIDENCE
- CORREL
- COUNT
- COUNTA
- COUNTBLANK
- COUNTIF
- COVAR
- CRITBINOM

COUNTIF(range,criteria)

Counts the number of cells within a range that meet the given condition.

3 Select the 'COUNTIF' function.

Range | Goals

4 The range to be analysed is called 'goals'.

Criteria | >20

5 Enter '>20' as a search criterion.

OK

6 Click on Finish.

Football teams	Goals		Statistics		
Manchester United	29		Most goals		34
West ham	19		Least goals		19
Manchester City	21				
Wimbledon	30		Average goals		27
Leeds United	29				
Arsenal	30		Number of teams		7
Tottenham	34		Teams having scored more than 20 goals		6

7 These are the teams which scored more than 20 goals.

Changing a formula

Football teams	Goals		Statistics	
Manchester United	29		Most goals	34
West ham	19		Least goals	19
Manchester City	21			
Wimbledon	30		Average goals	27
Leeds United	29			
Arsenal	30		Number of teams	7
Tottenham	34		Teams having scored more than 20 goals	6

Our little statistical analyses are now completed. Next match day, just change the figures. You will see how the statistics are adjusted automatically. If you want to change anything, it's easy. Let's take 'COUNTIF' as an example.

Clicking on the appropriate cell will display the formula in the formula bar. If you double-click with the left-hand mouse button,

Goals	Statistics	
31	Most goals	38
23	Least goals	23
24		
32	Average goals	30
32		
31	Number of teams	7
38	Teams having scored more than 20 goals	=B6:B12=COUNTIF(Goals,">20")

Excel will show you the range from which the analyses come, in blue. Up until now the formula 'COUNTIF (goals;'>20')' has applied. We are going to change this to '>30'. There is no need to run the Function Wizard. You can make the changes direct in the formula bar. Just replace the '2' with a '3'.

= =B6:B12=COUNTIF(Goals,">30")

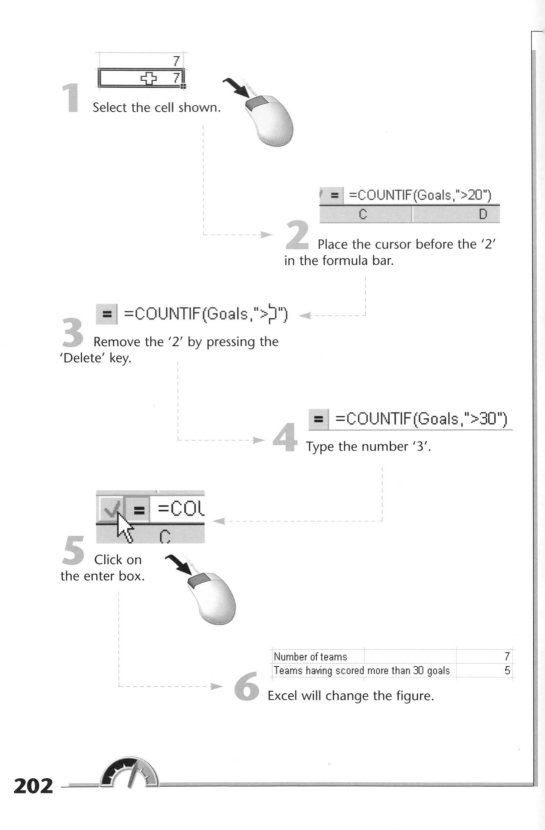

1 Select the cell shown.

=COUNTIF(Goals,">20")

| C | D |

2 Place the cursor before the '2' in the formula bar.

= =COUNTIF(Goals,">2")

3 Remove the '2' by pressing the 'Delete' key.

= =COUNTIF(Goals,">30")

4 Type the number '3'.

= =COL

C

5 Click on the enter box.

| Number of teams | | 7 |
| Teams having scored more than 30 goals | | 5 |

6 Excel will change the figure.

202

Another way to the same goal

It is not absolutely necessary to enter data in the Function Wizard in order to insert formulas. Naming cell ranges can also be dispensed with. There is another way! We

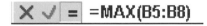

Statistics	
Most goals	
Least goals	
Average goals	

would like to show you another alternative. It is ultimately up to you which way you choose.

X ✓ = =MAX(B5:B8)   Let's assume that you have to analyse the statistics again. The maximum, i.e. the MAX function, is specified again. You click on the cell, run the Function Wizard and then the 'MAX' function.

MAX

Number1		▦ = number
Number2		▦ = number

=

Returns the largest value in a set of values. Ignores logical values and text.

Number1: number1,number2,... are 1 to 30 numbers, empty cells, logical values, or text numbers for which you want the maximum.

[?]   Formula result =   [OK]   [Cancel]

This time, don't make any entries. Just click on Finish.

Microsoft Excel

The formula you typed contains an error.

- For information about fixing common formula problems, click Help.
- To get assistance in entering a function, click OK, then click Function on the Insert menu.
- If you are not trying to enter a formula, avoid using an equal sign (=) or minus sign (-), or precede it with a single quotation mark (').

OK   Help

Excel will then display an error message, but we aren't going to take any notice of it. If you click on OK, Excel will insert part of the formula. Only the cells to be analysed are missing. The cursor will flash between the brackets ().

By pressing the mouse button you can specify the range to be considered. You will see a broken line around the cells. Once you  have covered all the cells, enter the formula. The process works for the other formulas too, not just for MAX.

Inserting a picture

Why not 'dress up' the statistics a bit? How about a picture? What could be better for goal statistics than a picture of a soccer player? You can find one by using the menu command Insert/Picture/Clip Art.

Football teams	Goals		Statistics	
Manchester United	31		Most goals	38
West ham	23		Least goals	23
Manchester City	24			
Wimbledon	32		Average goals	30
Leeds United	32			
Arsenal	31		Number of teams	7
Tottenham	38		Teams having scored more than 30 goals	5

You need the Clip Art tab, where you will find numerous categories. The pictures are classified as Household, Cartoons or Animals, for example. The All Categories option will show you all the Clip Art options. You can browse through them from top to bottom by using the scroll bar.

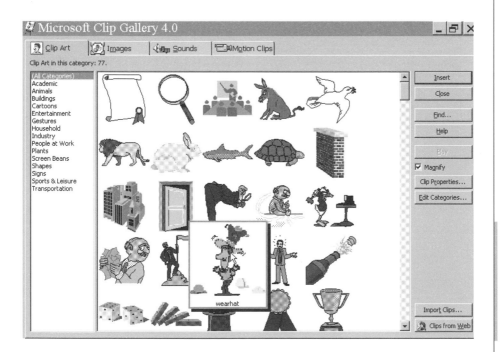

Select a picture by clicking on it with the mouse, though you can also use the arrow keys. A Clip Art picture will be inserted into your workbook when you click on the OK button. But there's a quicker way. Just double-click on the picture and it will be inserted into the document. You'll find our footballer under 'Sports and Leisure'.

soccer

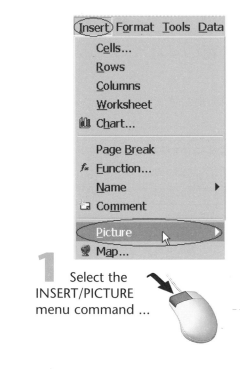

1 Select the INSERT/PICTURE menu command ...

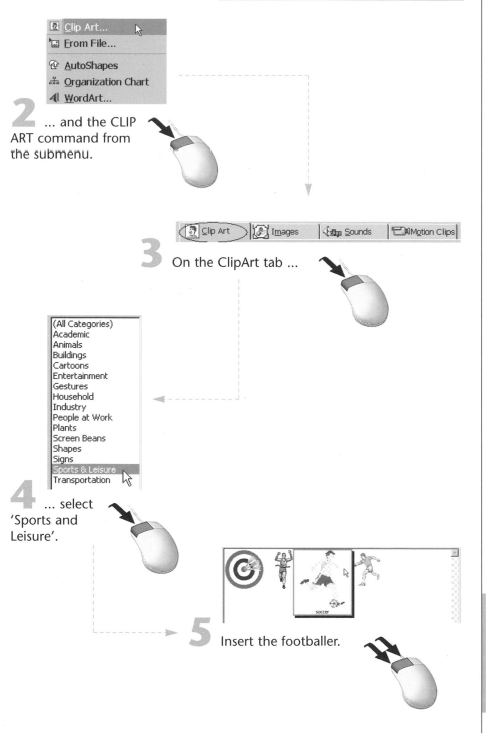

🖻 Clip Art...
🖼 From File...
🖲 AutoShapes
🔠 Organization Chart
4️ WordArt...

2 ... and the CLIP ART command from the submenu.

Clip Art | Images | Sounds | Motion Clips

3 On the ClipArt tab ...

(All Categories)
Academic
Animals
Buildings
Cartoons
Entertainment
Gestures
Household
Industry
People at Work
Plants
Screen Beans
Shapes
Signs
Sports & Leisure
Transportation

4 ... select 'Sports and Leisure'.

soccer

5 Insert the footballer.

207

Editing a picture

You will see little squares around the footballer. (They are called 'handles' – more about them later.) They show the precise border of the clip. You can remove the handles by clicking anywhere outside the picture. However, if you want to edit the

You must click on a picture in order to edit it.

picture, you must select it. To do this, click on the footballer and the squares will reappear.

When the clip appears on the screen, so will a graphics toolbar. You can use this to change the picture which you have inserted, e.g. its brightness or contrast. What is important to us is the Reset Picture button. If you click on this, the white background of the picture will disappear, or more exactly, it will become transparent.

1 Select the Clip Art picture (if you haven't already done so).

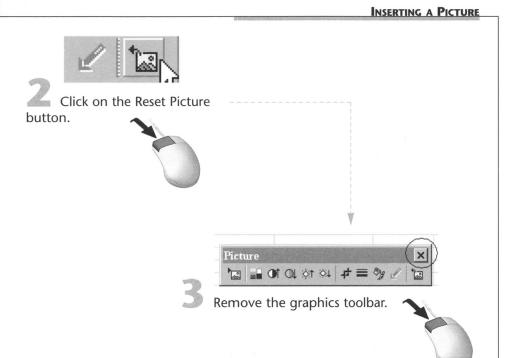

2 Click on the Reset Picture button.

3 Remove the graphics toolbar.

The footballer may now be offside in the workbook. He deserves to play in a better position. Click on the middle of the footballer and the

mouse pointer will turn into 'crosshairs'. If these are displayed, you can drag the picture to and fro in the workbook by holding down the left-hand button on the mouse. If you place the mouse pointer on a handle, you can change the size of the picture in the directions shown by the arrow.

209

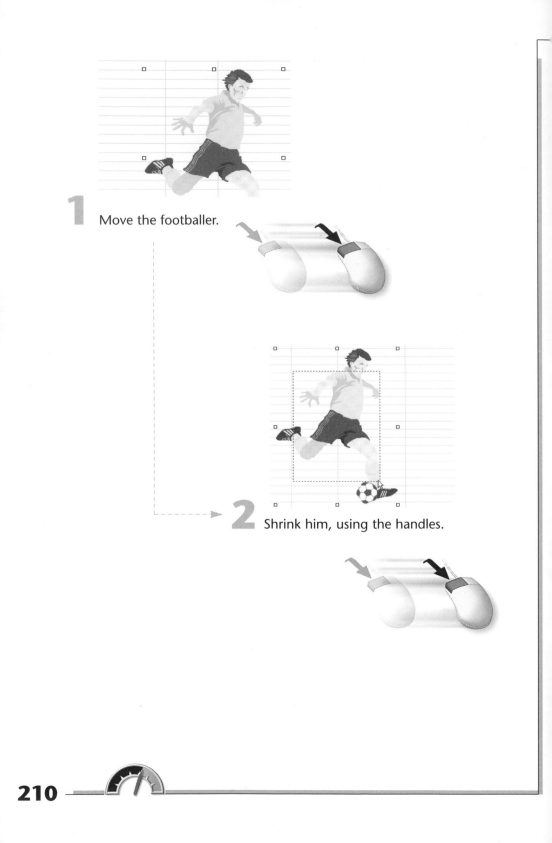

1 Move the footballer.

2 Shrink him, using the handles.

Full screen

Sometimes the Excel screen does not provide an overview. You can reduce the zoom by using VIEW/ZOOM. The Full Screen view is another option. You will find it on the VIEW menu. If you use the appropriate command, the section of the worksheet displayed on the screen will be increased. The title and toolbars will initially disappear from the screen. The menu bar will stay put. You can exit from 'Full Screen' by reselecting VIEW/FULL SCREEN.

Football teams	Goals		Statistics	
Manchester United	31		Most goals	38
West ham	23		Least goals	23
Manchester City	24			
Wimbledon	32		Average goals	30
Leeds United	32			
Arsenal	31		Number of teams	7
Tottenham	38		Teams having scored more than 30 goals	5

In the FULL SCREEN view, the toolbars and status bar can be displayed by placing the mouse pointer on the menu bar and pressing the right-hand button. Then click on the desired toolbars.

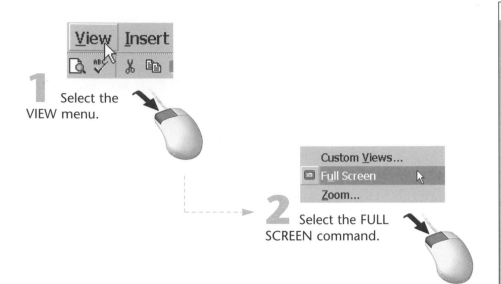

1 Select the VIEW menu.

2 Select the FULL SCREEN command.

Hiding and displaying gridlines

If the Excel gridlines are a distraction they can be hidden. They don't appear on the printout 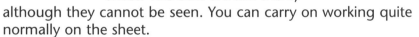 anyway. You will then have a white background on the sheet. The cells are still there, although they cannot be seen. You can carry on working quite normally on the sheet.

Select the menu command TOOLS/OPTIONS, then the VIEW tab. 'Uncheck' the Gridlines box under Window options. Display the gridlines by using the same procedure.

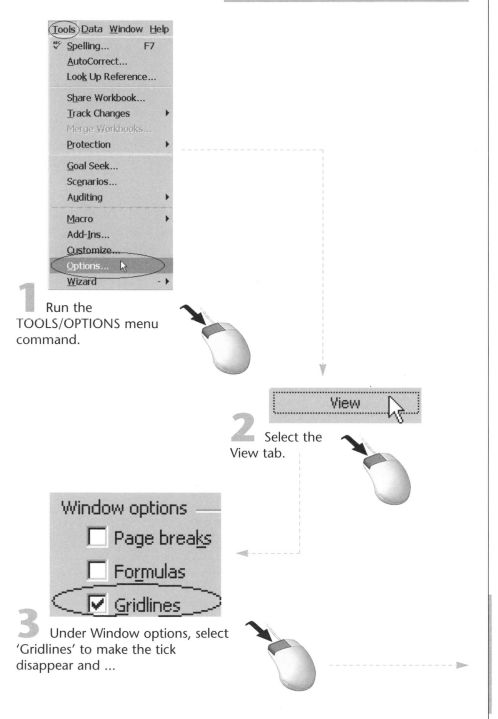

1 Run the TOOLS/OPTIONS menu command.

2 Select the View tab.

3 Under Window options, select 'Gridlines' to make the tick disappear and ...

213

4  ... confirm by clicking on OK.

Statistics

Most goals	38
Least goals	23
Average goals	30
Number of teams	7
Teams having scored more than 30 goals	5

Your worksheet will look a little unfamiliar without the gridlines, but this will not affect its use. You can carry on doing everything you have learned exactly as usual.

You must decide for yourself whether you prefer working with gridlines or without. It is certainly easier for a beginner to use gridlines.

As you were!

In order to carry on smoothly into the next chapter, we suggest that you deactivate 'Full Screen' and display the gridlines again (if you haven't already done so).

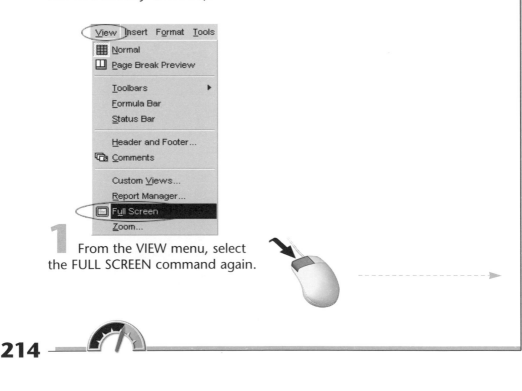

1 From the VIEW menu, select the FULL SCREEN command again.

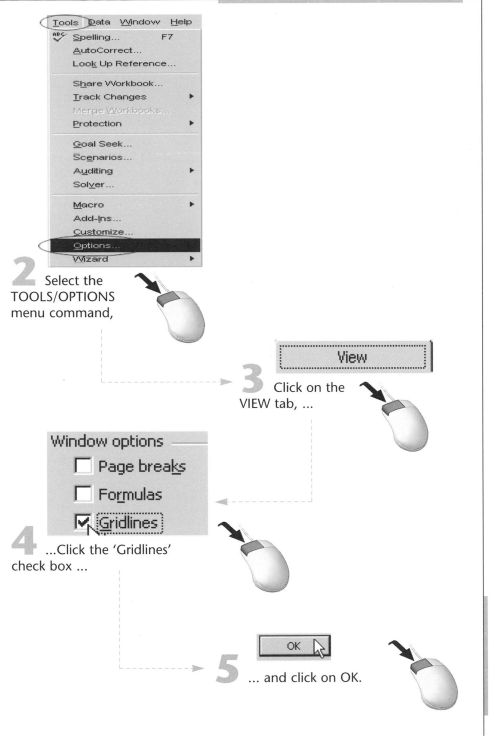

Tools D̲ata W̲indow H̲elp

✓ S̲pelling...   F7
A̲utoCorrect...
Loo̲k Up Reference...

S̲hare Workbook...
T̲rack Changes   ▶
Merge Workbooks...
P̲rotection   ▶

G̲oal Seek...
Sce̲narios...
A̲uditing   ▶
Sol̲ver...

Ma̲cro   ▶
Add-I̲ns...
C̲ustomize...
O̲ptions...
W̲izard   ▶

2 Select the TOOLS/OPTIONS menu command,

View

3 Click on the VIEW tab, ...

Window options
☐ Page brea̲ks
☐ Fo̲rmulas
☑ G̲ridlines

4 ...Click the 'Gridlines' check box ...

OK

5 ... and click on OK.

The Excel trainer

Of course, other figures besides goals have to be analysed. First we are going to obtain an overview. Enter the individual formulas by using the Function Wizard, which you can run by double-clicking on the appropriate button on the standard toolbar.

	Jan		
Brown	1,500.00	2,450.00	Jan 9,200.00
Jones	2,300.00	5,000.00	5,800.00
Mark	4,500.00	3,100.00	7,000.00
Smith	5,600.00	3,400.00	5,600.00
Barking	11,000.00	2,750.00	8,900.00
Peters	13,000.00	4,300.00	7,800.00
Thomas	500.00	4,200.00	12,000.00

1 Use the text in the cells and enter the months 'January', 'February' and 'March', using the AutoFill function.

	Jan		
Brown	1,500.00	2,450.00	Jan 9,200.00
Jones	2,300.00	5,000.00	5,800.00
Mark	4,500.00	3,100.00	7,000.00
Smith	5,600.00	3,400.00	5,600.00
Barking	11,000.00	2,750.00	8,900.00
Peters	13,000.00	4,300.00	7,800.00
Thomas	500.00	4,200.00	12,000.00

2 Enter the sales figures.

Highest sales	
Lowest sales	
Average sales	
Sales greater than £1,000	
Sales greater than £5,000	

3 Enter the criteria for analysis.

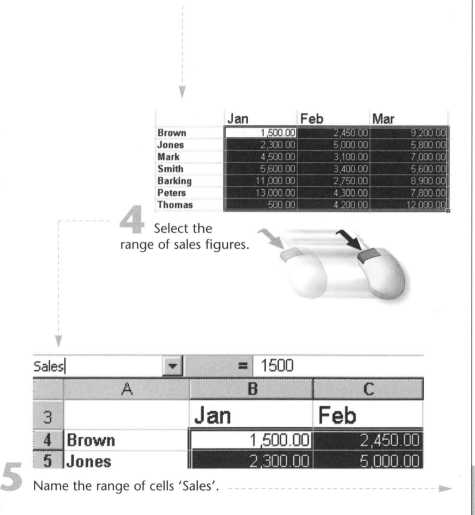

	Jan	Feb	Mar
Brown	1,500.00	2,450.00	9,200.00
Jones	2,300.00	5,000.00	5,800.00
Mark	4,500.00	3,100.00	7,000.00
Smith	5,600.00	3,400.00	5,600.00
Barking	11,000.00	2,750.00	8,900.00
Peters	13,000.00	4,300.00	7,800.00
Thomas	500.00	4,200.00	12,000.00

4 Select the range of sales figures.

Sales		=	1500
	A	B	C
3		Jan	Feb
4	**Brown**	1,500.00	2,450.00
5	**Jones**	2,300.00	5,000.00

5 Name the range of cells 'Sales'.

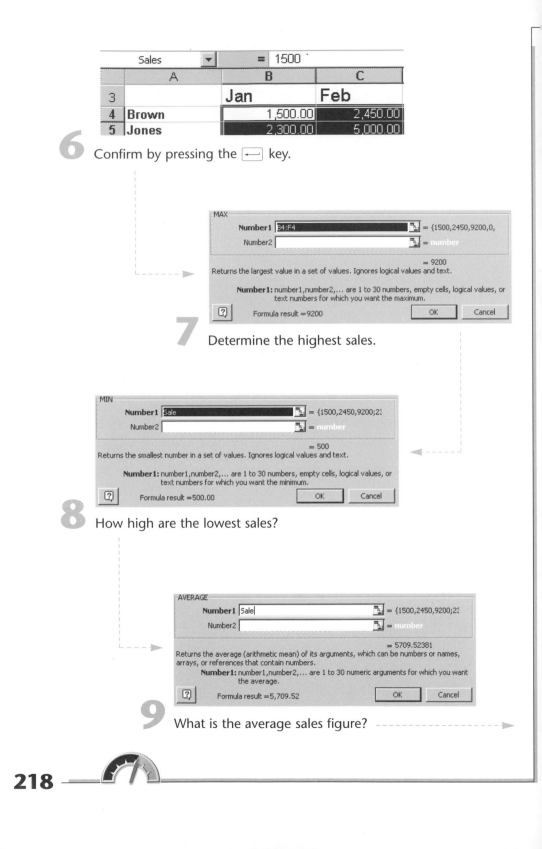

	A	B	C
	Sales	▼	= 1500
3		Jan	Feb
4	Brown	1,500.00	2,450.00
5	Jones	2,300.00	5,000.00

6 Confirm by pressing the ⏎ key.

MAX

Number1 B4:F4 = {1500,2450,9200,0,

Number2 = number

= 9200

Returns the largest value in a set of values. Ignores logical values and text.

Number1: number1,number2,... are 1 to 30 numbers, empty cells, logical values, or text numbers for which you want the maximum.

Formula result =9200   OK   Cancel

7 Determine the highest sales.

MIN

Number1 Sale = {1500,2450,9200;2:

Number2 = number

= 500

Returns the smallest number in a set of values. Ignores logical values and text.

Number1: number1,number2,... are 1 to 30 numbers, empty cells, logical values, or text numbers for which you want the minimum.

Formula result =500.00   OK   Cancel

8 How high are the lowest sales?

AVERAGE

Number1 Sale = {1500,2450,9200;2:

Number2 = number

= 5709.52381

Returns the average (arithmetic mean) of its arguments, which can be numbers or names, arrays, or references that contain numbers.

Number1: number1,number2,... are 1 to 30 numeric arguments for which you want the average.

Formula result =5,709.52   OK   Cancel

9 What is the average sales figure?

```
COUNTIF
       Range  Sale                          ▦  = {1500,2450,9200;2:
     Criteria  >1000                          ▦  =
                                          =
Counts the number of cells within a range that meet the given condition.

       Criteria is the condition in the form of a number, expression, or text that defines
                which cells will be counted.
  [?]     Formula result =                    [  OK  ]   [ Cancel ]
```

10 How many of the sales figures are over £ 1,000?

```
COUNTIF
       Range  Sale                          ▦  = {1500,2450,9200;2:
     Criteria  >5000                          ▦  =
                                          =
Counts the number of cells within a range that meet the given condition.

       Criteria is the condition in the form of a number, expression, or text that defines
                which cells will be counted.
  [?]     Formula result =                    [  OK  ]   [ Cancel ]
```

11 How many of the sales figures exceed £ 5,000?

Highest sales	13,000.00
Lowest sales	500.00
Average sales	5,709.52
Sales greater than £1,000	20.00
Sales greater than £5,000	10.00

12 Here's the result. Now change some of the sales figures.

What's in this chapter?

Whether for sales figures, elections or food packaging, percentages are part of daily life, like death and taxation. They help you to recognise proportions more easily. Which is the better deal percentage-wise £1,800 out of £4,500 or £3,120 out of £7,800? Well, you can get more Smarties at the corner shop for £3,120, but the percentages are the same – 40%. But is there a quick way to get percentages? Yes, Excel has a fast track.

Amount	Percentage
£1,000.00	12%
£500.00	6%
£300.00	3%
£2,300.00	27%
£4,500.00	52%
	0%
	0%
	100%
£8,600.00	

Total

You already know:

Your are going to learn:

As a percentage

In this chapter you are going to make a simple calculation, with no tricks. You are going to make a list of figures, find their sum and give the individual figures as percentages. The sum is always 100%, that's easy. But what are the percentages of the other figures? First you need the figures for the calculation.

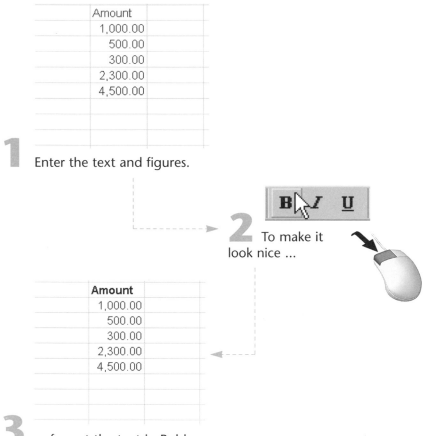

1 Enter the text and figures.

2 To make it look nice ...

3 ... format the text in Bold.

This could represent a sales presentation, cost analysis or whatever. Enter the abbreviation £ here, though the units could be anything, litres (of beer or petrol consumed), miles (of road built) or even eggs laid on a hen farm.

Select the corresponding cells and click on the Currency Style button. For any other units, select the FORMAT/CELLS menu command and the Number tab.

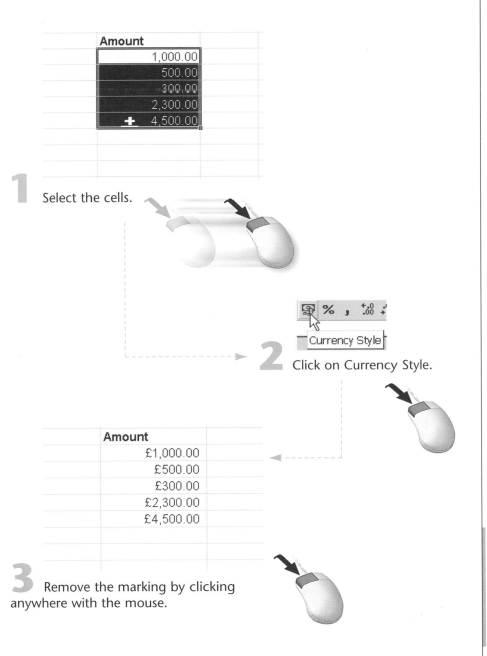

1 Select the cells.

Currency Style

2 Click on Currency Style.

3 Remove the marking by clicking anywhere with the mouse.

Summing Up

To determine percentages, you need the total, or sum of the figures. Select the cell in which you want the result to appear. Click on the Sum button and Excel will select the cells above with a broken line. Press the ⊖ key and the result will be inserted.

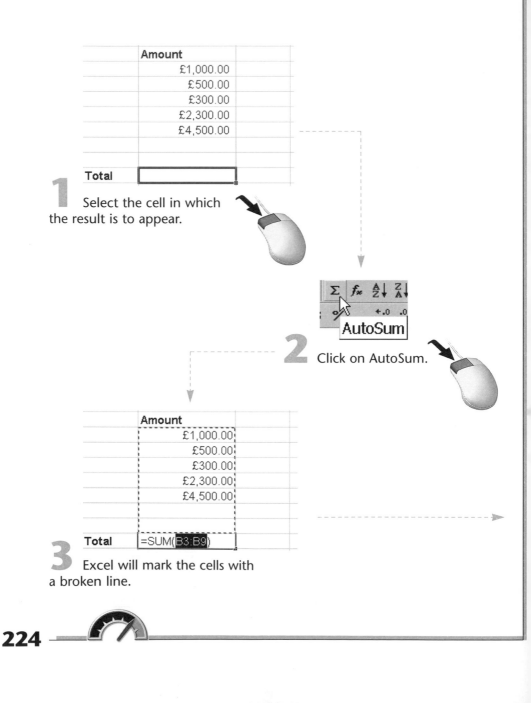

1 Select the cell in which the result is to appear.

AutoSum

2 Click on AutoSum.

3 Excel will mark the cells with a broken line.

	Amount	
	£1,000.00	
	£500.00	
	£300.00	
	£2,300.00	
	£4,500.00	
Total	£8,600.00	

4 Confirm by pressing ⏎.

Naming a cell

We now come to the percentages. To determine these individually, we need the sum of the amounts we are going to refer to. Naming the cell makes things a lot simpler. In order to name a cell, you must first click on it.

Now place the cursor in the Name box at the top. Enter the name. We are using 'Total'. This has the advantage that you can always refer back to the 'Total' cell when making calculations.

	Amount	
	£1,000.00	
	£500.00	
	£300.00	
	£2,300.00	
	£4,500.00	
Total	£8,600.00	

1 Click on the cell containing the total.

| | Total | | ▼ | | = | =SUM(B3:B9) |

Book1

	A	B	C
1			
2		Amount	
3		£1,000.00	
4		£500.00	
5		£300.00	
6		£2,300.00	
7		£4,500.00	
8			
9			
10	Total	£8,600.00	

2 Select the Name box, type in 'Total' and confirm it by pressing the ⏎ key.

Back to school

Now all that remains is to enter the formula for calculating the percentages represented by the individual figures. So, it's back to school We need to apply what we learned, or should have done, in arithmetic lessons. Are you paying attention?

First, we take the result, the sum of all the figures, which is '8,600' in the example.

To find 1% of 8,600, 8,600 must be divided by 100:

$$1\% = \frac{8,600}{100}$$

If you want to know what £1,000 is as a percentage of £8,600, the formula must be as follows:

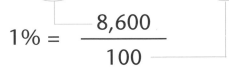

$$? \% = \frac{100 \times 1000}{8,600}$$

'£ amount' stands for the '1,000' which you want to determine. The '8,600' below the line represents the 'Total'. We have already named the relevant cell. If we now replace the numbers by the terms, we get the following formula:

$$? \% = \frac{100 \times £ \text{ amount}}{\text{Total}}$$

You will find the Percent Style button on the standard toolbar. This is used to specify that percentages should appear in this cell. If you click on it, Excel will automatically multiply the amount in the cell by 100.

This means that we do not need to multiply by 100. If we take this into account, we get the following formula:

$$? \% = \frac{£ \text{ amount}}{\text{Total}}$$

You need only click on the Percent Style button and divide the individual value by the total to express proportions as percentages.

In our example, you therefore only need to divide the £ amount by the total and click the Percent Style (%) button.

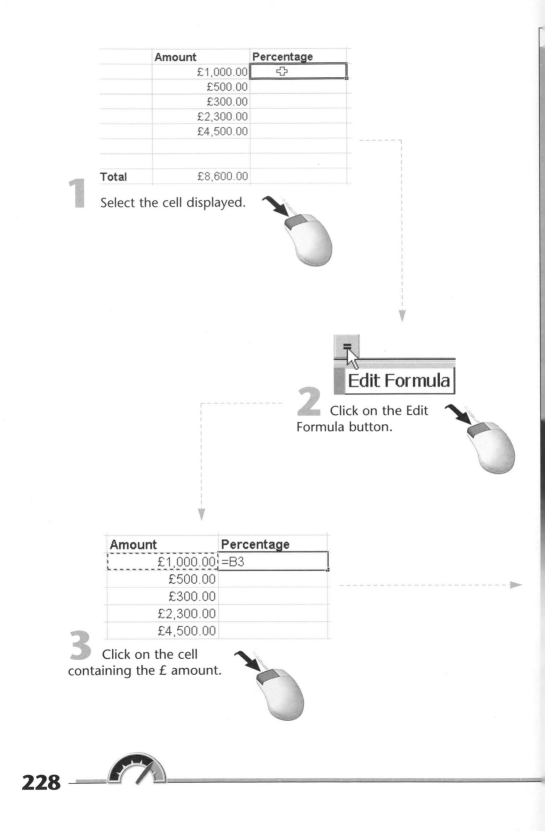

	Amount	Percentage
	£1,000.00	✛
	£500.00	
	£300.00	
	£2,300.00	
	£4,500.00	
Total	£8,600.00	

1 Select the cell displayed.

Edit Formula

2 Click on the Edit Formula button.

Amount	Percentage
£1,000.00	=B3
£500.00	
£300.00	
£2,300.00	
£4,500.00	

3 Click on the cell containing the £ amount.

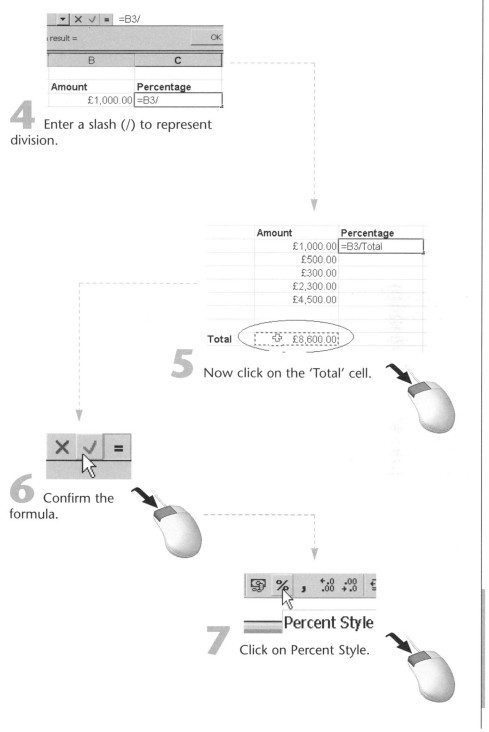

4 Enter a slash (/) to represent division.

5 Now click on the 'Total' cell.

6 Confirm the formula.

Percent Style

7 Click on Percent Style.

Copying formulas

You have determined percentages for one cell. The rest are still missing. All the calculations refer to the '£ amount' and the 'Total'. The formula need only be copied from one cell to the others.

Amount	Percentage
£1,000.00	12%
£500.00	6%
£300.00	3%
£2,300.00	27%
£4,500.00	52%
Total £8,600.00	100%

Move the mouse pointer to the fill handle and drag it downwards, holding the mouse button down.

Amount	Percentage
£1,000.00	12%
£500.00	
£300.00	
£2,300.00	
£4,500.00	
£8,600.00	

1 Place the mouse pointer on the fill handle.

Amount	Percentage
£1,000.00	12%
£500.00	
£300.00	
£2,300.00	
£4,500.00	
Total £8,600.00	

2 Copy the formula by dragging the mouse pointer downwards.

Hiding zeros

Rounding figures up and down may mean that you do not always get 100% exactly.

Our percentages have been calculated. The figure '100%' appears alongside the 'Total' cell. So everything is correct.

When you look at the exercise, only one thing is out of place: '0%' appears alongside the empty cells. Down with zeros! They are an occupational hazard, but they don't have to be. You can delete them. However, you might want to enter figures in the

Amount	Percentage
£1,000.00	12%
£500.00	6%
£300.00	3%
£2,300.00	27%
£4,500.00	52%
	0%
	0%
Total £8,600.00	100%

empty cells later on. Excel provides a possibility for suppressing zeros, such that if a cell contains the figure '0' it will not be displayed on screen or printed. From the TOOLS/OPTIONS menu go to the View tab and uncheck the 'Zero values' box (remove the tick). This

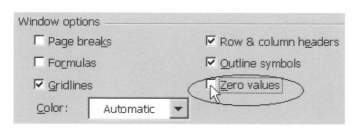

doesn't just apply to percentages, but also to all figures. The zeros will be suppressed until you select the same menu command again and recheck the box on the View tab.

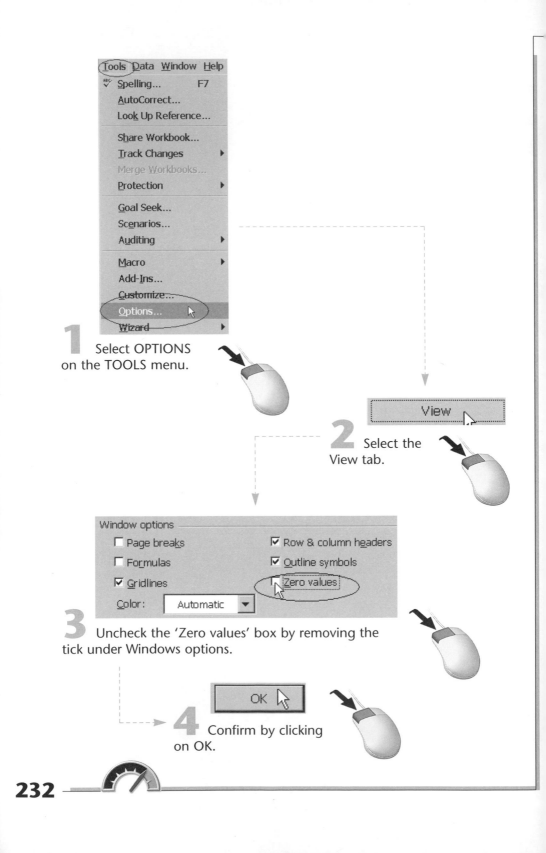

Tools Data Window Help

✓ᴬᴮᶜ Spelling...   F7
       AutoCorrect...
       Look Up Reference...

       Share Workbook...
       Track Changes   ▶
       Merge Workbooks...
       Protection   ▶

       Goal Seek...
       Scenarios...
       Auditing   ▶

       Macro   ▶
       Add-Ins...
       Customize...
       Options...   ▶
       Wizard   ▶

1 Select OPTIONS on the TOOLS menu.

2 Select the View tab.

View

Window options
   ☐ Page breaks   ☑ Row & column headers
   ☐ Formulas   ☑ Outline symbols
   ☑ Gridlines   ☐ Zero values
   Color: Automatic ▼

3 Uncheck the 'Zero values' box by removing the tick under Windows options.

OK

4 Confirm by clicking on OK.

232

No room for figures

Our little percentage calculation, which you can also use for larger exercises, is now finished. If you enter new amounts Excel will adjust the percentages automatically.

	Amount	Percentage
	£1,000.00	12%
	£500.00	6%
	£300.00	3%
	£2,300.00	27%
	£4,500.00	52%
Total	£8,600.00	100%

If you enter longer amounts, you may see this displayed: (##########) – gates but no figures. Don't panic! It's OK. These

	Amount	Percentage
	########	93%
	£500.00	0%
	£300.00	0%
	£2,300.00	2%
	£4,500.00	4%
Total	########	100%

characters do not mean that anything is wrong. They just mean there isn't enough display space in the 'Total' cell because you have entered longer figures.

Gates ######## mean that the column is too narrow to display the contents of the cell.

All you need to do is widen the column, by placing the mouse pointer on the column heading border between the column headings. You can widen the column by moving the mouse with the button held down, or, even quicker, by double-clicking. Excel will automatically adjust the column width to accommodate the longest entry.

	Amount	Percentage
	£1,000.00	9%
	£500.00	4%
	£300.00	3%
	£2,300.00	20%
	£4,500.00	39%
	£2,800.00	25%
Total	£11,400.00	100%

233

1 If the space in a cell is insufficient (shown by #####),

B	C
Amount	**Percentage**
£1,000.00	7%
£500.00	4%
£300.00	2%
£2,300.00	17%
£4,500.00	33%
£5,000.00	37%
########	100%

2 Place the mouse pointer on the column heading border.

Amount	Percentage
£1,000.00	7%
£500.00	4%
£300.00	2%
£2,300.00	17%
£4,500.00	33%
£5,000.00	37%
£13,600.00	100%

3 Adjust the column width by double-clicking.

The Excel trainer

Percentages, percentages, percentages! The Excel Trainer provides more opportunities for practice.

Products

	Items	Percentage of total
Brown	1,234	
Jones	4,555	
Mark	1,025	
Smith	3,578	
Barking	3,323	
Peters	4,023	
Thomas	4,506	
Cane	2,223	

1 Enter the text and figures.

Then:

☞ Determine the total number of items.

☞ Enter the name 'Total items' in the Name box for the cell.

☞ Click on the cell to the right of 'Brown's items'.

☞ Click on the equals sign to edit the formula.

	Items	Percentage of total
Brown	1,234	5%
Jones	4,555	19%
Mark	1,025	4%
Smith	3,578	15%
Barking	3,323	14%
Peters	4,023	16%
Thomas	4,506	18%
Cane	2,223	9%
	24,467	

2

 Divide the numbers under 'Items' by the total number of items.

 Click on the Percent Style button.

 Copy the formula down.

	Expenditure	Expenditure (%)
Stationery	£900.00	
Expenses	£170.00	
Mileage	£250.00	
Food	£520.00	
Software	£320.00	
Total		

1
Living is costly. Everything is getting more expensive! Enter the text and figures for the household budget.

Then proceed as follows:

 Determine the total costs.

 Enter the name 'Costs' in the Name box.

 Select the cell to the right of Accommodation/Expenditure.

 Click on the equals sign to edit the formula.

	Expenditure	Expenditure (%)
Accomodation	£900.00	42%
Extras	£170.00	8%
Travel	£250.00	12%
Food	£520.00	24%
Other	£320.00	14%
Total	£2,160.00	100%

2

➡ Divide the 'Expenditure' cell by 'Costs'.

➡ Click on the Percent Style button.

➡ Copy the formula down.

➡ Suppress the zero values (if present) (TOOLS/OPTIONS, View tab, Window Options).

Cashing in

What's in this chapter?

No dough, no go. Look at your finances. What can you see? Nothing! 'But there was still some money there yesterday!' you say, wiping the tears from your eyes. 'Where's it all gone? How shall I pay the rent?' By using an Excel cash book, you will always know where your money went. And not only that: you will be able to see how much money is left, without having to count every penny. Time is money! By using Excel you can determine your income and expenditure from month to month and from year to year.

Cash Book

| | | | | Income | | £1,290.00 |
| | | | | Expenditure | | £539.90 |

Company ABC, 51 Bond Street, London

| | | | | | | £200.00 |
| | | | | | | £950.10 |

Opening balance
Closing balance

No.	Text	Income	Expenditure	Cash	
1	Bank interest	£200.00			£400.00
2	Courier		£80.00		£320.00
3	Stationery		£200.00		£120.00
4	Travel		£29.95		£90.05
5	Facsimile	£115.00			£205.05
6	PC hardware		£200.00		£5.05
7	Bank interest	£400.00			£405.05
8	Consulting	£575.00			£980.05
9	Travel		£29.95		£950.10
10	Closing balance				£950.10

You already know:

Your are going to learn:

Inserting borders

Highlighting text

First you must decide what's what. We are making up a 'cash book' and that is what you are going to call it in Excel. You can highlight it by selecting a different font and font size. Once you have entered everything, confirm the entry.

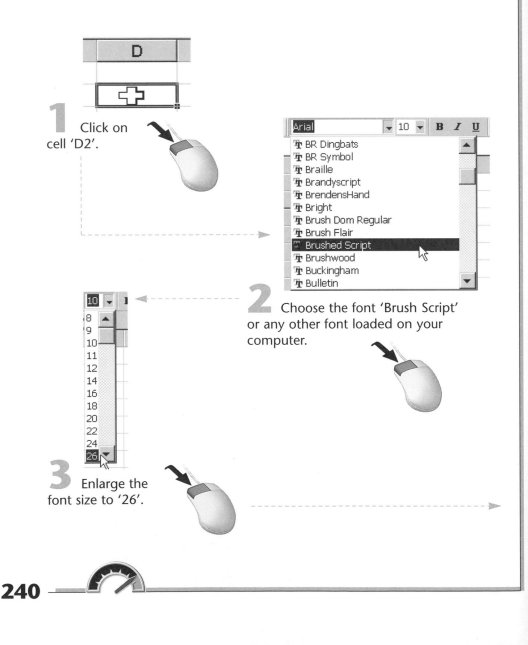

1 Click on cell 'D2'.

2 Choose the font 'Brush Script' or any other font loaded on your computer.

3 Enlarge the font size to '26'.

Cash Book

4 Type in 'Cash Book'.

× ✓ = Cash Book

Enter   D

5 Confirm the entry.

What's always needed in a cash book? The name of the firm! Enter it in cell 'B2'. What's a cash book supposed to do? To keep things simple, we have selected only 'income' and 'expenditure', otherwise we might not see the wood for the trees.

Excel will work out your VAT for you. The date of the invoice can also be entered. The design of your cash book depends on you. We are only providing the framework in this chapter. When it comes to actually building the 'pay kiosk' you can do it yourself.

In this example we are going to determine the current balance, but more of that later. We also want to establish the totals for 'income' and 'expenditure'. The monthly closing balance should be available at a glance. Every cash book also has an opening balance, so we shall enter it.

TIP

You should use the same cells for making up your cash book as the ones specified in this example.

So you will be entering the following text in the cash book: opening balance, monthly closing balance, income and expenditure. The figures will come later, when you enter the actual income and expenditure as amounts.

241

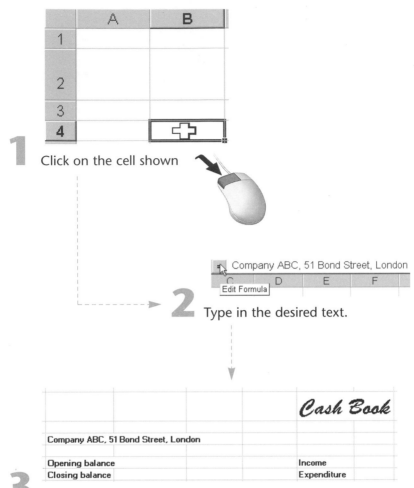

1 Click on the cell shown

Company ABC, 51 Bond Street, London

2 Type in the desired text.

			Cash Book
Company ABC, 51 Bond Street, London			
Opening balance		Income	
Closing balance		Expenditure	

3 Enter the other text in the appropriate cells.

'Bordering' cells

As already stated, we shall sort out the figures later. The amounts will then appear opposite the relevant text. In order to highlight the cells more strongly, we are going to border them. The border is the line around the cells.

Opening balance		Income	
Closing balance		Expenditure	

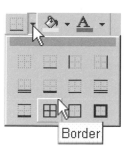

Select the Borders button on the standard toolbar and click on the arrow. A selection of possible borders will be displayed. You will see that the lines are black. This is exactly how you would draw the borders. You will see a black line on the left, on the right, at the top or at the bottom, or a combination of these. The button the mouse is pointing at here will place a border around more than two cells, i.e. all the cells selected will receive a border.

Highlight the cells for the opening and monthly closing balance in our cash book in precisely this way. First, select the two cells. Then select the border.

You cannot delete a border by using the ⌊Delete⌋ key. You have to select the Borders button again to do this. Then choose the border without any black lines.

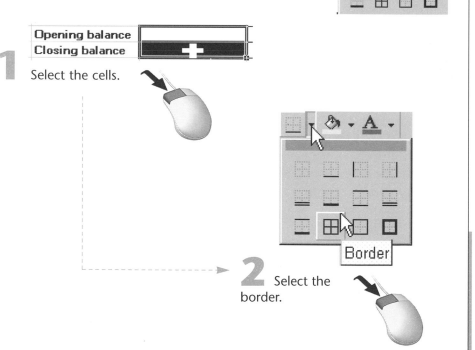

Opening balance	
Closing balance	

1 Select the cells.

2 Select the border.

The standard Excel toolbar will always display the most recently used border. If you want to use it again, you need not select the whole border menu again. Just click on the button. This border will be displayed until you select another one.

Use the same type of border as you originally selected for 'income' and 'expenditure' in our cash book.

| Income |
| Expenditure |

1 Select both cells.

2 Click on the button.

The 'heading' is finished. The actual income and expenditure now follow, but we want to distinguish visually

Company ABC, 51 Bond Street, London		
Income		
Expenditure		

 between the upper and lower sections. You are going to use another border, though the term 'border' is a bit confusing, as you are going to select a form in which only the lower line of cells will be double-underlined.

Select a whole row. There is no need to select every cell. Just click the corresponding row number on the left-hand side of the screen. Of course, you can also select several rows simultaneously in this way. You need only drag the pointer up or down with the left-hand mouse button pressed down.

If you click on row no. 9 in the cash book the whole row will be selected. Then select the appropriate type of border.

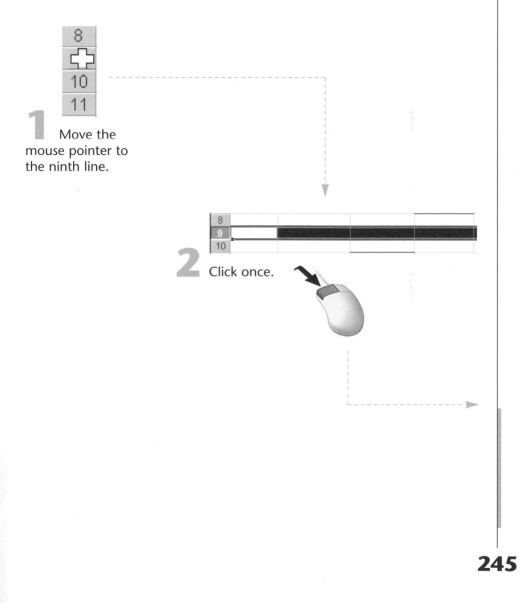

1 Move the mouse pointer to the ninth line.

2 Click once.

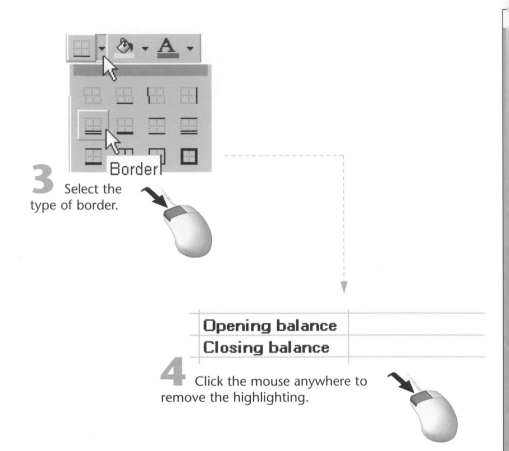

3 Select the type of border.

Opening balance	
Closing balance	

4 Click the mouse anywhere to remove the highlighting.

Preparing cells

The next step is to prepare cells for the cash form. Then you will only need to enter transactions as income or expenditure later.

Changing the column width

We now come to the lower section of the cash book. We have chosen to use consecutive number, text, income, expenditure and balance. Once again, you can select other entries for your cash book. These are only intended as examples.

To be able to work more easily with the cells later on, we are going to change the individual column widths now. Only one number will be entered for 'consecutive number'. This column does not need to be too wide, so we shall make it narrower. In contrast, the 'Text' column will certainly need more space later, so we shall widen it.

As we explained earlier, there is a quick way to change the column width. Place the mouse pointer at the top, between two columns, or more precisely, on the column header border. The mouse pointer will change its appearance. As soon as it changes into a 'double arrow' you can change the respective column width with a click.

	A	B	C	D	E	F	G
3							
4		Company ABC, 51 Bond Street, London					
5							
6		Income					
7		Expenditure					
8							
9							
10							
11			Text				

1 Enter the text in the cells.

2 Position the mouse pointer.

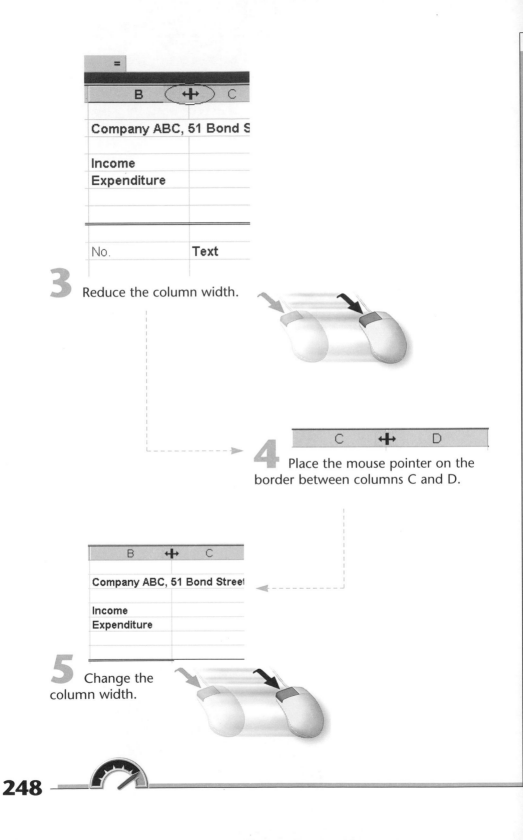

B	⟨✛⟩ C
Company ABC, 51 Bond S	
Income	
Expenditure	
No.	**Text**

3 Reduce the column width.

C	✛	D

4 Place the mouse pointer on the border between columns C and D.

B	✛	C
Company ABC, 51 Bond Street		
Income		
Expenditure		

5 Change the column width.

You have now changed the column width. If you see a broken line on the right-hand side of your worksheet, Excel is telling you that this is the limit, i.e. the edge of the worksheet. Anything that you enter beyond this line will be printed on a separate page. You will see this broken line not only on the right-hand side of the sheet, but also at the bottom. This means that the end of the page has also been reached. This is just mentioned in passing.

Back to the cash book. You have entered the first row. Place a border round the cells: the style of border will be shown on the button, because you used it last time. So, select the cells again and click on the Borders button. We cannot select a whole row this time because we only want to place a border around certain cells.

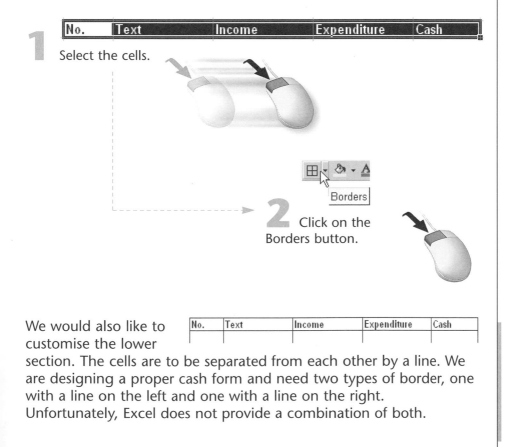

1 Select the cells.

| No. | Text | Income | Expenditure | Cash |

Borders

2 Click on the Borders button.

We would also like to customise the lower

No.	Text	Income	Expenditure	Cash

section. The cells are to be separated from each other by a line. We are designing a proper cash form and need two types of border, one with a line on the left and one with a line on the right. Unfortunately, Excel does not provide a combination of both.

249

You could select the cells now and select the appropriate border. But let's do it differently. Both methods take as long as each other and produce the same result.

Click on a row. Then select one border style (line on the left), then the other (line on the right). Of course, you could do it the other way round. After all, we don't want to be accused of political bias.

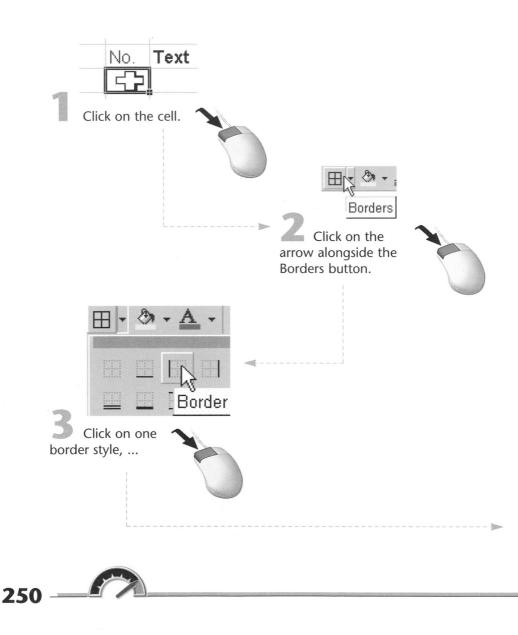

1 Click on the cell.

2 Click on the arrow alongside the Borders button.

3 Click on one border style, ...

4 ... click on
the arrow again ...

5 ... and click on
the other border style.

The borders have been selected. Move the mouse pointer onto the
fill handle. Hold the button down and drag it into the other cells.
This will copy the border style.

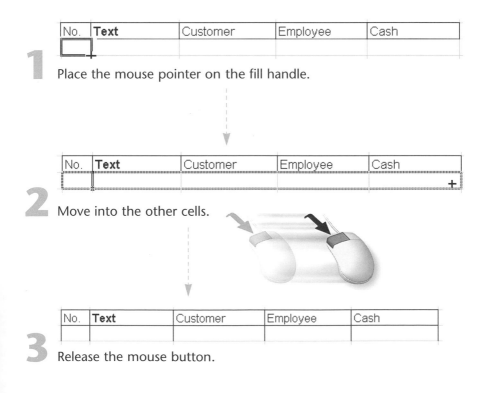

No.	Text	Customer	Employee	Cash

1 Place the mouse pointer on the fill handle.

No.	Text	Customer	Employee	Cash

2 Move into the other cells.

No.	Text	Customer	Employee	Cash

3 Release the mouse button.

251

Now be patient and don't enter any more text and figures yet. We'll tell you why later (It's a secret). If you were to put in figures now, you would look silly. No one would know what they meant – eggs, pears, apples or what? In a British cash book we give the amounts in pounds, of course – at least until the Euro arrives.

Format the cells for Currency Style. You do not need to enter any figures to do this. Income and expenditure are not

Company ABC, 51 Bond Street, London					
Income		200			
Expenditure					

No.	Text	Customer	Employee	Cash	
1	Bank cheque	200			

always round figures: pence can occur too. For this reason the cells must be formatted for two decimal places.

Click on the cell and press the right mouse-button. A context-sensitive menu will appear. You can also select the FORMAT/CELLS menu command. It comes to the same thing.

    ✂ Cu<u>t</u>
    🗐 <u>C</u>opy
    📋 <u>P</u>aste
       Paste <u>S</u>pecial...

       <u>I</u>nsert...
       <u>D</u>elete...
       Clear Co<u>n</u>tents

    📷 Insert Co<u>m</u>ment

    🖘 <u>F</u>ormat Cells... ▶
       Pic<u>k</u> From List...

WHAT'S THIS?

The name context-sensitive menu means that the menu commands depend on what you are doing when you press the right mouse-button. Every command can also be run from the menu bar, but the context-sensitive menu is quicker.

In this case, click on FORMAT CELLS. The format of cells is determined on the Number tab. You will recognise the individual options under Category, where you will also find the entry 'Currency'. Our 'pounds' are also entered under Symbol, by the abbreviation '£', but you can equally show the cells in other currencies. For example, if you are buying tulips from Amsterdam, apply 'HFL' (Dutch Guilders) to the cells.

Don't forget to enter the decimal places, i.e. the numbers after the decimal point. You will need '2' for pence. Exit from the Cells dialog box by clicking on OK.

Number	Alignment		Font	Border	Patterns	Protection

Category:

Sample

£200.00

General
Number
Currency
Accounting
Date
Time
Percentage
Fraction
Scientific
Text
Special
Custom

Decimal places: 2

Symbol:

£ English (United Kingdom)

Negative numbers:

-£1,234.10
£1,234.10
-£1,234.10
-£1,234.10

Currency formats are used for general monetary values. Use Accounting formats to align decimal points in a column.

OK   Cancel

It gets complicated if you want to delete a cell format. This is not done with the [Delete] key, but by using the method above to enter the Cells dialog box. Under Category, select 'Standard'. This is the only way to return to a 'normal' number format.

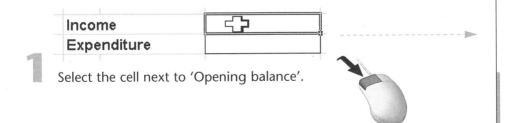

Income	✛
Expenditure	

1 Select the cell next to 'Opening balance'.

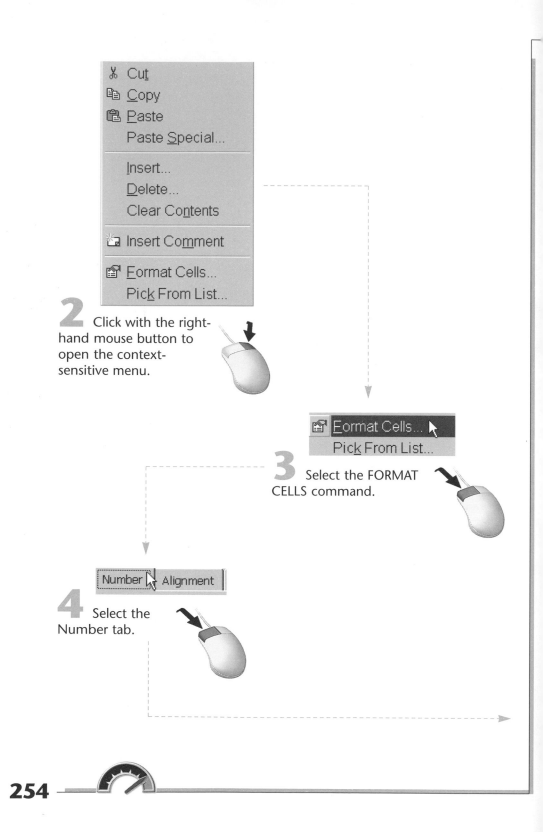

✂ Cu_t_
📋 _C_opy
📋 _P_aste
Paste _S_pecial...

_I_nsert...
_D_elete...
Clear Co_n_tents

📝 Insert Co_m_ment

📄 _F_ormat Cells...
Pic_k_ From List...

2 Click with the right-hand mouse button to open the context-sensitive menu.

📄 _F_ormat Cells... ▶
Pic_k_ From List...

3 Select the FORMAT CELLS command.

Number ▶ Alignment

4 Select the Number tab.

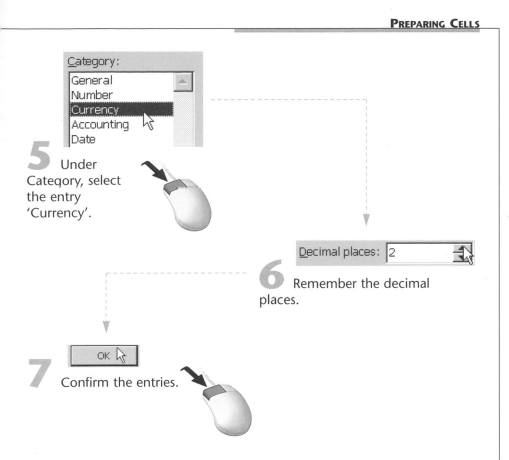

5 Under Category, select the entry 'Currency'.

6 Remember the decimal places.

7 Confirm the entries.

Copying formats

Don't enter any numbers yet! If you do, Excel will think, 'Aha, this cell gets the £ currency style with two decimal places'. But this is not the only cell for which this format must be specified. The 'income' cell would still be 'bare'. The cells for 'expenditure' and 'balance' still have to be formatted. You don't need to carry out the same procedure again and again. Once is enough.

Income	£200.00
Expenditure	

No.	Text	Customer	Employee	Cash
1	Bank cheque	£200.00		

On the standard toolbar is a brush. You can use this to copy the currency style into (including the two decimal places) into the other cells. Clicking the mouse once will only copy the style once. However, as several cells are to be formatted, double-click on the brush (Format Painter) button. The function will remain active until you click on the button again or press the [Esc] key.

 If you click on the Format Painter button a brush will appear alongside the mouse pointer. Excel is telling you that you can copy formats, which is exactly what we are going to do now.

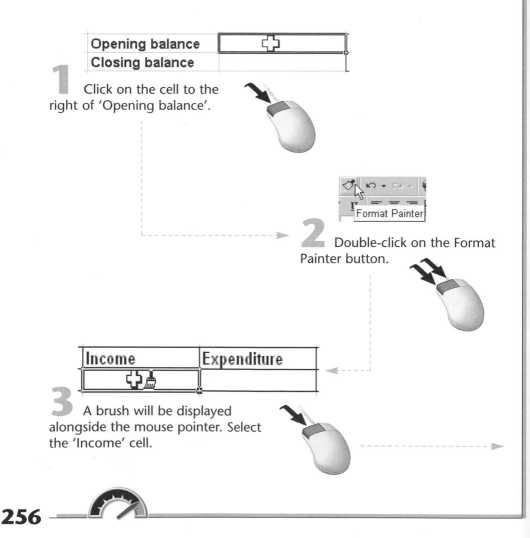

| Opening balance | 🛠 |
| Closing balance | |

1 Click on the cell to the right of 'Opening balance'.

Format Painter

2 Double-click on the Format Painter button.

| Income | Expenditure |
| 🛠 | |

3 A brush will be displayed alongside the mouse pointer. Select the 'Income' cell.

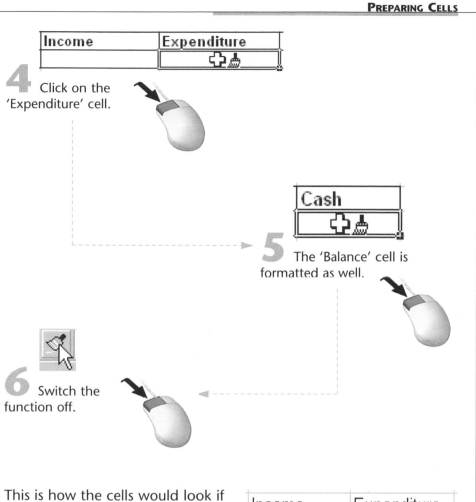

4 Click on the 'Expenditure' cell.

5 The 'Balance' cell is formatted as well.

6 Switch the function off.

This is how the cells would look if you were to enter figures now. But don't enter any figures yet!

Income	Expenditure
£200.00	£100.00

257

Changing font colours

Expenditure can make you see red!
What could be more appropriate than
making figures for expenditure red?
But you have a choice of several

Income	Expenditure
£200.00	£100.00

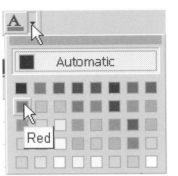

colours. You will find the Font Color
button on the standard toolbar. Click on
the arrow alongside and you will see a
pallet of different colours. For example,
you could select yellow for postal items.
You can format the activated cell by
clicking the mouse on the desired colour,
in this case red. The colour most recently
chosen will appear on the Font Color
button. If you want to cancel a colour,
select Automatic.

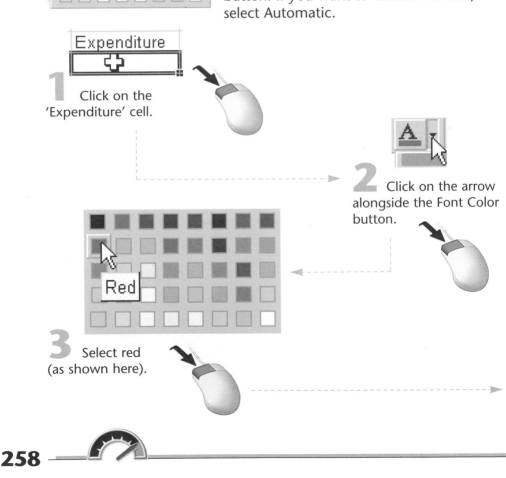

1 Click on the
'Expenditure' cell.

2 Click on the arrow
alongside the Font Color
button.

3 Select red
(as shown here).

If ... then ... else ...

If you were to enter the first transaction now, as shown here, the cash book would look like this. But we aren't going to enter any figures yet That comes later.

Company ABC, 51 Bond Street, London				
Opening Balance	£200.00		Gross	
Expenditure			Expenditure	
No.	Text	Revenue	Expenditure	Cash
1	Bank cheque	£200.00		

The formulas still have to be entered. There is only one, namely for the current balance. In the first case the 'Opening balance' and the 'Income' must be added together. However, as we do not know whether the first transaction will be income or expenditure, it may be that the opening balance is reduced by the expenditure.

We provide Excel with the following rule in a formula: if income is involved, addition must take place; if expenditure is involved, subtraction must take place.

You will need a formula whatever the circumstances. Use the Function Wizard. You will find the button on the standard toolbar. If you click on it, the Function Wizard will run. Various options are listed under Category. We need the function 'IF', which you will find under 'Logical'. If you don't know the category in which to find a particular function, select 'All', which contains a list of all the functions in Excel. If you have already used the function, it is advisable to use the category 'Most Recently Used'. This is not the case here, so choose the category 'Logical'. You will see 'IF'. Run it by double-clicking.

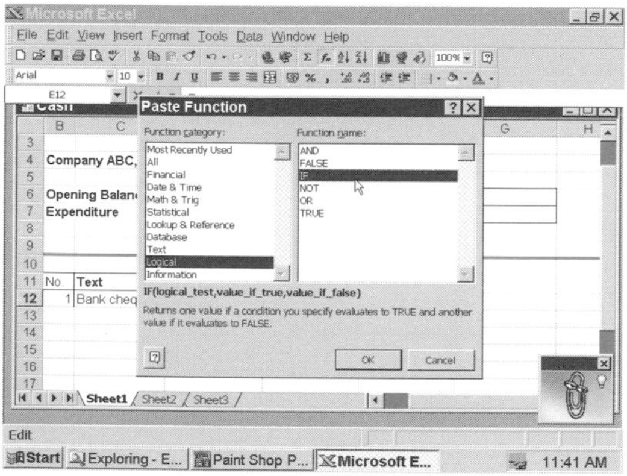

Expenditure	Cash
	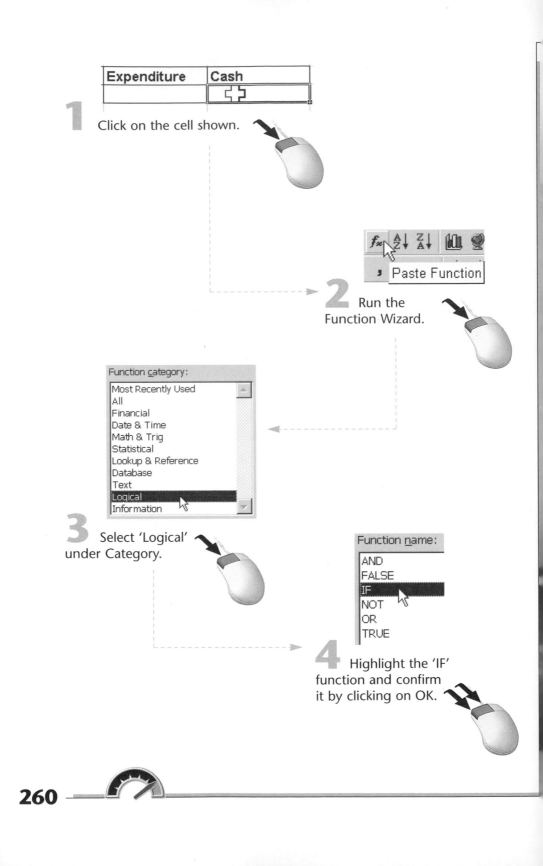

1 Click on the cell shown.

f_x A↓ Z↓ 🏛 🌐

⌐ Paste Function

2 Run the Function Wizard.

Function category:

Most Recently Used
All
Financial
Date & Time
Math & Trig
Statistical
Lookup & Reference
Database
Text
Logical
Information

3 Select 'Logical' under Category.

Function name:

AND
FALSE
IF
NOT
OR
TRUE

4 Highlight the 'IF' function and confirm it by clicking on OK.

Moving a dialog box

We are not going to enter any formulas yet. Our worksheet must be more clearly designed. We need the cells that are covered by the dialog box, so we are going to shift it. To move it around the worksheet, just click on a grey surface. Hold the mouse button down. The mouse pointer will change into an arrow. During movement you will see a broken line outlining the dialog box. Drag it to its new position in the worksheet. When you run the Function Wizard again later the dialog box will reappear in its former position. Moving it only applies to the job in hand.

IF

Logical_test		= logical
Value_if_true		= any
Value_if_false		= any

=

Returns one value if a condition you specify evaluates to TRUE and another value if it evaluates to FALSE.

    Logical_test is any value or expression that can be evaluated to TRUE or FALSE.

[?]	Formula result =		OK	Cancel

If it doesn't work the first time, just keep moving it, until you have found the ideal position.

1   Place the mouse pointer on a grey surface within the dialog box.

IF

Logical_test		🔢 = logical
Value_if_true		🔢 = any
Value_if_false		🔢 = any

=

Returns one value if a condition you specify evaluates to TRUE and another value if it evaluates to FALSE.

Logical_test is any value or expression that can be evaluated to TRUE or FALSE.

| ❓ | Formula result = | | OK | Cancel |

10					
11	No.	Text	Revenue	Expenditure	Cash
12	1	Bank cheque	£200.00		=IF()

2 Hold down the mouse button and drag the dialog box ...

Opening Balance Expenditure	£200.00		Gross Expenditure	

No.	Text	Revenue	Expenditure	Cash
1	Bank cheque	£200.00		=IF()

IF

Logical_test		🔢 = logical
Value_if_true		🔢 = any
Value_if_false		🔢 = any

3 ... until it is underneath the cells which we are going to need next.

If ...

...it wasn't for the word 'if'! The entry still looks a bit empty. The first thing you will notice is Logical

IF

Logical_test		🔢 = logical
Value_if_true		🔢 = any
Value_if_false		🔢 = any

test. This is where you enter the condition. The computer will only recognise two cases, or conditions: true and false. What is not a woman must be a man for this program. Software knows no alternative. So we need a condition like this for our example. What is not income can only be expenditure. There is no middle ground.

Condition	Condition inapplicable
Man	Woman
Hearing	Deaf
Sighted	Blind
Death	Life
In	Out
Income	Expenditure

In this case, enter the following condition for Logical test: 'Revenue>0'. If a value is entered for 'Revenue', Excel will know that it is a receipt and must be added on. If it is not income, Excel will know that it can only be expenditure.

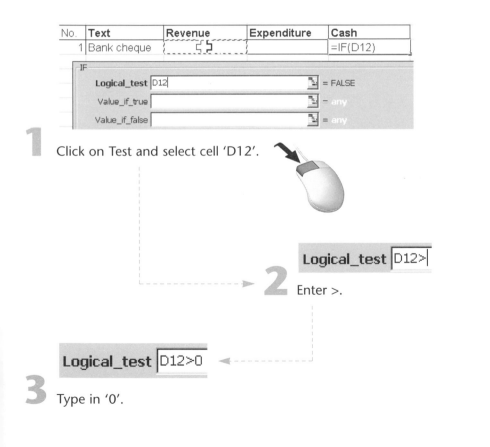

1 Click on Test and select cell 'D12'.

2 Enter >.

3 Type in '0'.

... Then

If income is involved, the opening balance and the income must be added together. You need not enter the '+' sign. If you do not enter any signs, Excel will know that the cells which you have clicked are to be added together.

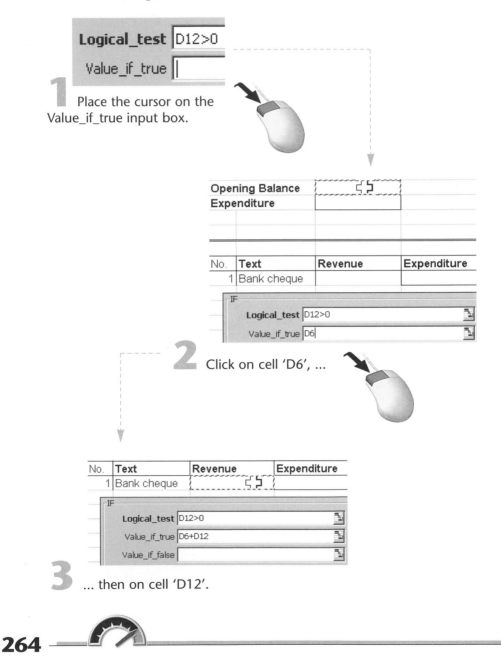

1 Place the cursor on the Value_if_true input box.

2 Click on cell 'D6', ...

3 ... then on cell 'D12'.

... Else

If no income is involved, it is expenditure to Excel. The opening balance will also be reduced by the expenditure. Now click on the Value_if_false box and select the cells. Use the '-' sign for subtraction.

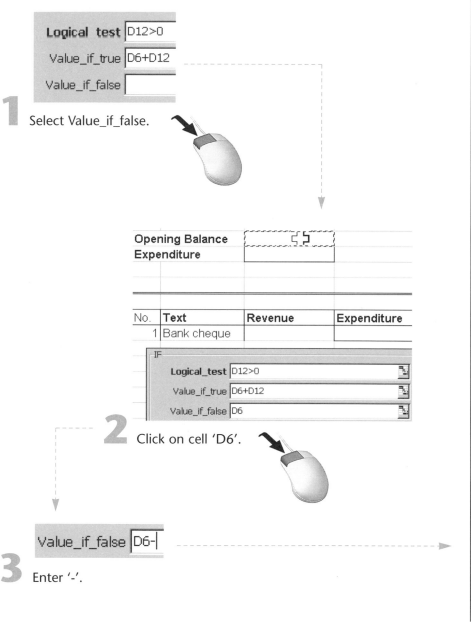

Logical test | D12>0
Value_if_true | D6+D12
Value_if_false |

1 Select Value_if_false.

| Opening Balance | |
| Expenditure | |

No.	Text	Revenue	Expenditure
1	Bank cheque		

IF
Logical_test | D12>0
Value_if_true | D6+D12
Value_if_false | D6

2 Click on cell 'D6'.

Value_if_false | D6-|

3 Enter '-'.

No.	Text	Revenue	Expenditure
1	Bank cheque		55

IF

Logical_test	D12>0
Value_if_true	D6+D12
Value_if_false	D6-E12

4 Click on cell E12.

= =IF(D12>0,D6+D12,D6-E12)

5 Confirm entry of the formula.

After you have entered the formula, you will see a balance of £ 0.00. This is correct, because we have not yet entered anything. We'll do that later. The

Cash	
	£0.00

The structure of a formula is called its syntax.

formula box shows that there is a formula in the cell. This is called the syntax and is the structure of the 'IF' formula. Individual instructions are separated from each other by a semicolon (;).

= =IF(D12>0;D6+D12;D6-E12)

Here is a translation into plain English:

= =IF(D12>0,D6+D12,D6-E12)

Expression	Meaning
If	(If ...
(D12>0,	(... income (cell D12) is greater than zero, then ...
D6+D12,	(add the opening balance (cell D6) and the income (cell D12) together; otherwise ...
D6-E12)	(subtract the expenditure (cell E12) from the opening balance (D6).

If you enter a transaction now, Excel will calculate correctly. In this case you have an opening balance of £200.00 and income of £200.00 (200 + 200 = 400).

Cash Book

Company ABC, 51 Bond Street, London

| Opening Balance | £200.00 | Gross |
| Expenditure | | Expenditure |

No.	Text	Revenue	Expenditure	Cash
1	Bank cheque	£200.00		£400.00

You will also get the right result for expenditure. In this case you have an opening balance of £200.00 and expenditure of £100.00 (200 – 100 = 100). If your Excel cash book looks like this, the calculation will work.

Opening Balance Expenditure	£200.00		Gross Expenditure	
No.	Text	Revenue	Expenditure	Cash
1	Bank cheque	£0.00	£100.00	£100.00

But don't enter any figures yet! We shall need the blank cash book forms later. However, there is one entry you can make. Enter the number '1' under 'Consecutive number'. Then select the whole row and copy it down one row by using the fill handle. You will notice that Excel counts consecutively upwards from '1' to '2'.

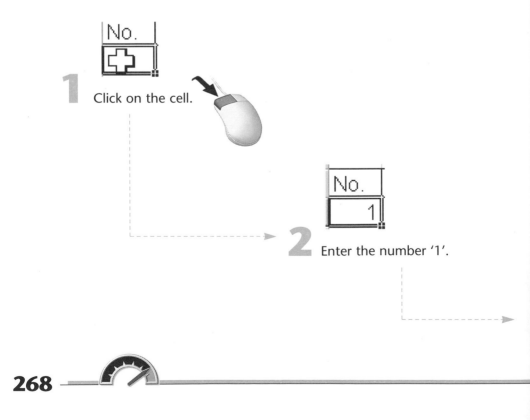

1 Click on the cell.

2 Enter the number '1'.

No.	Text	Revenue	Expenditure	Cash
1				£0.00

3 Select the cells.

Cash
£0.00

4 Move the mouse pointer onto the fill handle.

No.	Text	Revenue	Expenditure	Cash
1				£0.00

5 Drag one row down.

If you want to dispense with the 'Consecutive number' column, it is quite sufficient to copy the formula from the cell 'balance' (cell 'F12') downwards.

269

Changing a formula

An error now occurs in the formula. The Balance is not determined in the same way from the second line onwards. The first line really represents an exception, as it is the only one which refers to the opening balance.

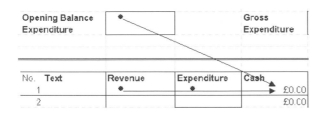

Opening Balance Expenditure			Gross Expenditure

No.	Text	Revenue	Expenditure	Cash	
1					£0.00
2					£0.00

Another cell and a correct balance

Revenue	Expenditure	Cash	
			£0.00
			£0.00

From the second line onwards, the current balance is always determined from the previous one, so the formula must be changed. But this is quite simple. You only need click on the cell to edit the formula. You no longer need the 'Opening balance', only cell 'D6'.

= =IF(D13>0 D6+D13;D6-E13)

We need cell 'F12', in which the current balance is shown. However, there is no need to run the Function Wizard again. You can make all the changes in the formula bar, remove the wrong cells and enter the right ones.

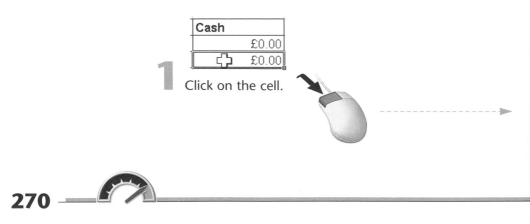

Cash
£0.00
£0.00

1 Click on the cell.

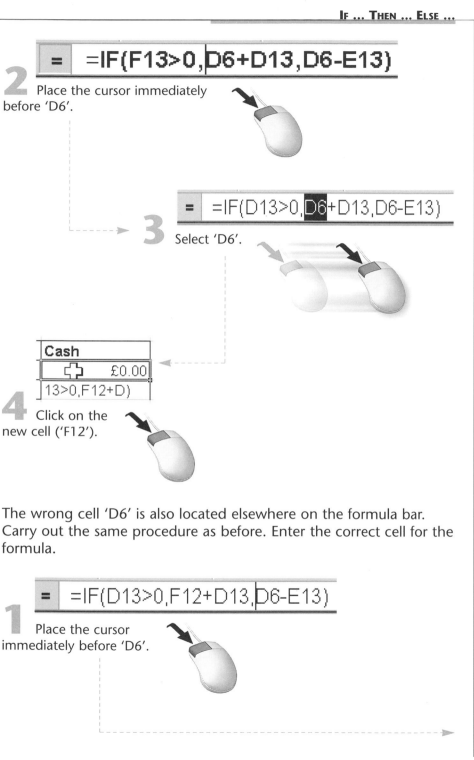

= **=IF(F13>0,D6+D13,D6-E13)**

2 Place the cursor immediately before 'D6'.

= =IF(D13>0,D6+D13,D6-E13)

3 Select 'D6'.

Cash

£0.00

13>0,F12+D)

4 Click on the new cell ('F12').

The wrong cell 'D6' is also located elsewhere on the formula bar. Carry out the same procedure as before. Enter the correct cell for the formula.

= =IF(D13>0,F12+D13,D6-E13)

1 Place the cursor immediately before 'D6'.

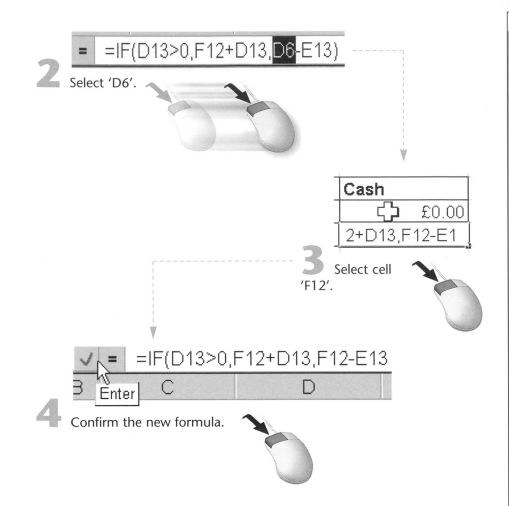

2 Select 'D6'.

=IF(D13>0,F12+D13,D6-E13)

Cash

£0.00

2+D13,F12-E1

3 Select cell 'F12'.

=IF(D13>0,F12+D13,F12-E13

B	Enter	C	D

4 Confirm the new formula.

From now on you can enter the transactions and everything will be determined correctly. But don't enter any figures yet! We'll explain why we keep telling you this in a minute. Is your patience running out?

Using the sheet tabs

The sheet tabs are located at the bottom of the screen and show the name of the worksheets in the workbook.

You will probably want to use your cash book for several months rather than just one. You will recognise the Excel sheet tabs below.

You can rename the individual worksheets here, creating one for 'January', one for 'February', and so on. In practice this is like having a folder marked 'Cash Book 1998'. This is where you file the individual cash sheets for 'January', February', 'March', etc. Excel works in exactly the same way. This you can record your income and expenditure throughout the whole year.

You are going to rename the first worksheet, in which you entered your income. Call it 'January'. To change the sheet tab, move the mouse pointer onto it (it says 'Sheet 1') and click the right-hand mouse button. Select the command RENAME from the context-sensitive menu which will be displayed. The sheet tab 'Sheet 1' will be highlighted in black. Type in 'January'. Terminate the entry by clicking anywhere on the worksheet.

1 Move the mouse pointer onto the sheet tab.

273

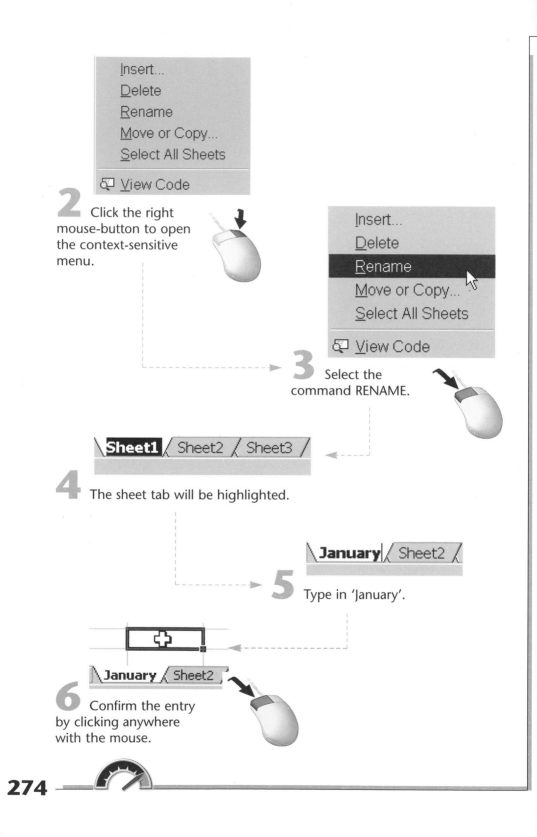

Insert...
Delete
Rename
Move or Copy...
Select All Sheets

⊡ View Code

2 Click the right
mouse-button to open
the context-sensitive
menu.

Insert...
Delete
Rename
Move or Copy...
Select All Sheets

⊡ View Code

3 Select the
command RENAME.

Sheet1 ╱ Sheet2 ╱ Sheet3 ╱

4 The sheet tab will be highlighted.

January ╱ Sheet2 ╱

5 Type in 'January'.

January ╱ Sheet2

6 Confirm the entry
by clicking anywhere
with the mouse.

Up until now you have only developed one type of blank form for the cash book. There is a reason for this. We would like to insert the existing form into a new worksheet, which we are going to call 'February'. In this way we only need to design the cash book once and then copy it for the other months.

Copying a worksheet into another one is easy. Place the mouse pointer on the sheet tab, in this case 'January'. If you hold down the left-hand mouse button a small sheet will appear alongside the mouse pointer. You can use this to move the content of January into a new sheet. But this is not what we want. We want to make a copy. Press the Ctrl key together with the left-hand mouse button. A plus sign (+) will then appear on the sheet at the end of the mouse pointer. Now you can make a copy. Drag it from one sheet tab to the next.

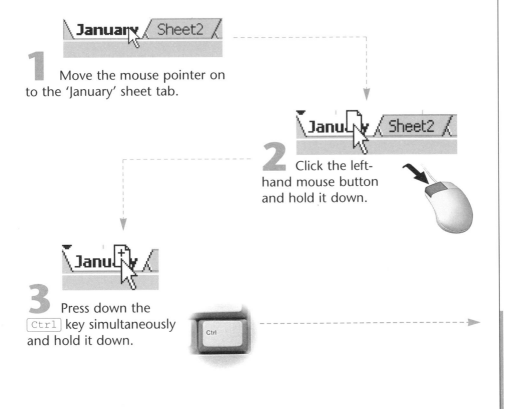

1 Move the mouse pointer on to the 'January' sheet tab.

2 Click the left-hand mouse button and hold it down.

3 Press down the Ctrl key simultaneously and hold it down.

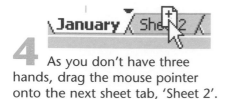

4 As you don't have three hands, drag the mouse pointer onto the next sheet tab, 'Sheet 2'.

Excel will automatically jump to the next worksheet and display its contents. You will have noticed that a new sheet tab has been created. It is called 'January (2)'. Of course, it needs to be called 'February', so we shall rename it. Carry out the same procedure as you did for the 'January' sheet tab.

Cash Book

Company ABC, 51 Bond Street, London

Opening balance	£200.00	Income	£1,290.00
Closing balance	£950.10	Expenditure	£539.90

No.	Text	Income	Expenditure	Cash	
1	Bank interest	£200.00		£400.00	
2	Courier		£80.00	£320.00	
3	Stationery		£200.00	£120.00	
4	Travel		£29.95	£90.05	
5	Facsimile	£115.00		£205.05	
6	PC hardware		£200.00	£5.05	
7	Bank interest	£400.00		£405.05	
8	Consulting	£575.00		£980.05	
9	Travel		£29.95	£950.10	
10	**Closing balance**			£950.10	

1 Move the mouse pointer on to the 'January (2)' sheet tab.

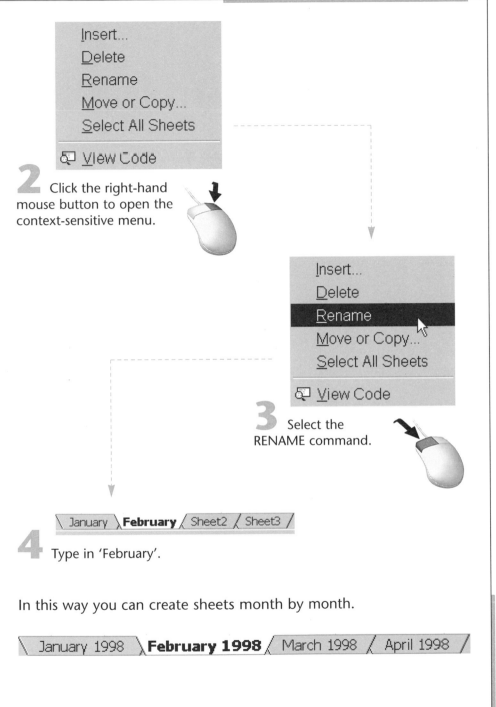

2 Click the right-hand mouse button to open the context-sensitive menu.

3 Select the RENAME command.

4 Type in 'February'.

In this way you can create sheets month by month.

You can also place the mouse pointer on a sheet tab and press the right-hand button. Then select INSERT and enter the name.

Of course, you need not just make entries month for month, but can use other filing systems as well:

Data for customers, suppliers, private addresses

Days of the week: Monday, Tuesday, etc. ...

Years: 1998, 1999, 2000, 2001

Calculating from worksheet to worksheet

One thing still has to be entered on the 'February' worksheet. The opening balance for the month is obtained from the closing balance for January. Click on the opening balance for February, enter the equals sign to select the beginning of a formula and use the sheet tabs to change to January. You only need to click on the closing balance for the month.

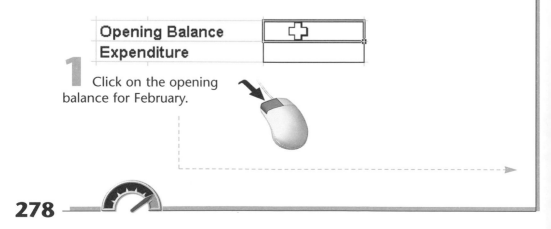

1 Click on the opening balance for February.

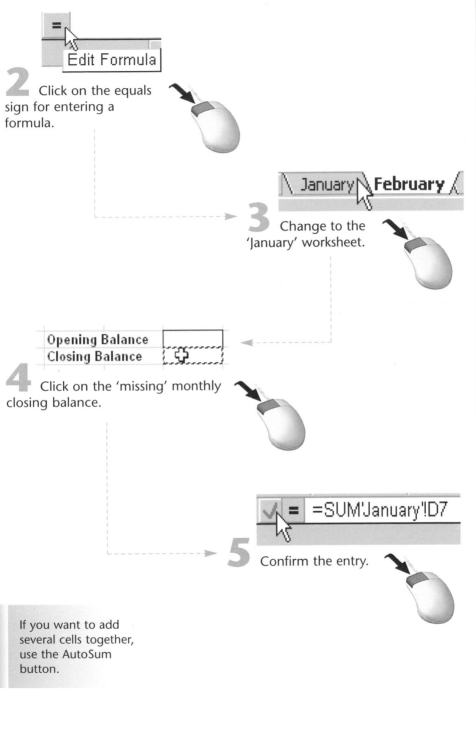

Edit Formula

2 Click on the equals sign for entering a formula.

\ January \ **February** /

3 Change to the 'January' worksheet.

| Opening Balance | |
| Closing Balance | ⊕ |

4 Click on the 'missing' monthly closing balance.

√ = =SUM'January'!D7

5 Confirm the entry.

If you want to add several cells together, use the AutoSum button.

279

Opening balance	£0.00
Closing balance	

Excel will jump back to 'February' as soon as all the entries have been made. You will see the figures '0.00' against the opening balance. This is quite correct, as we have not yet entered any figures for January. If you click on the cell, you will see the following formula on the formula bar. The term 'January!' means that the formula refers to the 'January' worksheet. The exclamation mark (!) shows the worksheet in which the calculation takes place. Then the cell (in this case 'D7') is specified.

= `=January!D7`

Entering transactions in the cash book

Now you can move on to the hard facts at last. The advantage of the methods used so far is obvious. Now all you need to do is enter the transactions. The cash book will do the rest by itself. First, change back to 'January'. Watch how the cash book fills the cells automatically while the figures are being entered.

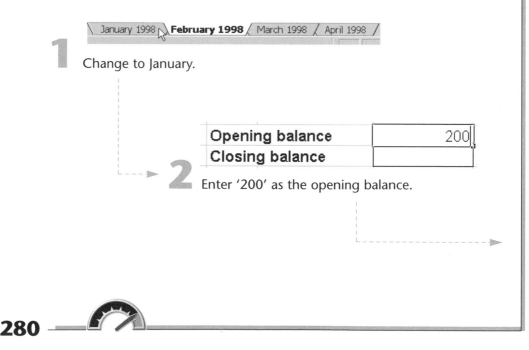

1 Change to January.

Opening balance	200
Closing balance	

2 Enter '200' as the opening balance.

Company ABC, 51 Bond Street, London	
Opening balance	£200.00
Closing balance	

3 Confirm by pressing the ⏎ key.

No.	Text	Revenue	Expenditure	Cash
1		£200.00		£400.00

4 Enter the first transaction.

The first transaction will certainly not be the last. Otherwise we wouldn't have gone to all this trouble! First, select the second line in the cash book and drag the fill handle downwards. Why? Excel will number the cells in the 'Consecutive number' column automatically and copy the formula for the current balance into the next row.

No.	Text	Revenue	Expenditure	Cash
1		£200.00		£400.00
2				£400.00

1 Select the second row.

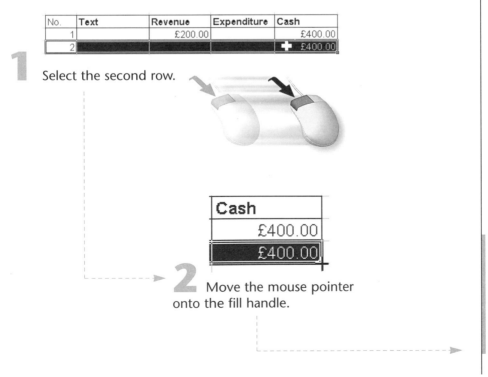

Cash
£400.00
£400.00

2 Move the mouse pointer onto the fill handle.

No.	Text	Revenue	Expenditure	Cash
1		£200.00		£400.00
2			£80.00	£320.00
3				£320.00

3 Drag one row downwards and enter the second transaction.

You can go on managing your cash book in this way. It is also possible to enter several transactions at once. Continue like this day by day; week by week, and the month will soon be over.

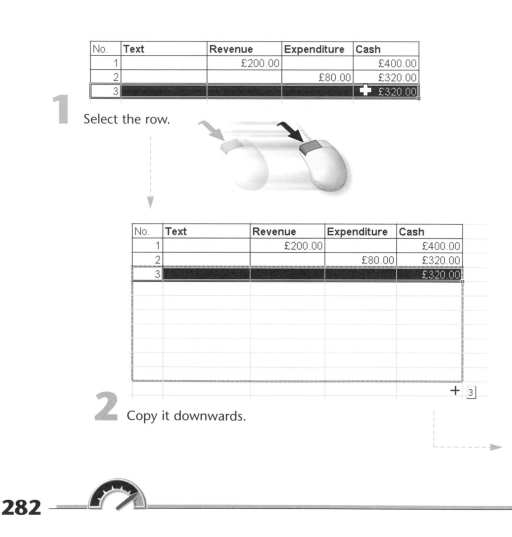

No.	Text	Revenue	Expenditure	Cash
1		£200.00		£400.00
2			£80.00	£320.00
3				£320.00

1 Select the row.

No.	Text	Revenue	Expenditure	Cash
1		£200.00		£400.00
2			£80.00	£320.00
3				£320.00

2 Copy it downwards.

No.	Text	Income	Expenditure	Cash
1	Bank interest	£200.00		£400.00
2	Courier		£80.00	£320.00
3	Stationery		£200.00	£120.00
4	Travel		£29.95	£90.05
5	Facsimile	£115.00		£205.05
6	PC hardware		£200.00	£5.05
7	Bank interest	£400.00		£405.05
8	Consulting	£575.00		£980.05
9	Travel		£29.95	£950.10
10	**Closing balance**			£950.10

3 Enter the income and expenditure.

9	Travel		£29.95	£950.10
10	**Closing balance**			£950.10

4 The month is over. Enter 'Closing balance' in the last row.

How time flies! How quickly a month passes. All that remains to be done is to identify the cells for our 'cash book heading': the 'Monthly closing balance', i.e. the sum of the income and expenditure.

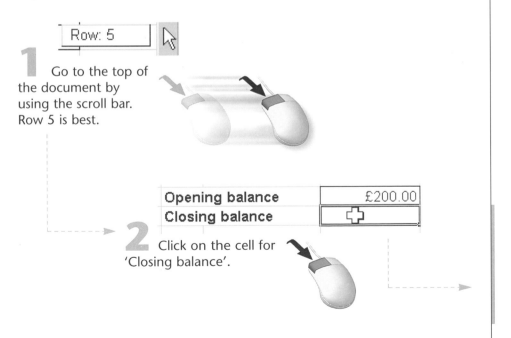

Row: 5

1 Go to the top of the document by using the scroll bar. Row 5 is best.

Opening balance	£200.00
Closing balance	

2 Click on the cell for 'Closing balance'.

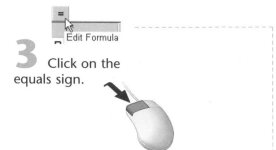

3 Click on the equals sign.

a result =1900.2		OK	Cancel	
Opening balance	£200.00		**Income**	
Closing balance	=F22+F22		**Expenditure**	

No.	Text	Income	Expenditure	Cash
1	Bank interest	£200.00		£400.00
2	Courier		£80.00	£320.00
3	Stationery		£200.00	£120.00
4	Travel		£29.95	£90.05
5	Facsimile	£115.00		£205.05
6	PC hardware		£200.00	£5.05
7	Bank interest	£400.00		£405.05
8	Consulting	£575.00		£980.05
9	Travel		£29.95	£950.10
10	**Closing balance**			£950.10

4 Click on the cell containing the last balance ('F21').

5 Confirm.

The total income must now be determined. Select the cell and click on the AutoSum button. Select the cells that are to be added together.

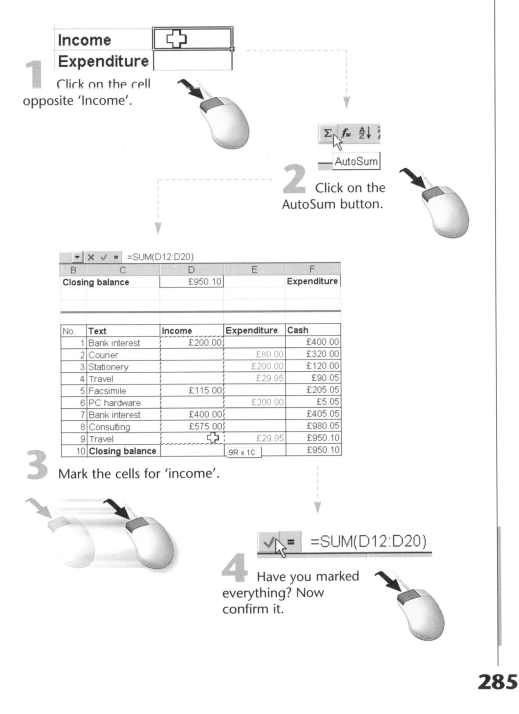

1 Click on the cell opposite 'Income'.

2 Click on the AutoSum button.

B	C	D	E	F
	Closing balance	£950.10		Expenditure
No.	Text	Income	Expenditure	Cash
1	Bank interest	£200.00		£400.00
2	Courier		£80.00	£320.00
3	Stationery		£200.00	£120.00
4	Travel		£29.95	£90.05
5	Facsimile	£115.00		£205.05
6	PC hardware		£200.00	£5.05
7	Bank interest	£400.00		£405.05
8	Consulting	£575.00		£980.05
9	Travel		£29.95	£950.10
10	Closing balance			£950.10

=SUM(D12:D20)

9R x 1C

3 Mark the cells for 'income'.

=SUM(D12:D20)

4 Have you marked everything? Now confirm it.

285

Now do the same for expenditure. Select the cell, click on AutoSum and mark the corresponding cells.

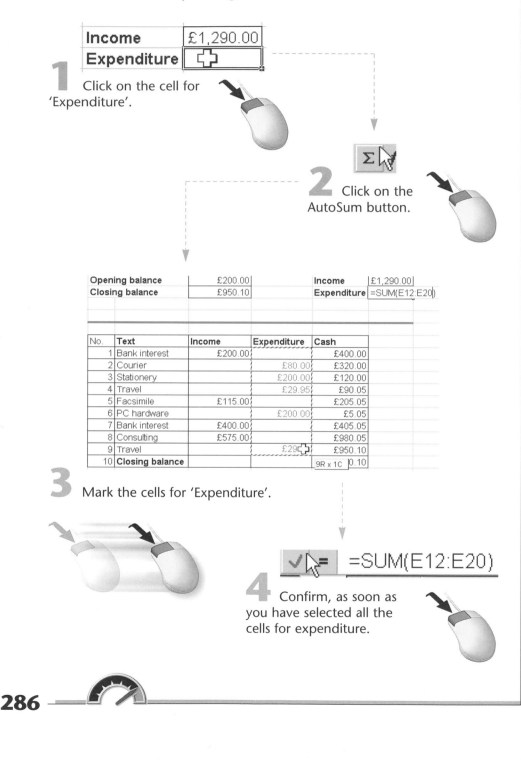

Income	£1,290.00
Expenditure	

1 Click on the cell for 'Expenditure'.

2 Click on the AutoSum button.

Opening balance	£200.00		Income	£1,290.00
Closing balance	£950.10		Expenditure	=SUM(E12:E20)

No.	Text	Income	Expenditure	Cash	
1	Bank interest	£200.00		£400.00	
2	Courier		£80.00	£320.00	
3	Stationery		£200.00	£120.00	
4	Travel		£29.95	£90.05	
5	Facsimile	£115.00		£205.05	
6	PC hardware		£200.00	£5.05	
7	Bank interest	£400.00		£405.05	
8	Consulting	£575.00		£980.05	
9	Travel		£29	£950.10	
10	**Closing balance**			9R x 1C	0.10

3 Mark the cells for 'Expenditure'.

=SUM(E12:E20)

4 Confirm, as soon as you have selected all the cells for expenditure.

Cash Book

Company ABC, 51 Bond Street, London

| Opening balance | £200.00 | | Income | £1,290.00 |
| Closing balance | £950.10 | | Expenditure | £539.90 |

No.	Text	Income	Expenditure	Cash
1	Bank interest	£200.00		£400.00
2	Courier		£80.00	£320.00
3	Stationery		£200.00	£120.00
4	Travel		£29.95	£90.05
5	Facsimile	£115.00		£205.05
6	PC hardware		£200.00	£5.05
7	Bank interest	£400.00		£405.05
8	Consulting	£575.00		£980.05
9	Travel		£29.95	£950.10
10	**Closing balance**			£950.10

Believe it or not – the cash book is complete! January is finished and filed: February is still to come. Use the sheet tab to change to February.

January 1998 / February 1998 / March 1998 / April 1998 /

You will recognise the amount in '£' as the opening balance. It is the closing balance from January. So everything is OK. Now we can start on February!

Cash Book

Company ABC, 51 Bond Street, London

| Opening balance | £950.10 | | Income | |
| Closing balance | | | Expenditure | |

287

What's in this chapter?

You can't live without money, and bills need to be settled. But first a bill must be prepared, so the customer knows it's time to pay. We are going to create a form for this. Our company logo will appear at the top. To obtain the money, we are going to give the bank details at the bottom. And, to save precious time later, we are going to produce a form that can be used over and over again. Excel has a suggestion ready for you!

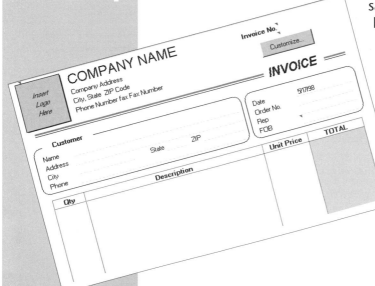

You already know:

Your are going to learn:

Templates

In this chapter we shall be dealing with templates. These are (blank) forms such as invoices, order forms or consignment notes, which you can use again and again. You need only update the respective data. Excel provides a template for an invoice. You will see an Invoice icon on the Spreadsheet Solutions tab, under FILE/NEW. Open this template by double-clicking its icon. A template is a normal workbook, but it has already been edited by the folk at Microsoft for your convenience.

CAUTION

You can only open a template from FILE/NEW, not by using the New button on the toolbar.

Excel will tell you that the 'workbook' contains macros. These are sequences of commands which the Excel programmers have included, so you must click on Enable macros for the template to work. Excel will prompt you to test for viruses when you run the template for the first time.

WHAT'S THIS?

Computer viruses are like human illnesses. Some will destroy data on the hard disk. For early diagnosis, don't ask the doctor or chemist, but buy an anti-virus program. Excel will test for viruses, but new ones could appear inside 'third party' workbooks.

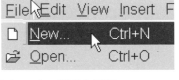

1 Select the FILE/NEW menu command.

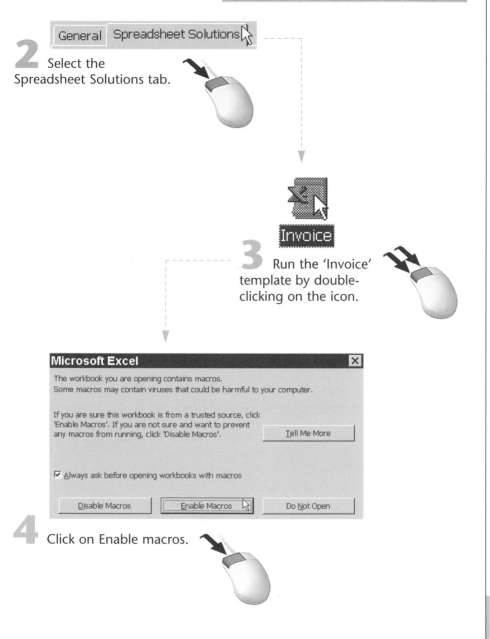

General   Spreadsheet Solutions

2 Select the
Spreadsheet Solutions tab.

Invoice

3 Run the 'Invoice'
template by double-
clicking on the icon.

Microsoft Excel   ☒

The workbook you are opening contains macros.
Some macros may contain viruses that could be harmful to your computer.

If you are sure this workbook is from a trusted source, click
'Enable Macros'. If you are not sure and want to prevent
any macros from running, click 'Disable Macros'.   Tell Me More

☑ Always ask before opening workbooks with macros

Disable Macros   Enable Macros   Do Not Open

4 Click on Enable macros.

291

An invoice form will appear on the screen. It will contain expressions such as the company name, address, town, postcode, etc. Your name should go here.

MOONPIE FILMS

16 St. Josephs Boulevard
Timbuctoo, Herts TB3 2IT
Tel: (01727) 873330 Fax: (01727) 888123

Insert Logo Here	**COMPANY NAME** Company Address City, State ZIP Code Phone Number fax Fax Number		Invoice No. Customize...

=== **INVOICE** ===

Customer

Name			Date	5/17/98
Address			Order No.	
City	State	ZIP	Rep	
Phone			FOB	

Qty	. Description	Unit Price	TOTAL

If you place the mouse pointer on Customize, it will turn into a pointing hand. If you then click on the button you will be able to enter your personal

Customize...

details. You will see 'Customizing Your Invoice' at the top. The template includes buttons and notes. A small red triangle indicates a note and supports you when making entries.

CUSTOMIZE YOUR INVOICE

Lock/Save Sheet

CUSTOMIZING YOUR INVOICE
Use this sheet to enter all of your company information to be used by subsequent worksheets in this template. The template will format this information for you and place it on the Invoice sheet. You can lock this sheet when you are finished with your customizations and save the template for future use.

Type Company Information Here...

Company Name	COMPANY NAME	Phone	Phone Number
Address	Company Address	Fax	Fax Number
City	City		
State	State		
ZIP Code	ZIP Code		

Treat the individual fields as normal cells. Click on them individually and enter your personal data. Once you have completed your entries, exit from 'Customizing Your Invoice' by using the sheet tab at the bottom of the screen. If you click on Invoice you will see your data on the invoice form. This is where you enter the details for the customer.

Customize Your Invoice / Invoice

In addition to the template, a toolbar will appear for editing the display on the screen.

Type Company Information Here...

Company Name	COMPANY NAME	Phone	Phone Number
Address	Company Address	Fax	Fax Number
City	City		
State	State		
ZIP Code	ZIP Code		

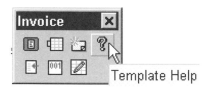
Template Help

If you click on the button marked with a question mark, you will get context-sensitive help for the template.

Save the template as normal. You can either use the Save button or store the workbook by using FILE/CLOSE and clicking on Yes to confirm. The original template will not be affected by saving as you have been automatically working on a copy the whole time. If you have not made any genuine entries, as in our example, click on No.

293

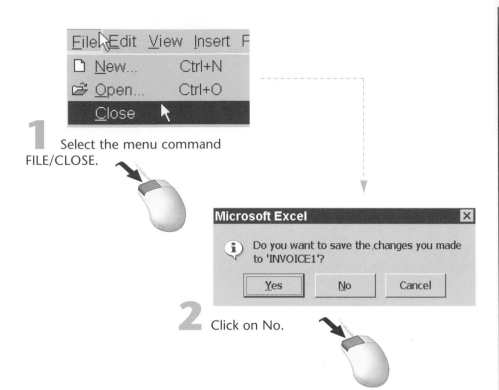

1 Select the menu command FILE/CLOSE.

2 Click on No.

Headers and footers

A human consists of a head, body, feet and everything in between. The invoice containing the figures is the body, but the workbook also contains a head and a foot. These are used to insert text at the top and bottom. As you know from experience, the company logo or its name will be at the top. Evidently, the bank details should be at the bottom of an invoice.

The header and footer can be specified by using the VIEW/HEADER AND FOOTER menu command.

The Headers/Footers tab is automatically activated in the Page Setup dialog box displayed. This is where you specify where the 'head' and 'foot' are to appear: on the left, in the centre or on the right. As we want to have the header and footer in the centre of the invoice, click on Center Section. We are going to create the header first.

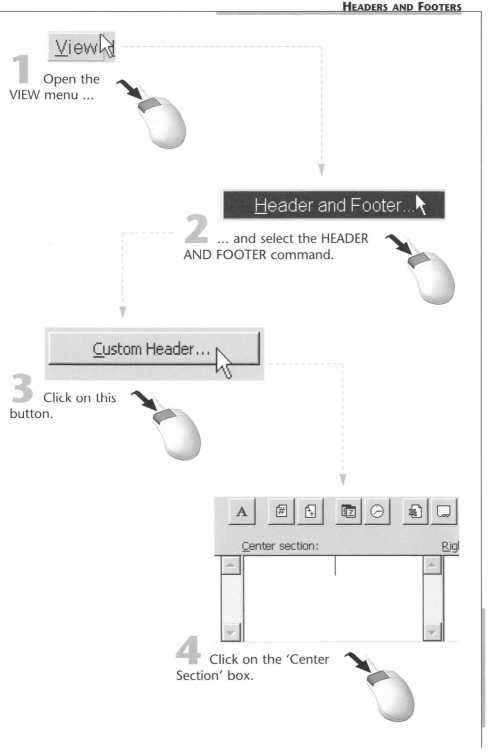

1 Open the
VIEW menu ...

2 ... and select the HEADER
AND FOOTER command.

3 Click on this
button.

4 Click on the 'Center
Section' box.

295

Before you enter the text for the header, you can highlight or format it. Click on the button to specify another font, select bold, italic, etc. In our example we are just going to change the font size.

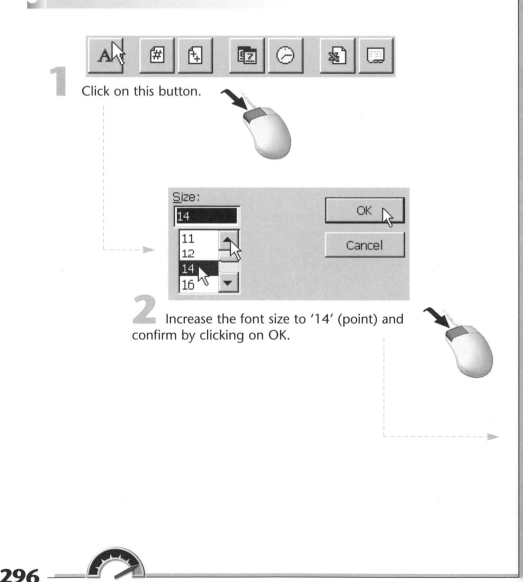

1 Click on this button.

2 Increase the font size to '14' (point) and confirm by clicking on OK.

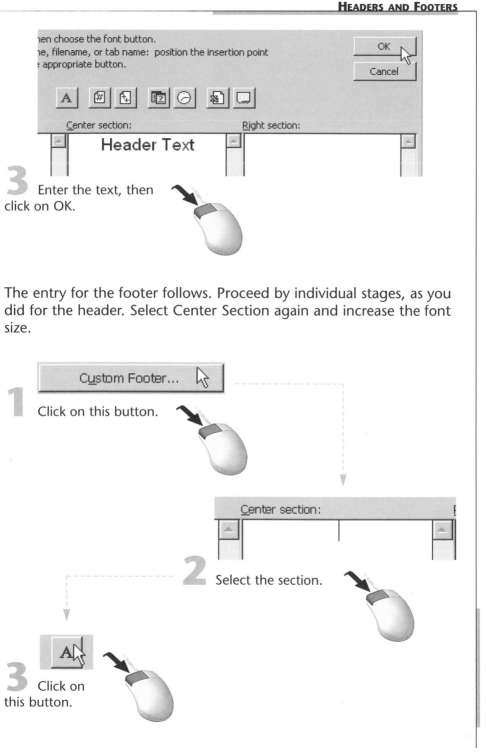

nen choose the font button.
ne, filename, or tab name: position the insertion point
e appropriate button.

OK

Cancel

A   #   ⊘

Center section: Right section:

Header Text

3 Enter the text, then
click on OK.

The entry for the footer follows. Proceed by individual stages, as you
did for the header. Select Center Section again and increase the font
size.

Custom Footer...

1 Click on this button.

Center section:

2 Select the section.

A

3 Click on
this button.

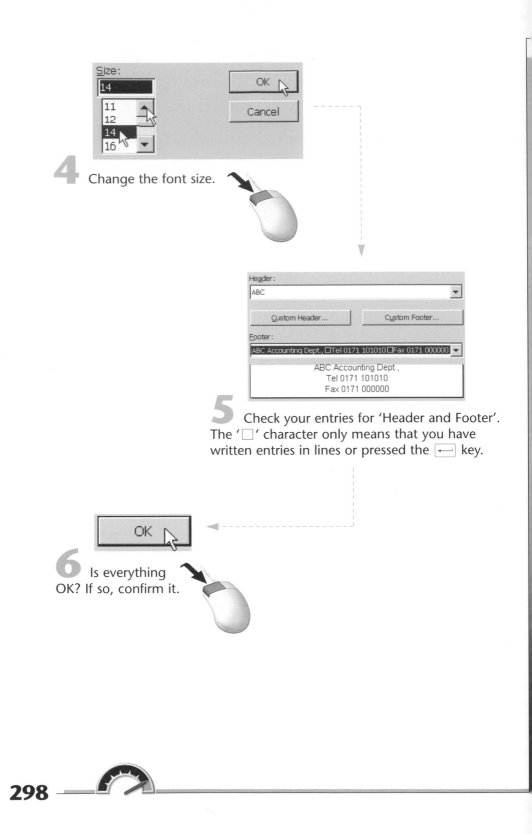

4 Change the font size.

5 Check your entries for 'Header and Footer'. The '☐' character only means that you have written entries in lines or pressed the ⏎ key.

6 Is everything OK? If so, confirm it.

Inserting a text box

As we are creating a form which we shall want to use again and again, we need to include an address box, where the addressee will be entered. This has the benefit that you will only need to enter the addressee's details such as name, street and town when you use the invoice form.

You can enter proper text passages in a workbook without having to worry about cells, rows and columns. To do this you need a text box, for which you must display the Drawing toolbar. If you click on the Drawing button on the standard toolbar, the drawing toolbar will appear. You will usually find it at the bottom of the screen. You will notice that it has several functions. Unfortunately, to explain them all is beyond th scope of this book.

As we want to enter a text box, you need this button on the toolbar. If you click on it, the mouse pointer will take on a rather peculiar appearance. Move this unusual mouse pointer to the point at which you would like to place the text box. Press the left-hand mouse button and hold it down. If you now move the mouse pointer, a text box will open. As soon as you let the mouse button go, it will assume the size displayed. You will see that a dash is flashing inside it. This is the cursor. It is used for entering the text.

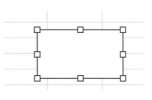

Editing a text box

Type your entries into the text box. You will see little squares and a frame. This is the edge. Get rid of the squares by clicking anywhere outside the box.

If you click on the text box, the squares and the frame will reappear. The squares are called 'handles'. If you place the mouse pointer on one, it will change its appearance. You can increase or reduce the size of the text box, depending on the direction of the arrow.

If you move the mouse pointer to the edge, it will turn into 'crosshairs'. Once these are displayed, you can drag the text box to and fro, holding down the left-hand mouse button.

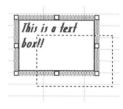

Now try to create a text box yourself. If it doesn't work, just remove it by clicking on the Undo button. By the way, if you keep to the following entries, your letters will always fit into a normal window envelope.

Enter your details in the text box. As we are creating a form, we are not going to use 'real' names, but pseudonyms, for 'company, first name, road, place, etc'. When you open the form, you need only overwrite the fictitious names with real details.

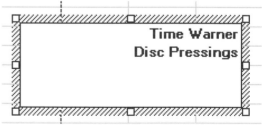

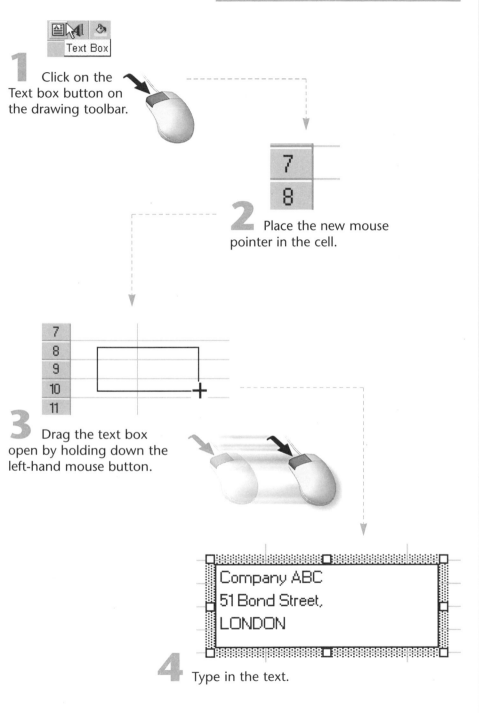

Text Box

1 Click on the Text box button on the drawing toolbar.

2 Place the new mouse pointer in the cell.

3 Drag the text box open by holding down the left-hand mouse button.

Company ABC
51 Bond Street,
LONDON

4 Type in the text.

The line colour

There is still a black frame around the text box. The black lines will not disappear, even if you click outside the text box with the mouse. But they're annoying! You need the button on the drawing toolbar with the brush (Line Color). Click on the arrow alongside it. No Line will remove the black lines around the text box. Of course, you could also border your text box in a different colour. As you please! If so, just click on the arrow alongside Line Color and choose a colour from the palette.

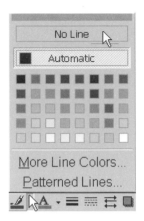

1 Click on the arrow alongside the Line color button.

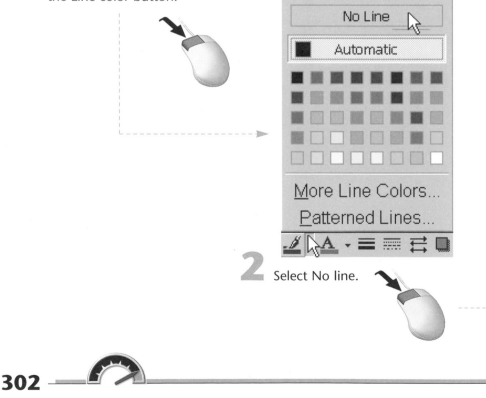

2 Select No line.

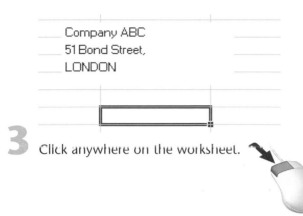

Company ABC
51 Bond Street,
LONDON

3 Click anywhere on the worksheet.

Return to Sender

Anything to add? The sender box always appears above the addressee in window envelopes. This way, Postman Pat always knows to whom the letter should be

Company ABC, 51 Bond Street,

Company ABC
51 Bond Street,
LONDON

returned if, for example, the addressee has moved away. You know how fussy the Post Office is. Create a second text box above the first and enter the sender's address. This is good practice for you, but it meant more work for your author.

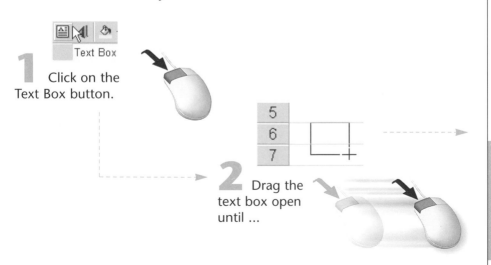

Text Box

1 Click on the Text Box button.

5
6
7

2 Drag the text box open until ...

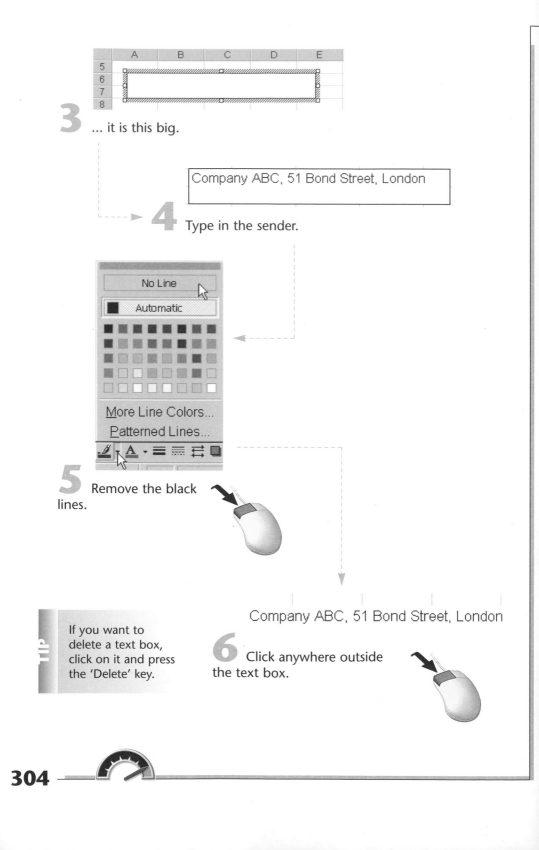

3 ... it is this big.

Company ABC, 51 Bond Street, London

4 Type in the sender.

No Line

■ Automatic

More Line Colors...
Patterned Lines...

5 Remove the black lines.

If you want to delete a text box, click on it and press the 'Delete' key.

Company ABC, 51 Bond Street, London

6 Click anywhere outside the text box.

Inserting dates

What must an invoice always include? Right – the date. First, enter the text 'Date and tax point' in a cell.

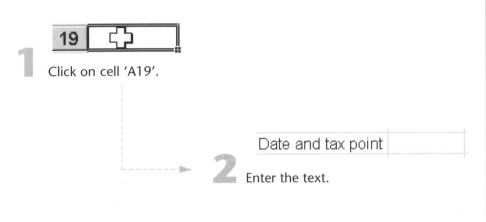

Click on cell 'A19'.

Date and tax point

2 Enter the text.

What's the date today?

The date will appear alongside the 'Date and tax point' cell. You can look at the calendar and enter the date, and that's it!

Date and tax point

However, as we are creating a template or form, it would be useful if Excel would insert the date for you. You could run the Function Wizard, but the formula is relatively easy, so you can set it up yourself in the twinkling of an eye. Whichever option you choose, enter the equals sign first, so that Excel will know that a formula is to follow. If you want to enter the date and time, enter 'now()'. The brackets () are important. They belong together like peaches and cream. The software will not recognise the formula without the brackets. By entering 'today()' you will get today's date.

| =now() | 10/08/98 14:01 |
| today() | 10/08/98 |

But Excel offers more. If you want to specify that the invoice should be paid within 30 days, enter 'today()+30'.

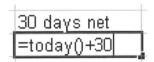

30 days net
=today()+30

Syntax	Result
=now()	Current date and time
=today()+7	Next week
=today()+30	Today's date + 30 days
=today()-7	Last week
=today()-30	30 days prior to today's date

How times change!

Your computer should always be up to date with the date and time. As a Windows 95 or NT user you will always know what time it is. You can see it at the bottom of the screen, on the status bar. But unless your computer is connected to a radio clock, there

Date/Time Properties [?] [X]

Date & Time | Time Zone

Date
May ▼ | 1998 ▲▼

S	M	T	W	T	F	S
					1	2
3	4	5	6	7	8	9
10	11	12	13	14	15	16
17	**18**	19	20	21	22	23
24	25	26	27	28	29	30
31						

Time

10 : 44 : 36 AM

Current time zone: Sydney Standard Time

OK | Cancel | Apply

is, of course, no guarantee that the time or date displayed will be correct. Place the mouse pointer on the clock and double-click. Set the correct date and time on the Date and Time tab and confirm them by clicking on Adopt.

Windows 95 will change from summer time to GMT and vice versa automatically.

But now back to work!

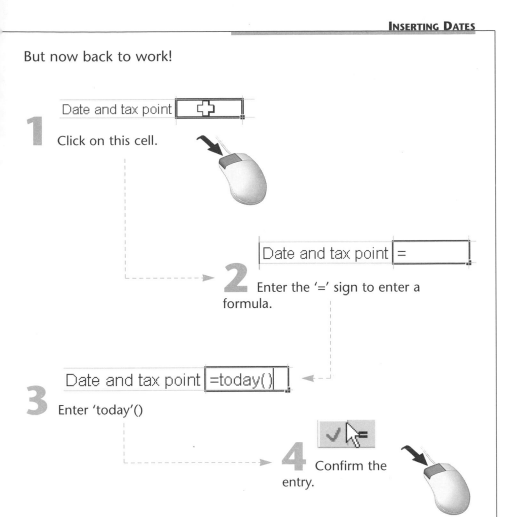

1 Click on this cell.

Date and tax point

2 Enter the '=' sign to enter a formula.

Date and tax point | =

3 Enter 'today'()

Date and tax point | =today()

4 Confirm the entry.

Formatting dates

The date is shown as '18.05.98', but you can display it differently.

Date and tax point | 18-May-98

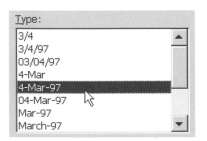

For example, you can change it to '18 May 1998'. Other forms of display are also possible. You only need to change the format. Under FORMAT/CELLS select the Number tab, and from Category, choose 'Date'. Under Format Codes you will

307

see the various forms which you can select. Don't be confused by the date shown – 4 March 1997. It's not a mistimed April Fool's joke. It is only meant to show the format of the date. Click on one of the options and you will see the format displayed in the Code box. Double-click to insert the new date format into your workbook.

Sample
18-May-98

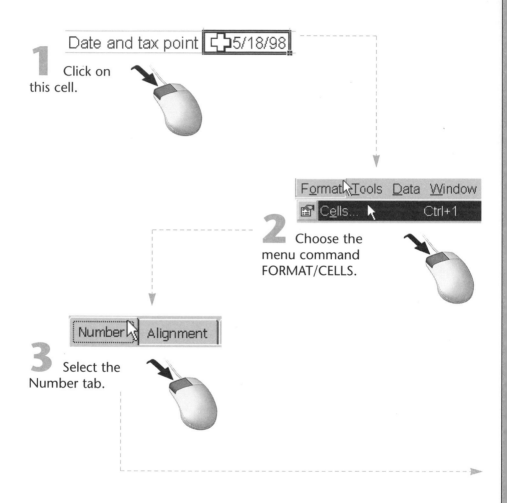

Date and tax point ⊕5/18/98

1 Click on this cell.

Format Tools Data Window

📝 Cells...   Ctrl+1

2 Choose the menu command FORMAT/CELLS.

Number Alignment

3 Select the Number tab.

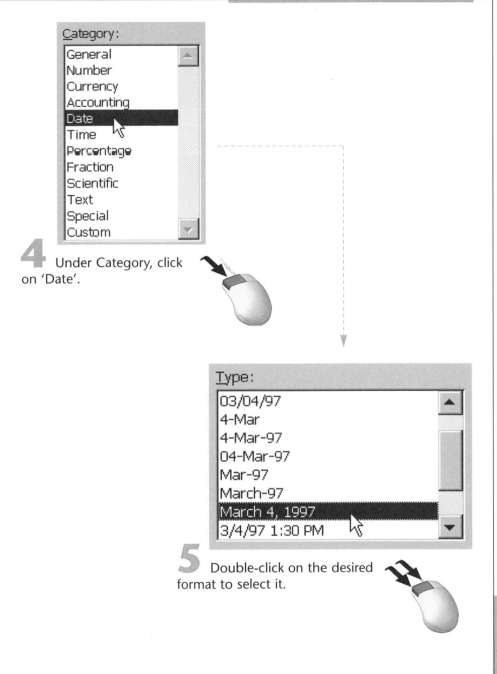

4 Under Category, click on 'Date'.

5 Double-click on the desired format to select it.

Preparing a template

As we are designing a form for future invoices, we are going to continue working on its 'blueprint'. Then you will only ever need to make a few entries yourself in the future. You will have more time to yourself and be able to concentrate on more important things in life.

Firstly, we are gong to create another text box, in which we are going to write a general text that applies to all recipients of invoices. We will leave space for the salutation, so that you can write 'Dear Mr', 'Dear Mrs' or 'Dear Sirs'. We are also going to enter headings for the items on the invoice, such as 'Item', 'Quantity' and 'Amount' on the form.

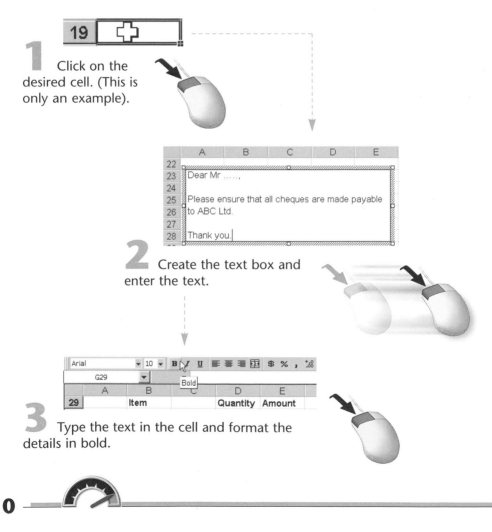

1 Click on the desired cell. (This is only an example).

2 Create the text box and enter the text.

3 Type the text in the cell and format the details in bold.

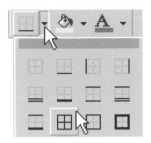

To highlight the items of the invoice later, apply a border to the appropriate cells now. Click on the arrow next to the Borders button and you will be offered a selection of borders. Click on the desired border style and the cells will be displayed accordingly. If you wish to remove a border later, select the display in which no lines are highlighted.

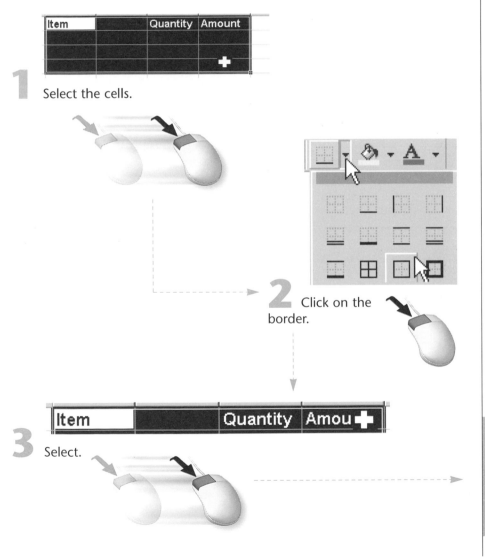

1 Select the cells.

2 Click on the border.

3 Select.

311

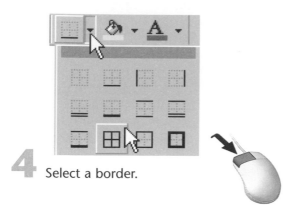

4 Select a border.

Using arithmetical signs in text

We are going to enter '+17.5% VAT' and 'Invoice total' in the invoice. But if we type the signs '+' and '=', Excel will

expect a formula whereas here the signs are meant to be text. So we insert an apostrophe (') before entering the text. Then Excel will know that text is on the way.

If you want to enter arithmetical signs such as = and + as text, use an apostrophe (') before the entry.

	A	B	C
34		+17.5% VAT	

1 Enter ' and type the text.

	A	B	C
34		+17.5% VAT	
35			
36		=Invoice total	

2 Make the next entry in the same way.

We are going to specify a different border style for the invoice amount, I.e. the gross total. Make the selection from Borders and choose 'double underlining' .

Item		Quantity	Amount

+17.5% VAT

=Invoice total

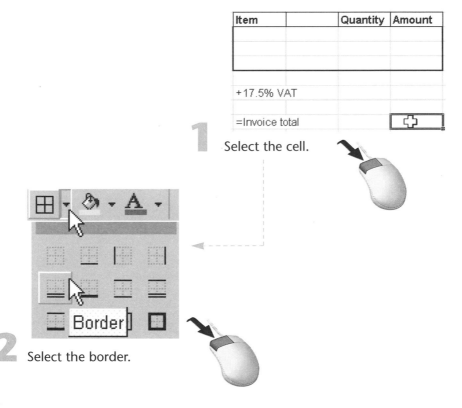

Item		Quantity	Amount

+17.5% VAT

=Invoice total

1 Select the cell.

2 Select the border.

313

We can also specify which currency applies to the amounts. As we want to have our money in pounds, select the cells and click on the Currency Style button.

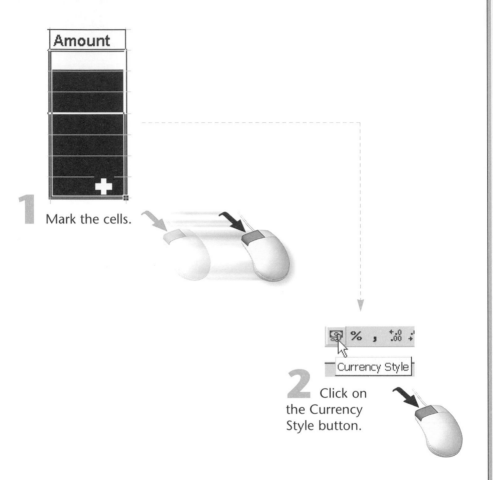

Mark the cells.

Currency Style

2 Click on the Currency Style button.

Pre-prepared forms

The next step is to enter the individual formulae for our calculations. You will then only need to enter the figures later and Excel will do the arithmetic automatically. First, we are going to enter the formula so that the government gets its share: the VAT. It is currently 17.5%. Should this change (i.e. go up), you must remove the '17.5' from the formula bar and enter the new tax rate.

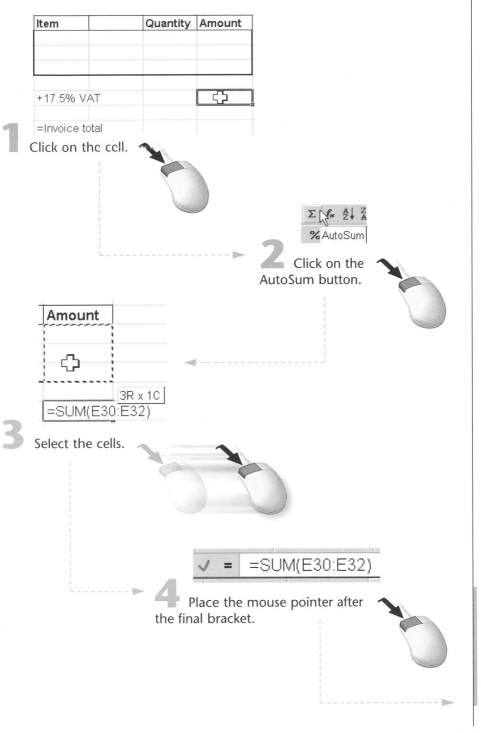

Item		Quantity	Amount
+17.5% VAT			
=Invoice total			

1 Click on the cell.

Σ f_x A↓ Z
% AutoSum

2 Click on the AutoSum button.

Amount

3R x 1C
=SUM(E30:E32)

3 Select the cells.

✓ = =SUM(E30:E32)

4 Place the mouse pointer after the final bracket.

315

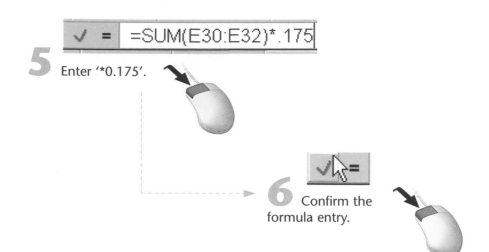

5 Enter '*0.175'.

6 Confirm the formula entry.

The gross total is determined after the VAT. Select the cell in which it is to appear, click on the AutoSum button and then select the cells from which the sum is to be added.

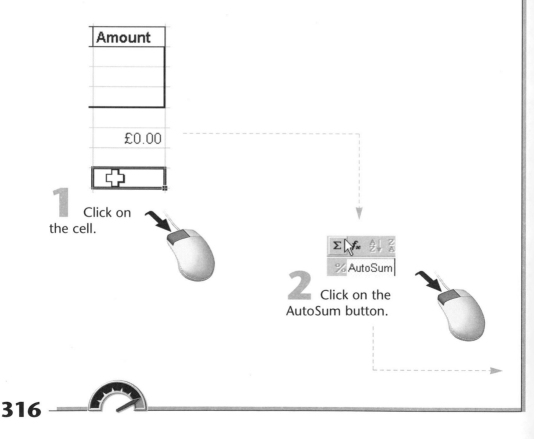

1 Click on the cell.

2 Click on the AutoSum button.

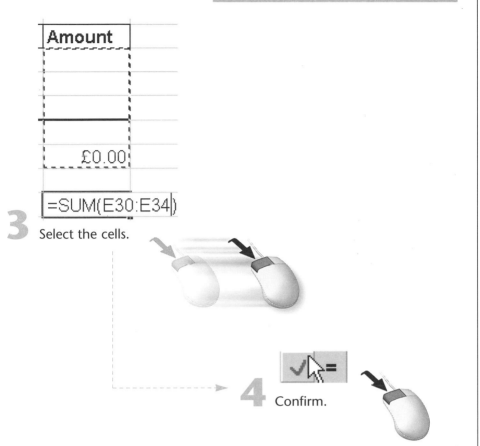

3 Select the cells.

4 Confirm.

Saving templates

Our form is finished! It only needs to be saved. Click on the Save button. In the Save As dialog box, highlight 'Template'. As soon as you have done this, Excel will automatically jump to the 'Templates' folder. Well done, you have created a form. Shout 'Template' and clap your hands. The files marked 'Template' fall out

317

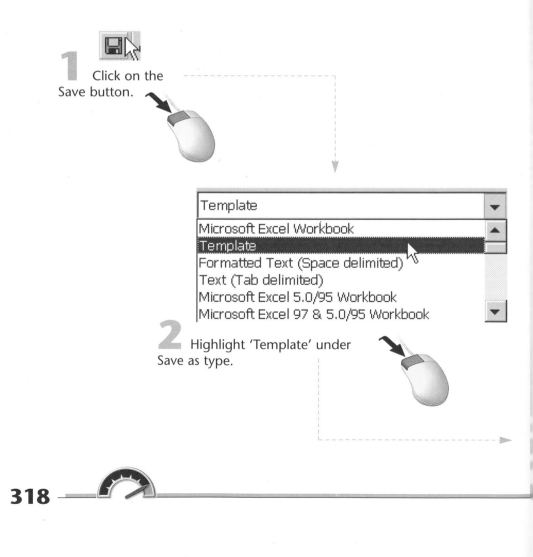

of the filing cabinets by themselves and open in front of you. You see the dividers, letters and faxes, miscellaneous documents, templates, etc. In Excel, the dividers in this file are the folders of the 'Templates' directory. You can now choose where you want to file – or save – your form. We are going to use the 'Spreadsheet Solutions' tab. The custom form will be filed there when you click on the Save button.

1 Click on the Save button.

2 Highlight 'Template' under Save as type.

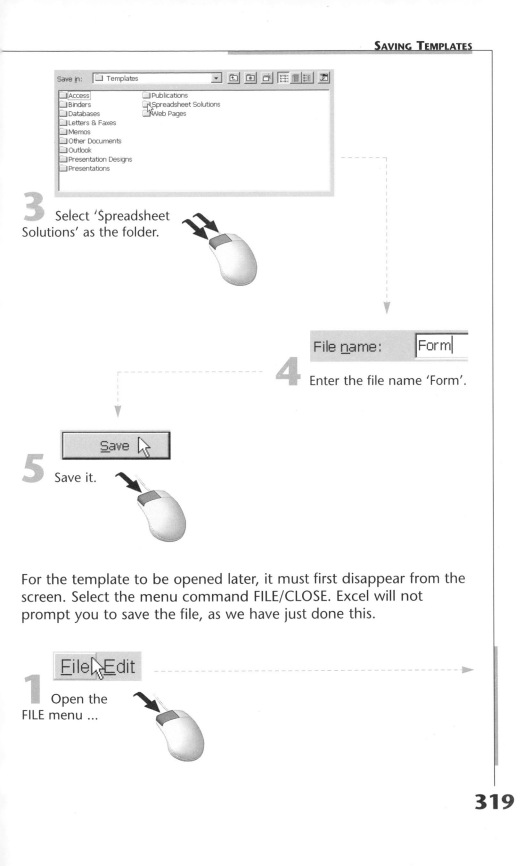

Save in: ☐ Templates

☐ Access   ☐ Publications
☐ Binders   ☐ Spreadsheet Solutions
☐ Databases   ☐ Web Pages
☐ Letters & Faxes
☐ Memos
☐ Other Documents
☐ Outlook
☐ Presentation Designs
☐ Presentations

3 Select 'Spreadsheet Solutions' as the folder.

File name: Form

4 Enter the file name 'Form'.

Save

5 Save it.

For the template to be opened later, it must first disappear from the screen. Select the menu command FILE/CLOSE. Excel will not prompt you to save the file, as we have just done this.

File Edit

1 Open the FILE menu ...

319

2 ... and select the command CLOSE.

What use is the template if you don't know how to get it back on the screen? Select the menu command FILE/NEW and the Spreadsheet Solutions tab. Remember? We saved our form in the Spreadsheet Solutions folder and that is exactly where we will find it. Reopen the template 'Form' by double-clicking on it.

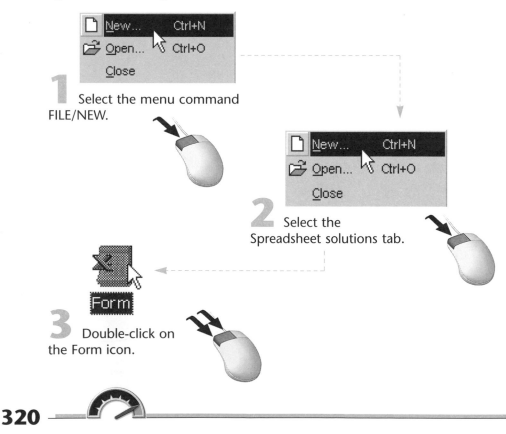

1 Select the menu command FILE/NEW.

2 Select the Spreadsheet solutions tab.

3 Double-click on the Form icon.

The template will appear on the screen. 'Form1' will appear on the title bar, i.e.

Microsoft Excel - Form1

you are working on the top copy. If you opened it again, a new template, 'Form2', would appear here.

Now, to enter text and figures, just follow the 'Excel trainer' steps below.

The Excel trainer

After you have opened your 'own' template, make the following entries. An invoice is required and you are going to 'fill in' the individual items.

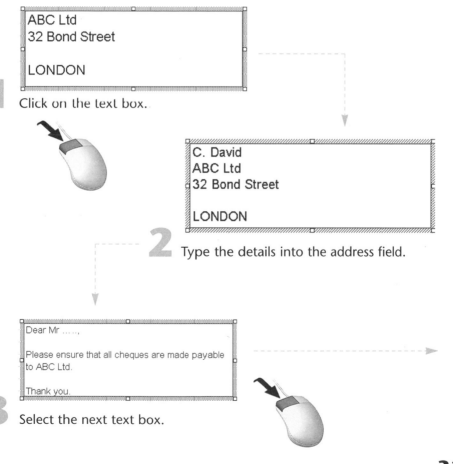

ABC Ltd
32 Bond Street

LONDON

1 Click on the text box.

C. David
ABC Ltd
32 Bond Street

LONDON

2 Type the details into the address field.

Dear Mr ......,

Please ensure that all cheques are made payable to ABC Ltd.

Thank you.

3 Select the next text box.

> Dear Mr C.David,
>
> Please ensure that all cheques are made payable to ABC Ltd.
>
> Thank you.

4 Just enter the name.

That's it. Now enter how much money you want.

Item		Quantity	Amount

1 Click on the cell.

Item		Quantity	Amount
Swivel chair		1	£450.00
Desk		1	£1,800.00
+17.5% VAT			£393.75
=Invoice total			£2,643.75

2 Enter the individual items in the cells. Watch how the 'VAT' and the 'Amount of the invoice' are calculated automatically from the formulas already entered.

Save the invoice. Then you will always know that an invoice has been issued and, more importantly, how much money you are due from the client.

CAUTION

If you want to file a workbook such as an invoice, note the date. If you have entered the formula '=today()', Excel will adjust the date automatically. Later you will not be able to see when you issued the invoice. In this case it is advisable to type in the date manually.

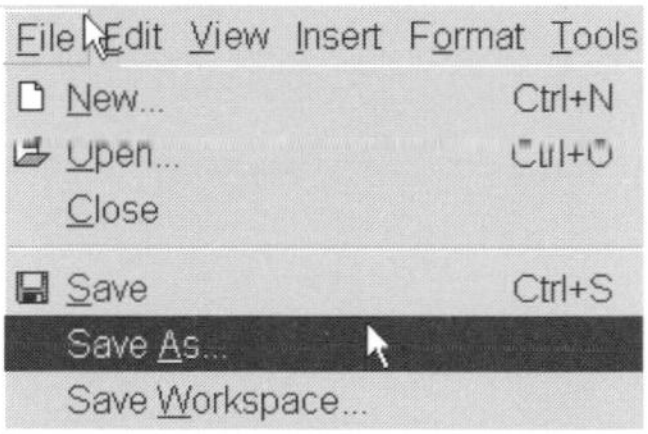

File	Edit	View	Insert	Format	Tools
New...					Ctrl+N
Open...					Ctrl+O
Close					
Save					Ctrl+S
Save As...					
Save Workspace...					

1 Select the menu command FILE/SAVE AS.

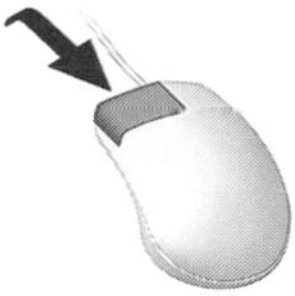

File name: ABC

2 Name the invoice.

Save

3 Save it.

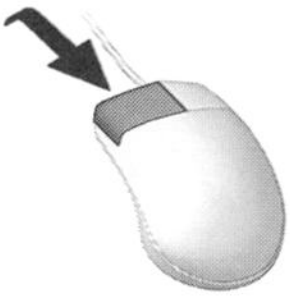

11

The address book

What's in this chapter?

Bye-bye Post-Its! Are you one of those people who keep the addresses and telephone numbers of your nearest and dearest, friends and acquaintances on any scrap of paper which comes to hand? What was the address of Mr A from Z? Forget it! We are going to create a clear address list with Excel and sort it from A to Z. Or from Z to A, if you really want. There will be a lot of filtering in this chapter – AutoFilter, custom filters and advanced filters.

Name	First name	Street	Postcode	City
Peterson	Kevin	2 Havard St.	SW1	London
Major	Jenny	10 Gilbert Ave.	SW2	London
Thatcher	Paul	4a Shakespeare Place	SW3	London
Prescot	Stuart	10 Portland Street	SW4	London
Hofner	Ken	30 Garden City Street	SW5	London
Peters	Samantha	2 Edwin Road	SW6	London
Bowen	Susan	40 Grove Place	SW7	London
Paris	Maria	190 Penny Lane	SW8	London
Stevens	Mary	7 Glades Road	SW9	London
Jones	Paula	90 Green Street	SW10	London

<u>You already know:</u>

<u>Your are going to learn:</u>

Sorting a list

You enter lists In order to obtain overviews of addresses, articles, etc. Excel provides extensive help with their management.

A list is a closed range in a worksheet.

We are going to create an address list, which you can expand by adding birthdays, telephone numbers, etc., if you like. We are going to sort the list, to keep an overview.

You will find these two buttons on the standard toolbar. But you can only use them to sort what is in the first column.
In our list this would be the 'Name' column. However, as people can have the same surname in real life, we have to sort it by first names, like a telephone directory. The two buttons are not sufficient for this purpose.

You can specify further criteria by using the DATA/SORT menu command. Sorting takes place first by 'name', then by 'first name'. You can use a total of three criteria for sorting.

Sort by	Example
Name	Adams, Peter, Birmingham Adams, Harry, Manchester Adams, Harry, Aberdeen Ballantine, Pauline, Edinburgh
First name	Adams, Harry, Manchester Adams, Harry, Aberdeen Adams, Peter, Birmingham
Place	Adams, Harry, Aberdeen Adams, Harry, Manchester

It is important that the 'Header Row' option button is checked for the sorting process, because our list

My list has

◉ Header row   ◯ No header row

actually has a header row. If the option button was not checked, Excel would sort the header row as well.

	A	B	C	D	E	F
1						
2						
3		Name	First name	Street	Postcode	City
4		Peterson	Kevin	2 Havard St.	SW1	London
5		Major	Jenny	10 Gilbert Ave.	SW2	London
6		Thatcher	Paul	4a Shakespeare Place	SW3	London
7		Prescot	Stuart	10 Portland Street	SW4	London
8		Hofner	Ken	30 Garden City Street	SW5	London
9		Peters	Samantha	2 Edwin Road	SW6	London
10		Bowen	Susan	40 Grove Place	SW7	London
11		Paris	Maria	190 Penny Lane	SW8	London
12		Stevens	Mary	7 Glades Road	SW9	London
13		Jones	Paula	90 Green Street	SW10	London

1 Enter the list.

Data Window Help

↓| Sort...

Filter ▶

2 Select the DATA/SORT menu command.

Sort by

Name   ◉ Ascending
  ◯ Descending

Then by

  ◉ Ascending
  ◯ Descending

3 Click on the arrow...

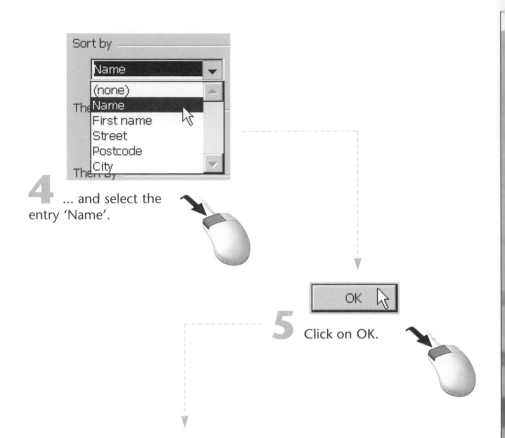

Sort by

| Name | ▼ |

(none)
Name
First name
Street
Postcode
City

4 ... and select the entry 'Name'.

OK

5 Click on OK.

Name	First name	Street	Postcode	City
Bowen	Susan	40 Grove Place	SW7	London
Hofner	Ken	30 Garden City Street	SW5	London
Hutcheson	Paul	4a Shakespeare Place	SW3	London
Jones	Paula	90 Green Street	SW10	London
Major	Jenny	10 Gilbert Ave.	SW2	London
Paris	Maria	190 Penny Lane	SW8	London
Peters	Samantha	2 Edwin Road	SW6	London
Peterson	Kevin	2 Havard St.	SW1	London
Prescot	Stuart	10 Portland Street	SW4	London
Stevens	Mary	7 Glades Road	SW9	London

6 The list has been sorted.

You can use key combinations to navigate through a list quickly and select cells.

Keys	Effect
Ctrl + ↑	Go to the first cell in a column
Ctrl + ↓	Go to the last cell in a column
Ctrl + ←	Go to the first cell in a row
Ctrl + →	Go to the last cell in a row
Ctrl + ⇧ + ↓	Select a column
Ctrl + ⇧ + →	Select a row
Ctrl + ⇧ + *	Select the entire list

Freezing panes

With very long lists, it is inconvenient to trudge through from A to Z. The header row will remain visible if the menu command WINDOW/FREEZE PANES is used. You can then scroll through the individual entries (addresses) with the scroll bar.

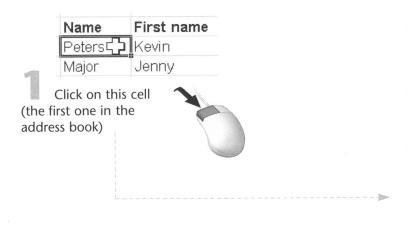

1 Click on this cell (the first one in the address book)

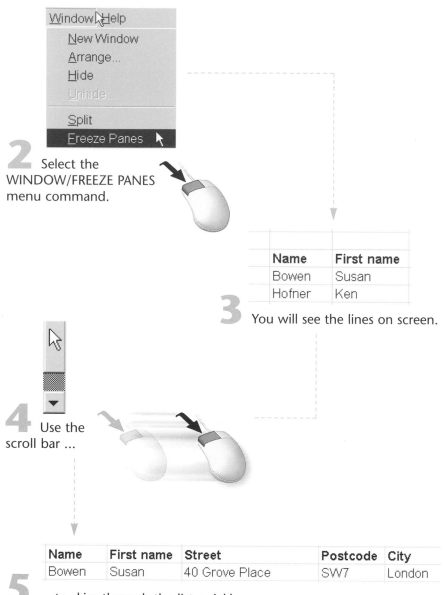

Window Help
New Window
Arrange...
Hide
Unhide...
Split
Freeze Panes

2 Select the
WINDOW/FREEZE PANES
menu command.

Name	First name
Bowen	Susan
Hofner	Ken

3 You will see the lines on screen.

4 Use the
scroll bar ...

Name	First name	Street	Postcode	City
Bowen	Susan	40 Grove Place	SW7	London

5 ... to skim through the list quickly.

Unfreeze the panes by using the menu command
WINDOW/UNFREEZE PANES.

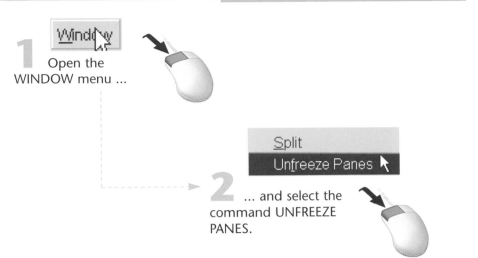

1 Open the
WINDOW menu ...

Split

Un<u>f</u>reeze Panes

2 ... and select the
command UNFREEZE
PANES.

The data form

A data set
consists of data
fields (name, first
name, road,
place, etc).

Excel has a convenient data form. A what? Click
on any cell in the list and select the menu
command DATA/FORM.

Name	First name	Street
Bowen	Susan	40 Grove Place
Hofner	Ken	30 Garden City Street
Hutcheson	Paul	4a Shakespeare Place

1 Click on any cell in
the list.

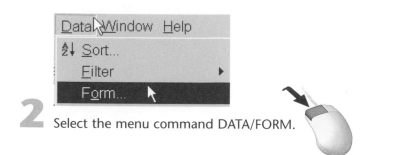

Select the menu command DATA/FORM.

You can also enter and edit your addresses from here.

| Sheet1 | | ? | X |

Name:	Bowen		1 of 10
First name:	Susan		New
Street:	40 Grove Place		Delete
Postcode:	SW7		Restore
City:	London		
			Find Prev
			Find Next
			Criteria
			Close

— Number of the data set

— Create new data set

— Delete data set displayed

— Restore the deleted data set

Looking for ...

You can select certain addressees by using the Criteria button. Click on it, and you can then enter the name to be displayed. If you only

| Name: | M* |

know the first letter of the name, use wildcards (*,?). If you enter M*, as shown here, only the data sets of people whose names begin with 'M' will be displayed.

Character	Entry	Effect
*	H*	All the people whose names begin with 'H' will be listed.
?	H???on	Excel will display Hendon, Hanson and Hatton, for example

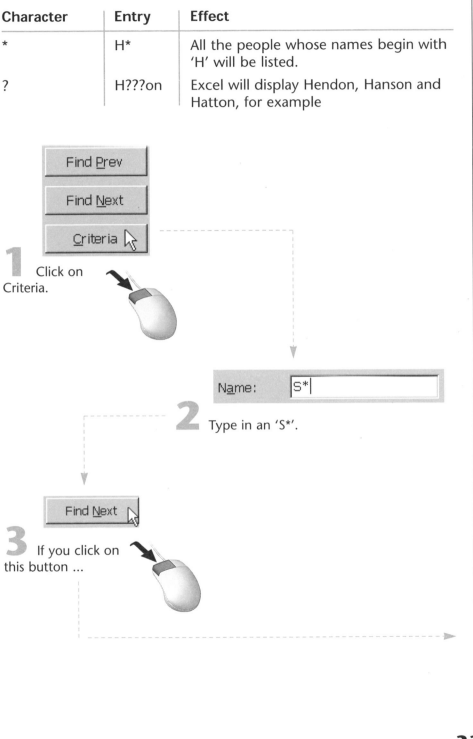

Find Prev

Find Next

Criteria

1 Click on Criteria.

Name: │S*│

2 Type in an 'S*'.

Find Next

3 If you click on this button ...

Na**m**e:	Stevens
Fi**r**st name:	Mary
S**t**reet:	7 Glades Road
Po**s**tcode:	SW9
Ci**t**y:	London

4 ... all the people whose names begin with 'S' will be displayed consecutively.

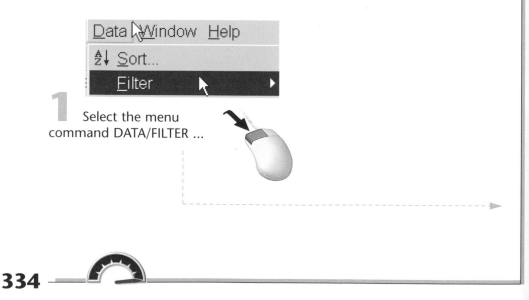

5 Close the dialog box.

Close

The AutoFilter

You can prevent certain addresses from being displayed by using the AutoFilter, which filters them out. You must enter criteria here too.

Data **W**indow **H**elp

$\frac{A}{Z}$↓ **S**ort...

Filter

1 Select the menu command DATA/FILTER ...

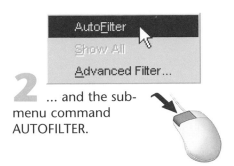

2 ... and the sub-menu command AUTOFILTER.

You will then see the following on screen. If you click on an arrow in a column, you can have certain data sets displayed. If you click on 'Hutcheson', you will see the addresses of all the people whose surnames are 'Hutcheson'.

Name	First Name	Street	Postcode	City
Bowen	Susan	40 Grove Place	SW7	London

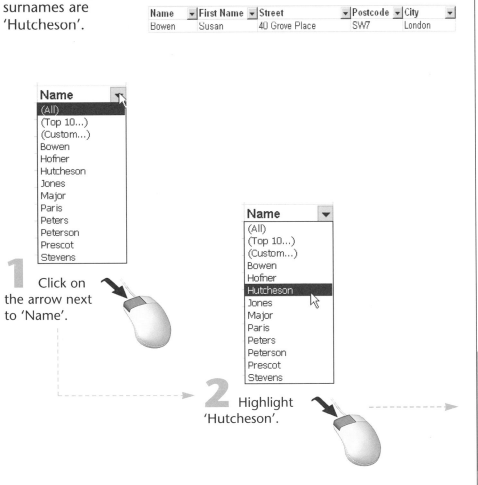

1 Click on the arrow next to 'Name'.

2 Highlight 'Hutcheson'.

335

Name		First Name		Street		Postcode		City	
Hutcheson		Paul		4a Shakespeare Place		SW3		London	

3 All the 'Hutchesons' will be displayed.

'(Top 10 ...)' will display the top ten in the selection: the highest figures, percentages, etc.

If you want to display all the data sets again, click on the arrow and highlight '(All)'.

Name	▼
Hutcheson	

1 Click on the arrow.

Name	▼
(All)	
(Top 10...)	
(Custom...)	

2 Select '(All)'.

336

Custom filters

A custom filter can be selected for every field in the list. In our example we would like to display all the places with a postcode between 'SW2' and 'SW5'.

Click on the arrow for the 'Postcode' column and select (Custom ...). Enter the criteria in the dialog box which appears. Combine the two by checking the And option button.

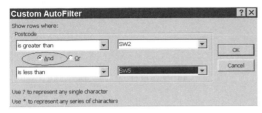

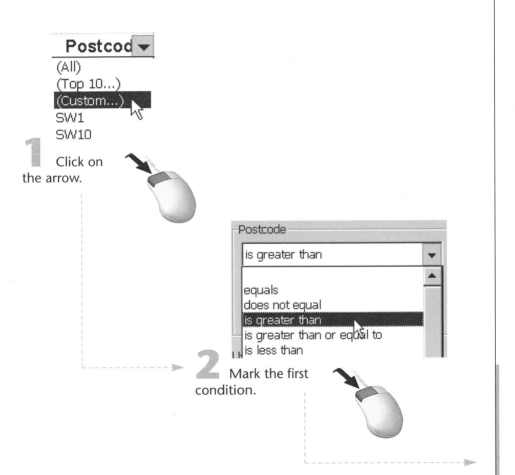

1 Click on the arrow.

2 Mark the first condition.

Postcode

| is greater than ▼ | SW2 ▼ |

3 Type in 'SW2'.

is less than ▼
equals
does not equal
is greater than
is greater than or equal to
is less than
is less than or equal to

4 Select the second condition.

| is less than ▼ | SW5 ▼ |

5 Type in 'SW5'.

OK

6 Click on OK.

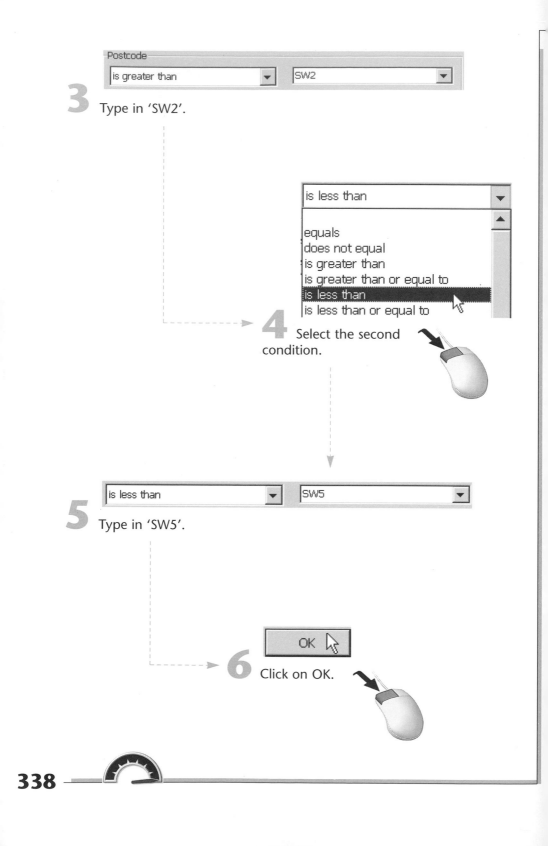

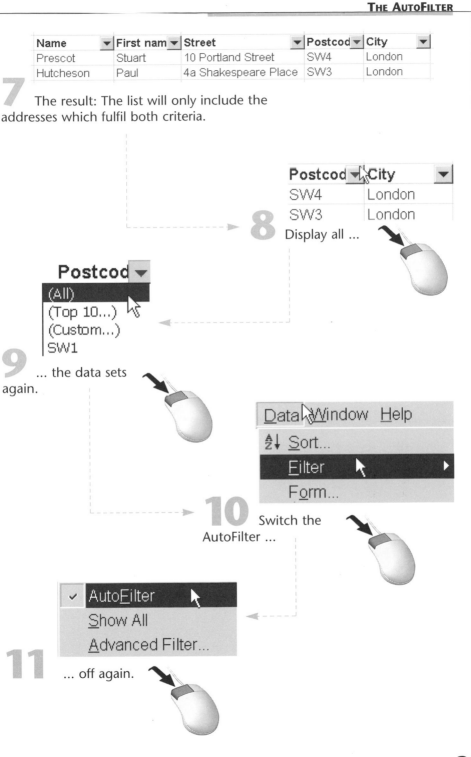

Name ▼	First nam ▼	Street ▼	Postcod ▼	City ▼
Prescot	Stuart	10 Portland Street	SW4	London
Hutcheson	Paul	4a Shakespeare Place	SW3	London

7 The result: The list will only include the addresses which fulfil both criteria.

Postcod ▼	City ▼
SW4	London
SW3	London

8 Display all ...

Postcod ▼

(All)
(Top 10...)
(Custom...)
SW1

9 ... the data sets again.

Data Window Help

↕ Sort...
Filter ▶
Form...

10 Switch the AutoFilter ...

✓ AutoFilter
Show All
Advanced Filter...

11 ... off again.

The advanced filter

One filter is left: the advanced filter. This gives you the opportunity of entering certain addresses on the worksheet. Data sets are filtered here too. You then copy the result into the worksheet.

In our example, we are going to 'Auchtermuchty' (wherever that is) next week. Only the people who live here are to be displayed. You enter 'Place' in one cell on the worksheet and 'Auchtermuchty' in another.

It is important that you then select the relevant list by clicking the mouse so that Excel knows what it is to filter. Click the cells for the individual dialog boxes under DATA/FILTER/ADVANCED FILTER. If the Advanced Filter dialog box covers up the cells in question, just move it by clicking on its title bar, holding the mouse button down and dragging it to somewhere else in the worksheet. Check the 'Copy to another location' option button to insert the result in the worksheet.

Advanced Filter	? X
Action	
● Filter the list, in-place	OK
○ Copy to another location	Cancel

McMahon	Lisa
Stoneham	Ian
Place	
Auchtermuchty	

1 Type the text into the individual cells.

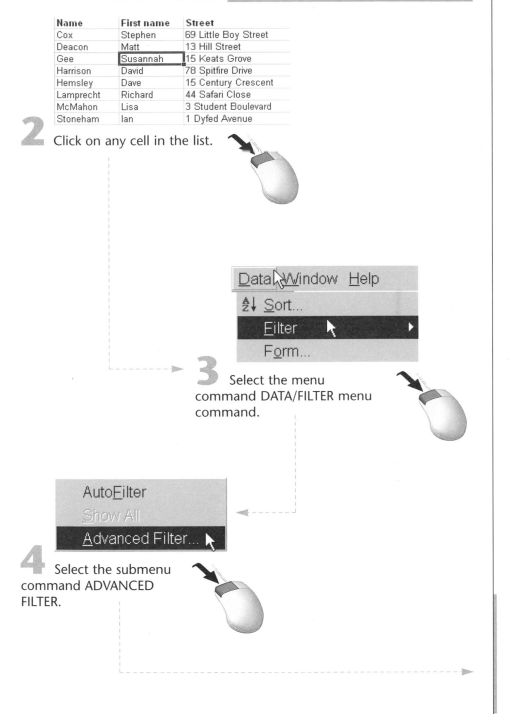

Name	First name	Street
Cox	Stephen	69 Little Boy Street
Deacon	Matt	13 Hill Street
Gee	Susannah	15 Keats Grove
Harrison	David	78 Spitfire Drive
Hemsley	Dave	15 Century Crescent
Lamprecht	Richard	44 Safari Close
McMahon	Lisa	3 Student Boulevard
Stoneham	Ian	1 Dyfed Avenue

2 Click on any cell in the list.

Data Window Help

A↓ Sort...

Filter ▶

Form...

3 Select the menu command DATA/FILTER menu command.

AutoFilter

Show All

Advanced Filter...

4 Select the submenu command ADVANCED FILTER.

Name	First name	Street	Postcode	City
Cox				
Deacon				th
Gee				
Harrison				uchty
Hemsley				
Lamprecht				uchty
McMahon				
Stoneham				

Advanced Filter   ? X

Action
- ⦿ Filter the list, in-place
- ○ Copy to another location

List range: `$B$2:$F$10`

Criteria range:

Copy to:

☐ Unique records only

OK   Cancel

Place
Auchtermuchty

5 Excel will select the list in the background.

⦿ Copy to another location

6 Check this option button.

List range: `$B$3:$F$13`

Criteria range:

Copy to:

7 Click on the Criteria Range box.

Place
Auchtermuchty

8 Select the cells.

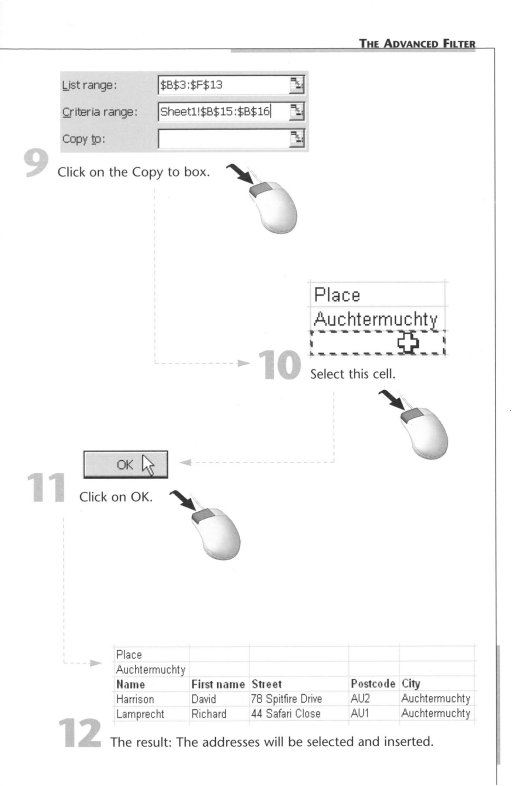

List range:	$B$3:$F$13	
Criteria range:	Sheet1!$B$15:$B$16	
Copy to:		

9 Click on the Copy to box.

Place
Auchtermuchty

10 Select this cell.

OK

11 Click on OK.

Place				
Auchtermuchty				
Name	**First name**	**Street**	**Postcode**	**City**
Harrison	David	78 Spitfire Drive	AU2	Auchtermuchty
Lamprecht	Richard	44 Safari Close	AU1	Auchtermuchty

12 The result: The addresses will be selected and inserted.

What's in
this chapter?

If you are drowning and can't swim, there's only
one thing for it. A brave lifesaver must pull you
out. Failing that, pray for
a lifebelt to drop from
the sky. Excel provides
lifebelts in the form of
extensive help. If
something doesn't
work, you don't have
to rely on miracles,
you can use the
Excel help facility.
It goes much
further than you
might think!

Installation

Most users will not be installing the Office 97 software themselves. If you are buying a PC, the dealer will often have done this for you. If you have to install Excel yourself, don't worry. Many things, for example, adjustment to your hardware (such as mouse, printer and monitor) were already entered when Windows 95 was installed. As you know, Excel 97 needs Windows 95 to run

If you insert the CD-ROM most things will be done automatically and the installation program – called Setup – will appear on your screen. The recommended functions will already have been selected and usually you will only have to confirm them.

You can choose between different types of installation. These include Standard, Custom and Run from CD-ROM. The standard version will, of course, take up the most space on your hard disk. It will install the program completely and almost fully automatically. In the case of custom installation, you specify the modules you would like to install. This is the recommended option if you are having to watch the space on the hard disk. If you use Run from CD-ROM you will have to start Excel from the CD-ROM every time. Although this takes up a little less storage space, you'll be forced to work at a snail's pace.

Subsequent reinstallation

You can always skip certain programs when you first install Excel. This is no problem. Just click on the appropriate option. A 'tick' means that it will be installed. If you remove the tick, the option will not be loaded. Also, if you decide to deinstall software later, insert the installation

Options:		Description:
☑ Microsoft Binder	2062 K	Microsoft Binder will be installed with only the selected options.
☑ Microsoft Excel	15685 K	
☑ Microsoft Word	25840 K	
☑ Microsoft PowerPoint	26119 K	
☑ Microsoft Access	29692 K	
☑ Microsoft Outlook	26617 K	
☐ Web Page Authoring (HTML)	9690 K	Change Option...
☑ Microsoft Bookshelf Basics	385 K	
☑ Data Access	6775 K	Select All
☑ Office Tools	15721 K	

345

CD-ROM before you select what you want to delete from the hard disk.

Space required on C:	154969 K
Space available on C:	47744 K

It is always important to keep an eye on the storage space on the hard disk. In this case it is insufficient. Any attempt at installation would be punished by automatic cancellation. In this case you must think carefully about other software that you could do without.

Only when you get confirmation that installation has been completed successfully can you run Excel.

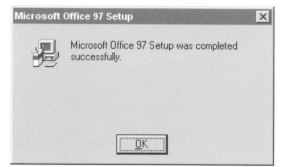

Only when you get confirmation that installation has been completed successfully can you run Excel.

Clippit – there to help you

One of the nice refinements in Excel are the amusing Office Assistants. If you click on ? on the standard toolbar, an assistant will appear.

In this case it is 'Clippit', the high-spirited paper clip which helps you work with Excel. If you move the mouse pointer onto the assistant and press the right-hand button, a menu will drop down.

You can select various commands. For example, you can use OPTIONS to specify which tips the assistant will give you.

After selecting the ANIMATE command you will get a short, spirited demonstration. Run it by pressing the left-hand mouse button.

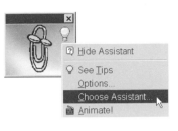

If you click on Choose Assistant a variety of helpers will appear. The Next button will show you the next one.

You are spoiled for choice between Clippit, The Dot, The Genius, Hoverbot, Office Logo, Mother Nature, Power Pup, Scribble and Sir William. If you decide to change the assistant you will have to insert the Office 97 CD-ROM.

Any questions?

If you have a question about Excel, just click on the assistant, enter your query and select Search. Your query need not be formulated as a question, but only entered so that your wizard can understand it. Keywords are usually enough. In this case we will enter 'Copying cells'..

What would you like to do?

 Format cells and lists quickly with styles or built-in table formats

● Edit cell contents

 Move or copy cell data

The result: several options for relevant solutions are provided. Pick the appropriate one.

In our case, if you click on Move or copy cell data, Excel will display its information and instructions on the subject.

Move or copy cell data

When you copy a cell by dragging or by clicking **Cut** ✂ or **Copy** 🗐, and **Paste** 🗐, Microsoft Excel copies the entire cell, including formulas and their resulting values, comments, and cell formats.

If the selected copy area includes hidden cells, Microsoft Excel also copies the hidden cells. If the paste area contains hidden rows or columns, you might need to unhide the paste area to see all of the copied cells.

If the selected copy area includes hidden cells, Microsoft Excel also copies the hidden cells. If the paste area contains hidden rows or columns, you might need to unhide the paste area to see all of the copied cells.

What do you want to do?

≫ Move or copy characters within a cell

≫ Move or copy part of a cell's contents into another cell

When the mouse pointer changes into a hand, click to get a fuller explanation of the subject.

More help

Additional help, which is not suitable for beginners, is also available in Excel. Open the Help menu and select CONTENTS AND INDEX. You need the Contents tab, on which you will find the individual help books.
Double-click on one of them. (Of course, you can also click on it once and then click on the Open button).You will get a selection of individual subjects. If you double-click on one of them you will get a comprehensive explanation of the selected subject.

Contents | Index | Find

Click a book, and then click Open. Or click another tab, such as Index.

- ◆ Key Information
- ◆ Getting Help
- ◆ Installing and Removing Microsoft Excel
- ◆ Creating, Opening, and Saving Files
- ◆ Working with Workbooks and Worksheets

Index to help

Search terms on which you need help can be entered on the Index tab (HELP/CONTENTS AND INDEX). If you enter your search term under 1. Type the first few letters ..., you will see how Excel jumps down the lower list as each letter is entered, selecting terms which could be of interest.

Contents | Index | Find

1 Type the first few letters of the word you're looking for.

Copying cells

2 Click the index entry you want, and then click Display

to numbers
copyfitting text
copying
  cell contents
  cell formats
  cells
  comments
  data entries
  data in outlined worksheets
  data to other programs
  filtered data
  formulas
  hidden data
  hyperlinks
  Microsoft Access records
  screen pictures

Display | Print | Cancel

Click on the Display button to get the desired explanations.

Context-sensitive Help

Everyone should know about context-sensitive help (otherwise known as the 'What's This?' feature). Open the Help menu and click on 'What's This?'.

 A question mark will appear next to your mouse pointer.

If you click on a button (in this case the Format Painter), you will get a comprehensive explanation, instead of the usual quick help. You can deactivate direct help by pressing the 'Esc' key.

> **Format Painter (Standard toolbar)**
>
> Copies the format from a selected object or text and applies it to the object or text you click. To copy the formatting to more than one item, double-click ✍, and then click each item you want to format. When you are finished, press ESC or click ✍ again to turn off the **Format Painter.**

 You can also get extra context-sensitive help in a dialog box. Click on the question mark in the top right-hand corner and a question mark will appear alongside the mouse pointer.

If you now click on a point, you will get the desired information. The explanation will disappear from the screen if you click again anywhere.

 You can also click on an option with the right-hand mouse button. A tiny 'What's This?' menu will appear, which you can click to read the explanation.

 The assistant can also be run from within a dialog box.

The Auditor

The auditor really has nothing to do with taxes and accounts. It should really be called Sherlock Holmes, because it looks for clues. As shown here, both cells produce '48%'.

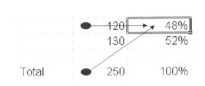

The 'auditor' is set to work by the TOOLS/AUDITING menu command. This will provide you with a selection. With TRACE PRECEDENTS you will obtain information to which the cell containing your formula refers. The TRACE DEPENDENTS option will show which cells depend upon the figure displayed. The SHOW AUDITING TOOLBAR command will display the toolbar on the screen.

⊞	Trace Precedents
◄	Trace Dependents
◇	Trace Error
ℛ	Remove All Arrows
	Show Auditing Toolbar

	120
	130
Total	250

1 Enter this small calculation. Click on the AutoSum button to determine the total.

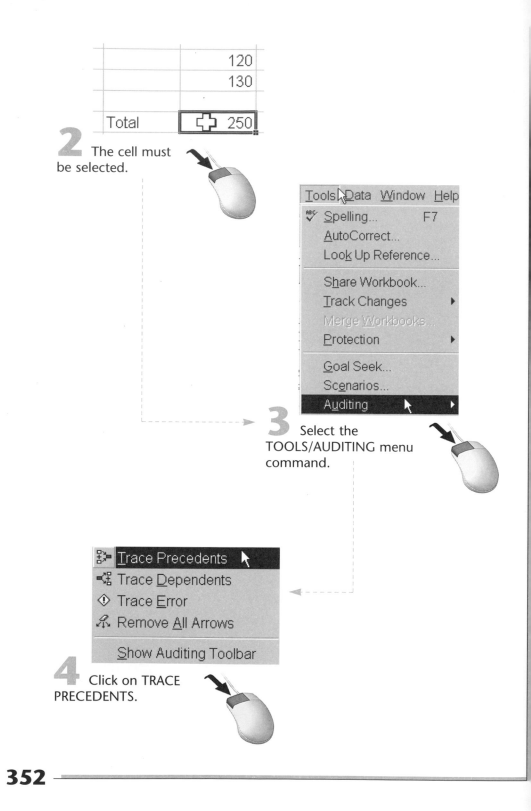

	120
	130
Total	250

2 The cell must be selected.

Tools	Data	Window	Help
✓ Spelling...			F7
AutoCorrect...			
Look Up Reference...			
Share Workbook...			
Track Changes			▶
Merge Workbooks...			
Protection			▶
Goal Seek...			
Scenarios...			
Auditing			▶

3 Select the TOOLS/AUDITING menu command.

⊞ Trace Precedents
⊞ Trace Dependents
◇ Trace Error
⋏ Remove All Arrows
Show Auditing Toolbar

4 Click on TRACE PRECEDENTS.

Excel will show you the values to which the formula refers. The range in question will be outlined in blue. This calculation is still clear.

●	120
	130
Total	▼ 250

In the case of larger calculations, it can be revealing to see how a figure was obtained, and from where. The dots mark the cells which affect the formula. The arrows point to the respective results.

Opening balance		£200.00		Income	£1,290.00
Closing balance		£950.10		Expenditure	£539.90

No.	Text	Income	Expenditure	Cash
1	Bank interest	£200.00		£400.00
2	Courier		£80.00	£320.00
3	Stationery		£200.00	£120.00
4	Travel		£29.95	£90.05
5	Facsimile	£115.00		£205.05
6	PC hardware		£200.00	£5.05
7	Bank interest	£400.00		£405.05
8	Consulting	£575.00		£980.05
9	Travel		£29.95	£950.10
10	Closing balance			£950.10

Removing the trails

Click on Remove all arrows under TOOLS/AUDITING to make all the trails disappear from the screen.

353

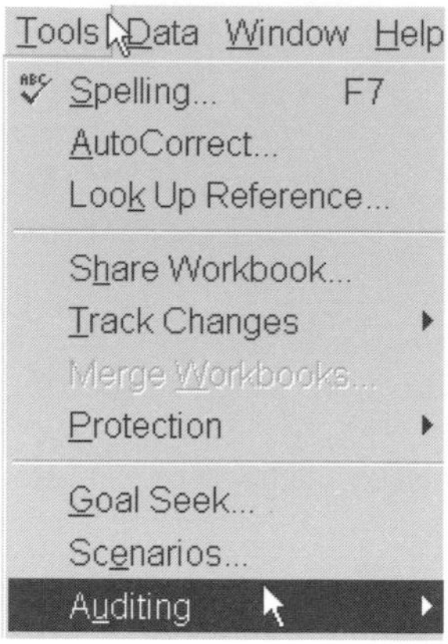

Tools Data Window Help
Spelling... F7
AutoCorrect...
Look Up Reference...
Share Workbook...
Track Changes
Merge Workbooks...
Protection
Goal Seek...
Scenarios...
Auditing

1 Select TOOLS/AUDITING and hide the trails by ...

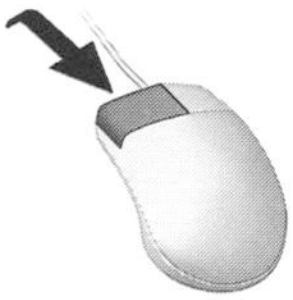

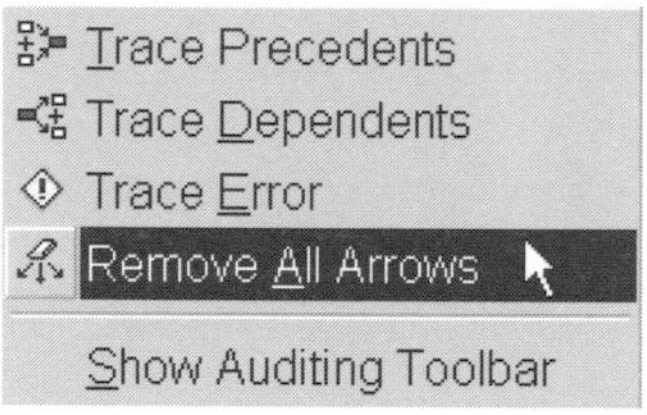

Trace Precedents
Trace Dependents
Trace Error
Remove All Arrows
Show Auditing Toolbar

2 ... using REMOVE ALL ARROWS.

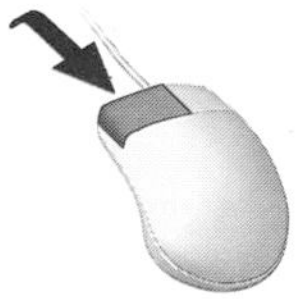

Hiding and displaying formulas

Excel provides you with further help by allowing you to display formulas. Up to now you have been able to see them on the formula bar by clicking on a cell. In this way you could see only one formula at a time. Select TOOLS/OPTIONS and then the View tab. Select 'Formulas' under Window options. Click with the mouse and a tick will appear in the box. As soon as you confirm by clicking on OK, you will see that the figures have disappeared from your workbook and the formulas are displayed.

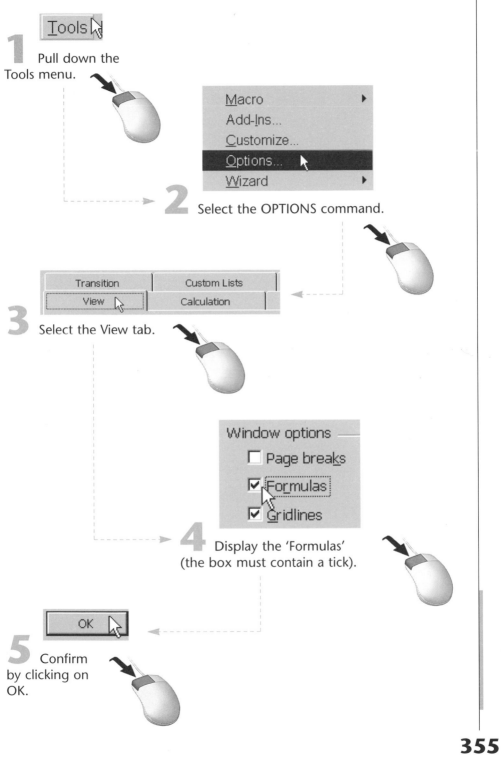

1 Pull down the Tools menu.

Tools

Macro ▶
Add-Ins...
Customize...
Options... ▸
Wizard ▶

2 Select the OPTIONS command.

Transition   Custom Lists
View   Calculation

3 Select the View tab.

Window options
☐ Page breaks
☑ Formulas
☑ Gridlines

4 Display the 'Formulas' (the box must contain a tick).

OK

5 Confirm by clicking on OK.

355

The formulas will be displayed on your screen. (There is not much point in doing this in the example shown on the right.) You could also check the content of the cell on the formula bar.

	120
	130
Total	=SUM(C6:C8)

It makes more sense in the case of several cells, each of which contains a formula. Here you can see what has been entered in each case. You can hide the formulas by clicking on Window options on the View tab under

Income	Expenditure	Cash
200		=IF(D12>0,D6+D12,D6-E12)
	80	=IF(D13>0,F12+D13,F12-E13)
	200	=IF(D14>0,F13+D14,F13-E14)
	29.95	=IF(D15>0,F14+D15,F14-E15)
115		=IF(D16>0,F15+D16,F15-E16)
	200	=IF(D17>0,F16+D17,F16-E17)
400		=IF(D18>0,F17+D18,F17-E18)
575		=IF(D19>0,F18+D19,F18-E19)
	29.95	=IF(D20>0,F19+D20,F19-E20)
		950.1

TOOLS/OPTIONS, thus removing the tick from the box.

Calculating and comparing in Excel

Symbol	Key	Meaning
+	+	Addition
-	-	Subtraction
-	-	Negative number
*	*	Multiplication
/	/	Division
%	%	Convert to percentage
^	^	Raise to the power of
=	=	Equals
<	<	Less than
>	>	Greater than

Symbol	Key	Meaning
<=	<=	Smaller than or equal to
>=	>=	Greater than or equal to
<>	<>	Not equal to

Error messages

Error messages always begin with the '#' character. Excel displays them in the cell in which the formula or instruction could not be implemented.

Message	Meaning	Suggested correction
#########	The column is too narrow to display the expression/figure.	Increase the column width.
#Div/0!	Mathematically incorrect: numbers cannot be divided by 0.	Check the cell content. All the figures must be greater than 0.
#Name?	Excel does not recognise the name in a formula.	You have entered an incorrect name (for cells/cell ranges). Correct it on the formula bar.
#Zero!	The individual cells or ranges do not agree.	Check the characters in the formula or function (;:) or the cell references (A1, B2, C3, etc).
#NV	A figure in a function or formula is not available.	Check the contents of the function, formula or cells.

357

Message	Meaning	Suggested correction
#VALUE!	The formula or function cannot be executed due to an erroneous entry.	You may have entered text instead of a figure.
#NUMBER!	Problem with a number.	Check the numbers in the formula, function or cells.

Answers

Chapter 1

Exercise I

Which toolbars are shown below?

Standard toolbar

Menu bar

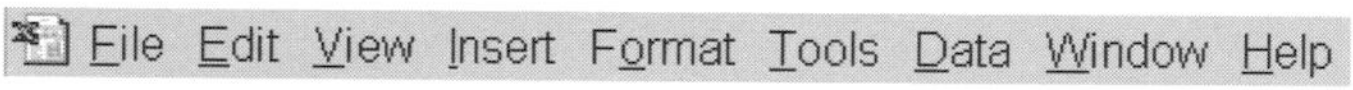

Formula bar

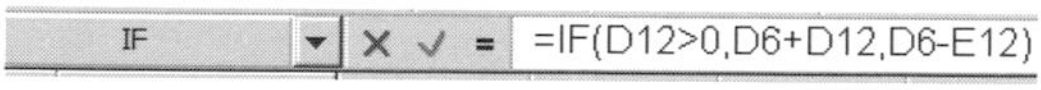

Formatting toolbar

Exercise III

Which key selects the menu bar?

☐   ⌫

X   Alt

☐   Alt Gr

☐   Ctrl

Which of the following command sequences will display Quick Help?

☐   FORMAT/DRAW/QUICK HELP

☐   VIEW/TOOLBARS/ADJUST/RESET/Quick Help tab

X   VIEW/TOOLBARS/RESET/Options tab/Display quick help on toolbars

What does your mouse pointer look like in the working area?

X

☐

How is a cell name made up?

☐   The cell is given first, then the column

X   The column is given first, then the row

☐   The row is given first, then the column

359

Chapter 2

Exercise V

When does Excel recognise the entry as a number (1) or text (2)?

Try it out on your screen.

(1)   234.56

(2)   23 dollars

(2)   ABC

(1)   - 34

(2)   34°

(2)   75.-

(2)   75 pounds

(1)   0.34

(1)   + 78

Exercise VI

Which characters are used for individual calculations in Excel?

                        - + * / \ x X

Division: /

Addition: +

Multiplication: *

Subtraction: -

Exercise VII

Which character must be inserted before a calculation?

  =

☐ No character need be entered

☐ ′

Chapter 3

Exercise IX

🔄	(4)	1.	Currency Style
I	(5)	2.	Italic
🔍	(7)	3.	Print Preview
<u>U</u>	(8)	4.	Underline
10 ▾	(9)	5.	Font Size
✂	(6)	6.	Cut
B	(10)	7.	Bold
☐	(3)	8.	New Workbook
🖨	(11)	9.	Print
💾	(2)	10.	Save Workbook
📋	(1)	11.	Paste

AutoFilter

You can reduce the number of data sets displayed by 'filtering them out' , using criteria.

Cell range

A combination of several cells forms a range.

Cells

The fields where columns and rows intersect are called 'cells' in Excel.

Clip Art

Excel contains a small library of ready-made graphics, the so-called ClipArt Gallery.

Clipboard

The Clipboard (also called the scrap) is usually used by Windows in order to move text from one point to another in the document, or to copy it. Text is placed on the clipboard by the commands Copy or Cut so that it can be inserted again (by using the Paste command) when required.

Combo-Box

In a combo-box entries can both be made and selected (e.g. for font and font size).

Context-sensitive menu

If the right-hand mouse button is pressed a context-sensitive menu will appear. The name shows that the menu options depend on the context, or situation, in which the button was pressed.

CPI

Abbreviation for 'characters per inch' (1 inch = 2.54 cm). This is the measurement for character density when printing.

Cue Cards

Provide information on what is behind the numerous icons in Excel. If the mouse pointer remains on an icon for more than one second, the explanation will appear.

Cursor

The position marker on the screen, in the form of a flashing rectangle or arrow. It marks the point at which the user's next entry will appear.

Data set

Consists of data fields ('name', 'first name', 'road', 'place', etc.) and is a constituent of a database such as 'addresses'.

363

Density

The density at which data is recorded on a diskette.

Desktop

The background of the screen in Windows 95 on which the windows, buttons and dialog boxes are displayed.

Dialog boxes

These are used for entering data and selecting commands. A dialogue thus takes place between you, as the user, and Excel 97.

Directory

Directories are like the drawers in a filing cabinet (the hard disk). All files which are related can be kept in the same drawer (Directory).

Dot matrix printer

Every character output by a dot matrix printer is composed of a number of dots. The dots are transferred to the paper by needles at the points at which the needles strike the ribbon.

Double-click

The mouse button is pressed twice in quick succession.

DPI

Abbreviation for 'dots per inch', the measurement for printer resolution.

Drag & drop

Name for pulling or moving. Graphic user interfaces such as Windows 95 provide this facility, in which you place the mouse pointer on an icon, press the left-hand mouse button and hold it down until the icon has been moved to another point and left there.

F1

Function key which activates help in Excel.

File

Composed of all the data stored on a data medium under one file name.

Folder

Allocation area on a data medium used for organising the files stored on it. Files can be stored in folders (see also Directories).

Formatting

Determines the appearance (bold, italics, font, etc) of a text on the screen and when printing.

Formatting toolbar

Using this toolbar you can undertake 'formatting'. i.e. you can, for example, select a different font, convert your figures into percentages or highlight text by making it bold or underlining it.

Formula

Calculation entered by an equals sign in Excel.

Formula bar

You can see the content of the selected cell here and edit cell entries (text, numbers and formulas).

Headers and footers

Designate the display of text at the top (head) or bottom (foot) of the document.

Icon

A symbol on the screen representing a computer function (e.g. the outline of a diskette, for saving) or for selecting a control facility in the program (e.g. an index card for retrieving a file).

Ink jet printer

Ink is sprayed at high pressure through nozzles onto the paper.

Italic

Italic is the name given to a font which slopes slightly to the right.

Laser printer

The printer works in a similar way to a photocopier. Individual dots on a roller are electrostatically charged by beams of light (laser) so that they attract toner (dye powder). The toner is then pressed onto the paper and fixed by heat.

List box

A list box offers a choice of several entries. The entry most recently selected is still displayed.

List

Closed range in a table.

Load

Expression for opening a worksheet.

Macro

Consecutively recorded or written commands which trigger actions and are processed in the order in which they are retrieved.

Master data

Data which is seldom, if ever, changed (such as name and address).

Menu bar

For running commands such as Save, Print, Close, etc, by clicking on them with the left-hand mouse button.

Option button

These buttons change the settings of Excel 97. They are usually operated from a tab.

Page break

The point on a worksheet at which one page ends and a new page begins.

Pagination

Expression for counting pages.

Pica

Typographical measurement. 1 Pica = 12 points (Pt) or approximately 4.2 mm.

Point

Point is an older unit for measuring the size of characters. A point is equal to 0.35 mm of character height.

Printer types

The most common types of printer are dot matrix, ink jet and laser.

RTF

Abbreviation for Rich Text Format, which is used to exchange text data and as a file type for saving.

Ruler

Measurement scale visible on screen.

Scroll bar

The scroll bar forms part of a document window and is used for faster flicking (scrolling) through documents.

Sheet tabs

These are located at the bottom of the screen and show the name of the worksheets in the workbook.

Shortcut

Combination of keystrokes for running a command.

Standard toolbar

The standard toolbar contains the buttons. They represent commands which can also be run from the menu bar.

Syntax

Name of the structure of a formula.

Tabs

In order to make dialog boxes somewhat clearer, many are shown as 'card indexes', containing various cards.

Tags

Tabs have 'tags' (on which the respective name is shown). They are used to bring a tab to the front.

Templates

These contain sheet templates and are used as a basis for new workbooks.

Text box

For extensive text. Entry is not in a cell, but in a box with a border.

TIFF

Abbreviation for Tagged Image File Format, a graphical format.

Times

A font in the baroque antiqua group. One of the most commonly used fonts.

Title bar

This will always show the workbook in which you are currently working, in other words, the title (name) under which you are working.

Top 10

Lists the first ten data sets following a selection, i.e. the highest numbers, percentages, etc.

Typography

The art of designing letters and fonts, and their use.

Wildcards

These are proxy characters which represent part of a file name and thus make it possible to list a group of files. The wildcards most commonly used are '?' for a single character and '*' for a whole file name or parts thereof.

WordArt

Microsoft WordArt is a supplementary application which is used to create special text effects.

Worksheet

A sheet which you prepare in Excel. Together they are called a 'workbook'.

Write-protection of diskettes

If the little black switch is raised, the diskette can only be read and not overwritten. In this way data on the diskette can be protected against accidental erasure. If the switch is moved down, the data can be overwritten.

Zoom

You can enlarge or reduce the view of the current worksheet with the Excel zoom function.

375

D

Data entry 36
Data field 331
Data set 331, 363
Date and time 305
- changing 306
Date, display 308
Date, format 308
Deactivating the menu bar 25
Decimal places 118, 195, 252
- decreasing 122
- increasing 122
Delete key 53
Deleting 53
- borders 243
- cells 53
- colours 94
- currency 78, 146
- decimal places 196
- font colour 258
- lists 158
- number formats 146, 253
- software 345
- text box 304
- trails 353
Density 363
Desktop 19, 363
Dialog box 364
- Save as 55
Dialog box help 350
Dialog boxes 28
Dialog window 28
- numbers 119
Direct help 350
- by clicking the right-hand mouse
  button 350
Directory 371
Diskette symbol 54
Display, date 308
- rows 70
Displaying, drawing toolbar 299
Displaying, formulae 354
- gridlines 212

Distinguishing between
  numbers/text 51
- copying/cutting 125
Division 50, 139
Dollar sign in cell references 132
Dollars 118
Dot matrix printers 364
Double underlining 65
Double-click 364
DPI 364
Drag & Drop 80, 82, 124, 139,
  364
- copying 125
- for charts 173
- formula area 129
Dragging points (see Handles)
Drawing 299
Drawing toolbar 299
Duplication with drag & drop
  124
- of cells 124
- of formulae 101

E

Editing bar 36, 362
Editing, ClipArt 208
- a chart 165
- a picture 208
- text boxes 300
Editing/Copying 125
Editing/Inserting 125
Else value 265
Ending the program 39
- from Excel 54
Enlarge, ClipArt 206, 208
Entering days of the week 153
Entering foreign currencies 118
- numbers 35
Entering formulae 47
Entering months 152
Entering numbers 35
Entering text, footers 296
- headers 296